THE
Fourth
World War

Also by the same authors:

By Count de Marenches:
Dans le Secret des Princes
(with Christine Ockrent)

Atlas Géopolitique
Editions Stock

By David A. Andelman:
The Peacemakers

THE
Fourth
World War

Diplomacy and Espionage in the Age of Terrorism

Alexandre de **Count de Marenches**
and
David A. Andelman

William Morrow and Company, Inc.
New York

oclc 24373159

This book, by Count de Marenches and David A. Andelman, is an updated and
adapted version of the original work *Dans le Secret des Princes,* published in 1986
by Editions Stock and signed Alexandre de Marenches and Christine Ockrent.

It is the policy of William Morrow and Company, Inc., and its imprints and
affiliates, recognizing the importance of preserving what has been written, to print
the books we publish on acid-free paper, and we exert our best efforts to that end.

Library of Congress Cataloging-in-Publication Data

    Marenches, Alexandre de, comte.
       The fourth world war : diplomacy and espionage in the age of
    terrorism / by the Count de Marenches and David A. Andelman.
        p.   cm.
      ISBN 0-688-09218-7
      1. World politics—1989– 2. Northern Hemisphere—Relations—Southern
    Hemisphere.   3. Southern Hemisphere—Relations—Northern
    Hemisphere. 4. Espionage. 5. Diplomacy. 6. Terrorism.
    I. Andelman, David A. II. Title.
    D806.M37 1992
    909.82′9—dc20   91-33604
                                                         CIP

Printed in the United States of America

First Edition

1 2 3 4 5 6 7 8 9 10

BOOK DESIGN BY LEON BOLOGNESE & ASSOCIATES, INC.

For Lillian
and to the memory of our son Anselme

Marenches

For my father and mother, Saul and Selma,
and my son, Philip . . .
the last generation who knew war, and the next . . . may he
never

Andelman

Acknowledgments

To David Andelman, whose patience and perception have helped the birth of this book. And to my dear cousin Thérèse de Saint-Phalle-Drouâs, without whom this book would not exist, with tenderness.

Marenches
Paris

From this side of the Atlantic, the debt is symmetrical. To my co-author, Alexandre—had he not lived every event in this book, there would have been no book. To his cousin, Thérèse de Saint Phalle-Drouâs, who was perceptive enough to have recognized in this humble servant an individual who would be compelled by the life of the Count de Marenches. To Robert Lescher, who never ceased to believe in me, and did what only the best agents can do—provide a sympathetic ear and a steady hand. And of course, to the editors at William Morrow, especially Connie Roosevelt, who embarked on the journey with me, Elisa Petrini, who saw it so skillfully to fruition, and her tireless assistant, Katherine Boyle. And finally, to an often unsung hero, the meticulous copy editor, David Falk, whose red-penciled labors in solitude must be credited with all the consistencies and none of the faults in this work.

There is a very special debt, as well, to those who helped all along with advice and encouragement, some of whom, still on station laboring in distant shadows for their country, may never be named. And above all, to Karen M., who must also for the moment remain nameless, but who taught me the most fundamental lesson—that the only true intelligence comes from the heart as well as from the mind.

Andelman
New York City

7

Contents

War is diplomacy by other means.

—Clausewitz, *On War*

CHAPTER

First the Cloak

hortly after he was elected President, before he even assumed office, at the end of 1980, I met with Ronald Reagan in California, where he was preparing to take over the presidency. Several friends and advisers to the President-elect had told him, as only Americans can exaggerate, that if there was one European he should see before assuming office, it was the Count de Marenches. I was, at the time, coming to the end of more than a decade of service as head of French Intelligence—a tenure that was the longest of any intelligence leader in French history. It was also the culmination of my lifelong preoccupation with the way the world worked and how the men who made it work ticked.

The President-elect had some immediate concerns; he was preoccupied with two critical events that were overshadowing his inauguration a month or so away—the taking of American hostages in Iran and the recent Soviet invasion of Afghanistan, a reflection of his larger concern about the implacable hostility of and danger presented by the Soviet empire.

Still, those concerns were merely a pale foreshadowing of a more cosmic sequence of events that was already unfolding and that no doubt neither he nor any of his principal advisers suspected at the time. Reagan and those he chose as his principal national security advisers were then just beginning to play out the endgame of the Third World War—or the cold war, as it had come to be known. They had been branded as "cold warriors," and would continue in many circles in the United States and abroad to carry that stigma. But the cold war they were fighting was every bit as much a world conflict as the Second World War, in which I had first learned the craft of war, espionage, and diplomacy; or the First World War, in which my father, the French aide-de-camp to General Pershing, had earned his spurs. The President-elect at that moment was trying his best to learn all he could about his adversaries, his allies, and the kind of world conflict they were fighting. He had not even begun to think about the next world war, which would totally overshadow the final years of his presidency—the South-North War, the Fourth World War—and which may yet prove to be the most deadly of all.

Our meeting took place in the sprawling Los Angeles home of Alfred Bloomingdale, one of the President-elect's closest and oldest friends; however, our host did not take part in the meeting. We sat in easy chairs in the huge living room, just the President-elect and I, and for part of the time—the conversation went on for more than three hours—my old friend Arnaud de Borchgrave, who had helped arrange this first rendezvous with Mr. Reagan. When we were introduced, the President-elect broke into a broad grin and shook my hand.

"Ah, here's the man who said the Russians would be arriving in Afghanistan at exactly the right hour and the right day!" Mr. Reagan exclaimed to me.

Borchgrave had been chief foreign correspondent for *Newsweek* magazine when he passed through Paris in December 1979, on the eve of the Soviet invasion. He had completed one reporting assignment and, before pushing on to another, came by to see me, as he sometimes did. After we'd finished lunch, he asked, just in passing, where I thought he should go next. I said I thought Afghanistan might prove interesting. We'd had some very good intelligence that the Soviets might be stirring the pot there. Without telling me, Borchgrave returned to his hotel—the Lancaster, just off the Champs Élysées—packed his bags, and headed for Kabul. He pitched up there three days later, late at night, exhausted after the grueling trip halfway around the world. He was awakened the next morning by the sound of the Soviet troop carriers landing at the Kabul airport. He was the only international journalist on hand to witness the Soviet invasion firsthand. And he never let me forget the reason why.

So, the introductions made, it was not surprising that our talk turned first to Afghanistan. It was clear from the first that while the President had done a great deal of thinking about the problem, he had no fundamental understanding of his adversaries, nor any real plan for dealing with them.

I had brought with me from Paris eight large maps of the world and I spread them out on the living room table. For the next three hours, we conducted a tour of the world. We talked about the strengths and weaknesses of the power blocs—East and West, North and South. I pointed out that of the eight strategic minerals essential for building the arsenal of a major power, the Americans had four within their borders, while the Russians had all eight. We touched on the pressures of population and religion, politics and power. At the end of the session, the President asked if he could keep the maps I had brought. I agreed.

This California session was only the first of a series I held with Mr. Reagan over the years of his presidency. But perhaps the most memorable was our second encounter, shortly after he assumed office. That time, we met in the Oval Office, and Afghanistan had become a major preoccupation.

"Mr. President," I began after some initial pleasantries, "there are several ways to fight this sort of war. There's a massive way, and there's the intelligent way. And since we cannot send an expeditionary force of a million men to Afghanistan, may I suggest that we launch what I will call Operation Mosquito?"

"Why Mosquito?" he asked.

"Because a mosquito cannot kill a bear, but it can pester the bear so that it won't sleep anymore, it won't eat anymore, and will be flabbergasted by all the buzzing. Nobody has ever seen a bear kill a mosquito. So a mosquito can be a very dangerous foe. What I'm saying now is that if we can use imagination and intelligence, perhaps we can do something in Afghanistan."

"So what *is* the intelligent thing to do?" he promptly shot back.

This time, we needed none of the maps I had brought to our first talk in California. We were talking about the battlefields of the mind.

"My service has done an analysis of the forces of our adversary," I continued. "They have an army based on old-fashioned spit and polish, so we must attack them on the discipline side. For example, I know a group of people in Paris, young people, with no resources whatsoever. They publish Russian Bibles, in Cyrillic characters, on hand-presses. They are small artisans. But they know what they are doing, on a very minor scale of course. They are building a small black market for Bibles among the Red Army soldiers stationed in Afghanistan. Imagine, on a large scale, how exquisite a blow this would deliver to the Soviet Army there. We should send Bibles in

Russian to the troops in Afghanistan. We should flood the bazaars of Kabul with them. Moreover, the soldiers in turn will smuggle them back to Mother Russia. You can't fight ideas with tanks and aircraft. And in this business of intelligence, what I call active intelligence, you must fight ideas with ideas, words with words, and sometimes even lies with lies. Let the air force fight planes with planes and the army fight troops with troops and the navy fight ships with ships. We are supposed to be intelligent, so we must use imagination."

The President was smiling and urged me to press on.

"The second part of my plan is equally simple," I continued. "We have a group of young journalists in Paris who have developed an exact copy of the Soviet Army newspaper [*Krasnaya Zvezda,* or *Red Star*]. The same paper, the same typeface, the same style, but completely subversive. It has the air of *Krasnaya Zvezda,* but it is not. The articles tell the truth about the Red Army, about its failures in Afghanistan and elsewhere in the world. It could become the Axis Sally or Tokyo Rose of the Afghan war. We should print that and distribute it to the Russian soldiers there. Moreover, you can sell these Bibles, these newspapers on the black market for three thousand percent of the price of production when you smuggle them in. So it's even self-liquidating. And it will help destroy the discipline and the morale of the Soviet Army."

By this time, the President was grinning—he loved it.

"The third element, Mr. President, is perhaps the most diabolical. What do you do with all the drugs seized by the DEA, the Coast Guard, the FBI, the Customs Service?" I asked.

"Well," the President said, "I don't know. I suppose we destroy them."

"That's a mistake," I replied. "We should distribute them for free."

"Ahaah!" He spoke with a low voice and said, "Oh my God, whew."

I continued, because I could see he was shocked. "It's exactly the same thing the North Vietnamese did in Vietnam to your GIs; they organized this. If this works, you will so upset the Russians, there will be considerable pressure on them to pack up and go home to avoid moral and physical disintegration. That's what Operation Mosquito is about. That's intelligence. And that's what it's designed to do. To fight wars without a shot being fired in anger."

I paused for effect. "Moreover, the entire operation can be organized for a million dollars, no more, and with a few trusted people.

For a million dollars, because if you have more, it won't work. You know what you've got to do in this business—you've got to take your goddamn brain and squeeze it like a lemon."

"This is great," he exclaimed. "No one has ever told me anything like that." He grabbed for the secure phone, and called William Casey at the Central Intelligence Agency. Casey had just taken over as director of central intelligence. But he was more than that—a friend and confidant whom Reagan relied on deeply for advice about the most sensitive and potentially embarrassing projects, the high-risk projects that had both big upsides and big downsides. Reagan described just briefly what we had been discussing and told Casey he had to see me.

Two days later, I went to see Casey and repeated the outlines of Operation Mosquito to him. He loved it. A bear of a man, he leaped from the chair and sliced at the air with his fists.

"Let's do it," I said. "But, excuse me for saying this, Bill, if you do it, it'll be fucked up. You'll put five thousand guys to doing it, when you only need five."

He paused for a minute and asked slowly, "Would you do it, Alex?"

"Yeah," I said. "But no Americans. You can see them a mile away. Also, I've had lots of problems with the CIA's discretion. They cannot keep a secret. In my eleven years with French Intelligence, you're the sixth director of the CIA I've dealt with.

"Many times in Paris, the CIA station chief would say to me, 'Please don't finish your sentence. If I report what I know you are about to tell me, there is no guarantee it will remain secret.' "

Casey, a lawyer and political operative by profession, with no major intelligence experience since his World War II service in OSS, was clearly shocked. "What's wrong?"

"Look," I replied. "Some eighty or ninety percent of the operations you do covertly, do them openly. The ten percent you do covertly, do them really covertly."

But Operation Mosquito was different. He would have serious problems explaining it to Congress if he was asked. Still, Casey desperately wanted to do it.

So he said, "How are we going to do it?"

"No Americans," I repeated. "Because you can't keep a secret. We need the Pakistanis."

I immediately flew to Pakistan and made contact with the Paks, as Bill Casey called the Pakistanis. "It's very simple," I told them.

"All I ask from you is that when I will be at such a day, such an hour, in such a place, just look in the other direction." We wouldn't want to embarrass them. They agreed. I returned shortly to Washington and Bill Casey.

"Bill," I began, "we will need a little money."

"Hah, we've got so much money," he replied. "But how do we get it out to you? The only way we can do it is to give it to the Paks and they will finance Operation Mosquito."

Finally, we were ready. We had identified our Pakistani operatives and the Afghan freedom fighters who would be responsible for infiltrating the country with the contraband, be it drugs or propaganda. In Paris, the printing operation, set up in the cramped one-time garage that was the headquarters and cover, was awaiting only the funding and the go-ahead. The journalists, with the help of some of our intelligence analysts, were boning up on Afghanistan to produce the most authentic counterpropaganda newspaper possible.

Finally, all was in place, though I was becoming increasingly worried about the growing number of Americans who had become aware of the operation. I returned to see Casey in Washington with the word, and a final caveat. "We're all set," I began. "But I have one more condition."

"And what might that be?" he asked carefully.

"Can you guarantee me that I won't have my picture at the end of this on the front page of *The Washington Post* or *The New York Times*?"

"No, I can't guarantee that," he said solemnly.

"Then, Bill, forget it. I won't do it."

That was the end of Operation Mosquito. How far America under Ronald Reagan would go in fighting this new Fourth World War had been clearly established. It was never as far as we were prepared to go—indeed, did go—time after time. In my view, after the experience during the Third World War of the Western intelligence services being repeatedly crippled by America's reticence to act, we can no longer afford any real limits to fighting the Fourth World War or we will lose it. And Western civilization, as we will see, is truly at stake.

For eleven extraordinary years, I wielded, in all but total secrecy, great power. It was not the power of life or death, though there were occasions when that, too, I held in my grasp. Nor was it the power of the nuclear destruction of our planet that a small number of our national leaders have wielded, more or less intelligently, for brief periods. Rather I wielded the power of knowledge—the power to know virtually everything that can be known about the most interesting subjects in the world, and how to turn events to the advantage of my country and our allies. Those who have been there will truly understand how heady that power can be. We—the heads of the world's most formidable intelligence organizations—are a small and select club. And because we have formed bonds of mutual friendship and trust, this power does not entirely cease when we surrender our identity cards. For once a member of the club, one retains a lifelong thirst for knowledge and for understanding events; one also inevitably retains the means to satisfy it. The quid pro quo for the counsel we are able to provide those who now wield this power is the wisdom we have accumulated through countless crises, countless challenges to the security and well-being of our free world.

Still, for much of my life, this power has been tempered by another, powerful compact—a code of silence. It is as profound as any blood fealty sworn by a tribal chieftain. With lives and the fate of nations at stake, the knowledge and power wielded by those in my chosen profession are accompanied by a need to guard our crown jewels in the most profound secrecy.

My reason for breaking silence now is simple—I want to put into print what I have been saying privately for most of my life. I believe we are at war. This may appear somewhat bizarre given the unprecedented rapprochement between East and West, the newfound democracy in some of the Eastern European countries, the apparently benign attitude of the former Soviet empire. But our enemy of the past three quarters of a century has been replaced by new enemies, more frightening, perhaps ultimately even more dangerous enemies whom we must understand if we are to cope. For the democracies of the West, for the newly emergent democracies of the East, even for the Soviet empire itself, the Fourth World War has already begun, and our enemies, the fanatics, from all parts of the world, and those who control and use them, are around and among us. If they succeed in their conquests, their first victims may well be the very Islamic moderates who are now our friends and allies. These fanatics, whatever their religious persuasion, are the terrorists who undermine our democratic institutions; the dictators who prey like vampires on the underprivileged of the third world and turn them against our civilization; the drug dealers who have infiltrated our cities and under the guise of producing a drug-induced escape from the world sell the seeds of our destruction to those too young or innocent or foolish to realize that they are destroying their own future, and ours, just as surely as any fifth column operative.

The world today is a somewhat different place from the one I spent much of my career navigating. The cast of characters has changed. In this new world, we must also learn to fight a new kind of war—the kind that operations like Mosquito are a basis for fighting. It is a war in which intelligence and imagination will count for far more than might, in which certitude will count for more than threats, in which our very survival will depend on our swift yet judicious use of the extraordinary military power wielded by the developed nations. We are at a critical moment in history—at what promises to be the opening skirmishes of the Fourth World War, the South-North War—when we need to rethink our most fundamental concepts of intelligence and defense, all the imperatives that have guided strategic thinking since the onset of the Third World War, the cold war. Indeed, we have embarked on what may perhaps be the most deadly war of any fought in recorded time—a war that, even more than the promise of nuclear holocaust held out by the Third World War, has the very real prospect of ending civilization, at least Western civilization, as we know it. Always, as long as there are nuclear, bacteriological, or chemical weapons on the earth, there is the possibility of the extinction of all human life, indeed of all but the most primitive life-forms.

The Fourth World War could be a conflict of frightening, indeed titanic proportions, using weapons of terror never even conceived in previous conflicts. Many will be weapons created for previous conflicts, but mutated grotesquely under control of individuals operating with none of the restraints of any civilization we know and understand.

In the First and Second World wars, the principal enemy for we Europeans was among us—Europeans like Hitler and Mussolini, whose aims may have been psychotic, but whose mind-set was fundamentally Western and Northern. Hatred, power, and territorial gain were their motivations.

The Third World War—the cold war—was a conflict between East and West. It was a war of rival political systems—one camp, freedom, and in the other, moral, intellectual, and physical slavery—our opponents at times masquerading as proponents of a new religion without God, as communism portrayed itself. The leaders of the two sides were, like their earlier counterparts, men and women of a Northern, even a European, mentality. My goal during much of my term in office was to understand our adversaries in the Third World War and how best to deal with them.

The efforts I spent battling this one enemy, the Soviet empire, might seem at this point worthy of being consigned to the dustbin of history. The term "Soviet empire" and all that it implies signify a reality that might one day be a relic. But the craft of intelligence—the need to understand the enemy deeply—is as vital in dealing with our new foes in the South-North context of the Fourth World War as it was in dealing with our opponent in the East-West context of the Third World War. Moreover, it is as useful to understand one's friends and allies as it is to understand one's enemies—especially when a particular ally, or at least an associate, was until so recently one's bitter enemy. As with Germany or Japan, after the Second World War, if we learn these lessons of history, we will be well on our way to converting what was once a monolithic Soviet empire into a network of friends and allies who will stand shoulder to shoulder with us as we move into the most deadly battles of the Fourth World War. Let us hope this is not a dream.

During the years that I had the vast resources of French Intelligence, and some of the data and resources of the intelligence apparatuses of much of the Western world, at my disposal, I developed a few precepts about these newfound friends.

First, it was clear that the Soviet empire was the last regime of the extreme Right—the last of the old-fashioned colonial systems that Europeans should understand most deeply, but do not. It was an old-fashioned empire in the classical sense, trying to keep 130 or more different peoples or tribes under the rule of the paramount Russian tribe of white European ethnic stock, and in thrall to the state religion, communism. Before it finally shattered, it was at times easy to forget that this empire—part of a continent that stretches from the Atlantic Ocean to the Ural Mountains—was run only by Europeans, but Europeans still living a century or more in the past. The other side of the Urals, the Asian regions of the Soviet Union that stretch to the Pacific Ocean, constitutes by far the single largest landmass in the world, dwarfing entire countries including the United States or Canada.

Until the very end, the Russians guarded jealously—indeed, without question, still harbor—the dreams of world domination that we have outgrown. Theirs was a dream inspired by a belief articulated by Lenin that there is no steady state in world politics—that a nation must maintain a dynamic of expansion or begin at once to atrophy or break apart. "Violence," said Lenin, "is the midwife of history." Clearly this is part of the dynamic that led to the end of the Soviet empire, and the end, too, of the Third World War. As the Soviet system has crumbled, it has become ever less a military threat to its traditional enemies, though it remains a formidable military force. The East European Communist states have been the first to leave the empire. And what next? The Soviet Union itself has disintegrated. Each of these hundred-plus ethnic or linguistic nations of the empire, it must be remembered, was incorporated only after the most fearsome bloodshed.

My second precept in dealing with the Soviet empire was the recognition that for decades the Russians succeeded because they had mastered a plain fact of life that is well known today not only to them but to our other, newer, and perhaps even more lethal enemies as well: the fact that it is not necessary to conquer territory to possess people—that it is enough to conquer the mind and the soul. The territory follows automatically.

We in the West must begin to play on these battlefields of the mind. For too long, we have been altogether too honorable. I am all for the rules drawn up by the Marquis of Queensberry, but if you go into the ring wearing boxing gloves and come up against a fellow with a submachine gun, you're done for. You may look noble and splendid for ten seconds, but only your obituary will call you a hero.

We must begin to take a measure of our opponents in the far corner. We are fighting a war of the mind, today, on many fronts, against many adversaries. Before we can defeat them, or coopt them, we must understand them.

The lesson of the proposed Operation Mosquito, for instance, was not lost on William Casey—he understood the value of working on the minds and the hearts of our opponents, and not merely attacking their physical defenses. But even though the redoubtable Casey had learned that lesson, only rarely in the succeeding years was he ever able to apply it. I am convinced that George Bush also, during his earlier tenure as director of central intelligence, understood the dimensions of the problem. But even Mr. Bush, during his stay, was unable to change the methods of the CIA. He tried, certainly, and described to me at times the lengths to which he went to move this enormous bureaucracy in a direction that would have created a more effective intelligence apparatus. He had many valuable ideas. But it would have taken years, rather than the time he was given, to put them into effect.

We on the Atlantic rim—Europeans and Americans—think in the most conventional terms of war and peace, of politics and diplomacy, whether we are dealing with Soviet leaders from the Kremlin, or Middle Eastern terrorists whose minds are embedded firmly in some twelfth-century, medieval hell of their own manufacturing. It is, perhaps, our greatest failing. The best intelligence professional is one who can put himself in the position of his enemies—understanding how they think, how they conceive reality, and how they are motivated.

The third and final precept that I learned during my years of study of the Soviet empire-builders was that one of their great strengths—one that they shared with the terrorist regimes of the Middle East, which they also helped organize—is that they do not have our notion of time. They had no clock, and no deadlines. This explains in part their economic backwardness. Economic development has a brutal pace and imperative of its own. But from the point of view of history, it is very important not to look at the clock. We in the West have time frames that are far more compressed—we deal in weeks or months, not decades. It is yet another weakness we must learn to master.

In the office of the director general of French Intelligence, we used to play a variety of war games. In one, we would line up on different sides of the room, in front of the walls hung with huge maps of the world—the principal masses of armed forces of different empires marked by small colored flags—and assume the roles of different nations. Much of the time, one side or another would take the part of our Soviet adversaries. At other times, depending on the nature or immediacy of events, one team would assume the role of other nations of the Middle East—Iran, perhaps, or Iraq, Syria, or Libya. It was a role-playing that, alas, only rarely anticipated the events of recent months and years.

Certainly, we believed the dissolution of the Soviet empire was inevitable, and that a major conflagration was conceivable in the Middle East. Our analyses were quite simply off on the time frame. We thought the conflagration would come sometime at the beginning of the next century, perhaps, in a distant future that was only rarely worth the attention of strategists preoccupied with immediate events and crises. Similar analyses were going on in the war rooms of every intelligence service from Langley, Virginia, to Dzerzhinsky Square in Moscow—and all failed to anticipate events as they really played out.

We were on what turned out to be the cusp of the Fourth World War, and we did not realize it at the time. That conflict, which we have now joined, is something else indeed. In its starkest terms, it is one of South against North, poor and disorganized nations against rich, organized nations. Soon, there will be more than four billion people in these Southern nations, one billion in Africa alone, against one billion in all of the North. Who will be our new allies, and our new enemies, in this Fourth World War, and what will be the greatest challenge for our systems of intelligence and analysis? There will rarely be the same cast of characters from one skirmish, one episode, to the next—and that is central to the problem. Our enemies are and will continue to exist in a constantly shifting kaleidoscope—projecting a fanciful landscape where it will be difficult, at times impossible, to tell the good guys from the bad.

To identify them, all we can do is attempt to understand just where the boundaries between South and North are drawn, so that we will know at least which direction to look toward from one moment to the next.

Included in what we call the North, there are our traditional NATO allies of Western Europe and Canada; as well as other nations of the developed world like that great economic power, Japan. But there will also be new allies alongside us in this Fourth World War, which we are only beginning dimly to understand.

First among them, we hope, will be Russia without its colonies. Our political strategy should be to assist in the liberation of the Ukraine following on the independence of the Baltic States, so that on the eastern frontier of Europe we have not a supergiant of three hundred million, but merely a giant of two hundred million people. That weakened, though by no means powerless, Russian nation could be an important ally.

The years and the effort we devoted throughout my career in intelligence trying to understand his enemy. In my first conversation with President Reagan, I told him that for years our goal had been to contain the Soviet empire for we knew that its own inefficiencies would lead to its ultimate implosion and collapse. Effectively, we won the Third World War through those years of containment. At the same time, we were accumulating the corpus of knowledge or the skills to acquire the knowledge that we will need to win the Fourth World War.

I am firmly convinced that in preparing for a defense against the new forces of the South arrayed opposite us, we will not be alone, for there is little love lost between the most politically and militarily powerful components of what had been the Soviet Union and the Southern world. Iran, driven by its radical Shiite Muslim religion, sits directly on the Soviets' most vulnerable southern frontier. As a result, the Kremlin for years understood the need to penetrate the ranks of the Shiite clergy—some eighty-five thousand strong. And the information we have developed indicates that they have had some considerable success.

The Kremlin fears the ayatollahs of Iran even more than we do; hence the Russians' ongoing, though hardly successful, attempts to "organize" the lower ranks of the Shiite clergy in an effort to coopt them. Those Shiite religious leaders remain a potential source of propaganda and instability for what had been the Soviet Union's most volatile regions, their southern, Muslim republics. It is telling that the first serious armed insurrections against Soviet rule began in those very regions—Azerbaijan and Uzbekistan—as a product of religious fanaticism and frustration. Both the Soviet and Russian leaderships understand religious fanaticism even better than we do. The Communist state was, after all, founded on a quasi-religious ideology. Soviet Communists feared any fundamentalist belief that diverged from their own. They understood the power, but feared its imperialist tendencies.

Lenin often said that it is better to enter the fortress carrying a white flag than to remain outside carrying a red flag. He, better than many of his Soviet successors, certainly better than nearly all his counterparts in the West, accepted the value of understanding his adversaries, and his allies—and of coopting them for his own use.

Many of the contemporary fundamentalist Islamic states, and many of those who act in their behalf, share goals, and above all a mentality that dates back eight hundred years. We cannot deal with them if we judge them as we have our adversaries of the last half of the twentieth century. We must put ourselves in the place of Europeans of the eleventh or twelfth century. I think then we might understand better what is going on in Iran and the Middle East.

Let's not forget some of the newly independent nations that

were once the chattel of the Soviet Union. Today, the term "union" itself is a misnomer. Whatever union prevailed since the earliest days of Lenin and Stalin, down through Khrushchev, Brezhnev, and their successors, was enforced by the KGB and the Red Army, as well as the now all but powerless Communist party. The disintegration of the Soviet empire represents the final step in the process that may be called decolonization. The French and the British lost their colonies earlier in this century, as did the Belgians, the Dutch, the Japanese, and even the Americans. Now this wave of decolonization has reached the Soviet empire. First its Eastern European colonies—Poland, Hungary, Czechoslovakia, Rumania, even the most reliable colonies of all, East Germany and Bulgaria—began splitting off. Now the colonies of the Soviet Union itself—the Baltic and Asian republics—have broken away—a prospect as profoundly revolutionary from the Kremlin's perspective as if California suddenly decided it deserved to be an independent nation.

We Western nations have been left with the economies of the Eastern European states in need of a lot of help. Poland, Rumania, Bulgaria, and to a lesser extent Hungary and Czechoslovakia, will tax our resources to the maximum. But we should help them, particularly if they are truly to abandon the concepts of communism that have been so deeply ingrained.

What we are really discussing here is the new shape of Europe. The new realities of power and the new dynamics of Europe will affect deeply the interplay of forces, the ability and desire of these nations to cooperate for the common good. The map of central Europe is being redrawn for a third time in our century.

As a young French liaison officer, I was a close witness, in my days beside Charles de Gaulle and the other Allied leaders at the end of the Second World War, to its last redrawing. But now we are entering the post-Yalta period, with a new balance of power on the Continent. There is, for instance, a new anchor to Europe—Germany. Today, the nation that has been divided for a half century is once again one state, one country, with one language, one culture, and one people driven by the same work ethic. It is home to eighty million Germans, and has become a major power concentrated in the center of Europe. If you add all the German-speaking and more or less German-thinking people all around these countries, including in the Soviet states, you get ninety million.

At each Olympics, when the results came into my office, I used to add the number of gold, silver, and bronze medals won by both

Germanies. Together, they always had won the most, more than the United States or the Soviet Union. That is a sign, a very important sign of German prowess.

Arrayed on the other side in the Fourth World War are the most pernicious forces of the South—pernicious in the sense of the violence they are prepared to unleash, at times in pure desperation; pernicious, too, in the sense of the imperatives of population, hunger, and poverty that drive them. They are the nations ruled and driven by dictators, not those Southern nations, our friends and allies, who believe that stability is the best means of achieving prosperity for their people, but nations like Iran, Iraq, and Libya, for instance. These countries' leaders have harnessed their populations and their oil revenues to the promotion of their own agendas that are fundamentally opposite to their Northern foes. On this side of the line there will be the new breed of superpowers of the South—every bit as powerful in their way as the old, traditional superpowers of the North.

In all of those Southern nations there are forces at work—pressures of population, hunger, disparate religious beliefs, historic prejudices, and hatreds—that we have never really experienced in dealing with our enemies of the First, Second, and Third World wars. They are centrifugal forces that may influence these nations' ability to wage war against the North as profoundly as internal political disagreements among the democratic nations of the West affected our ability to wage war against our enemies in past global conflicts. Those centrifugal forces of the new South will influence the entire definition of the terms of engagement.

But there is more at issue here than an exchange of one form of tyranny for another. Otherwise we would simply have a continuum, a seamless segue from one phase of the Third World War to the next. This time, the very essence of the enemy embodies a new form—which is what makes the Fourth World War so much more deadly, and desperate. Our enemy this time is the theological fanatic. Such a fanatic will never be happy as long as there is one member of his detested opposition left alive. That is the case in Lebanon, where Muslim fanatics are pitted against Christians. The fanatics will never be happy as long as there is one Christian left in their land. And after the Christians come the Jews. The Muslim fanatics want every other religion driven from their part of the world. This fanaticism is the heart of the civil war in Lebanon, of the Israeli-Palestinian conflict, of the recent Gulf war portrayed by Saddam

Hussein as Muslim against Christians and Jews. And it will be the heart of increasingly broader conflicts as the battles of the Fourth World War continue to spread. It is, effectively, the last act of the Crusades of the Middle Ages.

Today's South is producing the kind of irrational leader with whom we are not accustomed to dealing. Nikita Khrushchev could remove his shoe in the middle of the United Nations General Assembly session, pound it on the table, and scream, "We will bury you." The irony is that the Russians without the massive help of the West would bury themselves. That was theatrics. Khrushchev, and all his predecessors and successors, played fundamentally by rules that we were able to understand. They were European rules— Northern rules. Not Southern. Somehow, the same latitudes are on the same wavelength mentally, but not the same longitudes.

Along with our new enemies comes a whole new set of rules of the game that have been imposed by those nations that are waging the Fourth World War from the South. In many respects, we are marking a return to our most barbaric past—to a time before democracy when the rule of might was the only concept of government universally understood. There was no concept of right versus wrong. No real moral compass.

All our old assumptions of stability and security—the way we make war and guarantee peace—are going out the window on a daily basis as we plunge pell-mell toward the twenty-first century.

Throughout the history of warfare, it has never been possible to reply to new arms with old. At the time the bow and arrow was invented as a weapon, the human muscle provided the firepower. Then an obscure and nameless Italian invented something called the crossbow—an instrument that no longer depended on the arm of the archer, but on a mechanical device. It was believed at the time, in the mid-fifteenth century, that this was the ultimate weapon. For the first time, the chain-mail coat could be pierced by an arrow. Those who used the crossbow were ordered excommunicated by the church. Indeed, the Lateran Council of 1139 outlawed its use against Christians. Yet it was inevitable that this weapon would ultimately prevail. It ushered in a new form of warfare. Ever since, each new revolution in armament was to have as volcanic an effect on the stability of the world order.

Terrorism is the latest such weapon in the South-North conflict of the Fourth World War. It replaces, or could conceivably use in frightening new ways, the nuclear arms that were the ultimate weapons of the Third World War.

For the past forty years, our security was guaranteed by what has now become an all but archaic concept called Mutually Assured Destruction. MAD was a simple construct in its basic form, a balance of nuclear terror. If one side launched its nuclear weapons for whatever reason, the opposing side would have enough weapons in reserve after the initial salvo to launch its own nuclear missiles and destroy the other. Or the enemy could react quickly enough to launch its own missiles while the enemy's were in the air. Retaliation was entirely up to the President, who had a clear choice. If they fired their weapons, he pushed the button. He didn't have to go to Congress, to intelligence oversight committees, for permission. He just did it. He had only a matter of seconds, at best minutes, before the missiles hit. The system was inexorable and it was irrefutable. It worked largely because neither side was willing to test its assumptions. It worked because it was between nations who shared the same respect for the essential value of individual human life. It was all taken on faith. Above all, it worked because the consequences were so horrific.

The one eyeball-to-eyeball confrontation of the Third World War, the Cuban missile crisis, was really a very tame game of blindman's buff. Nobody really believed the Soviets would touch off the end of the world by dropping the Bomb. You could not cry wolf under MAD. You either pushed the button, or you didn't.

Today, the MAD of the nuclear age must give way to a new concept for the postnuclear age. Indeed, the unilateral decision by the Bush administration in September 1991 to do away with short-range nuclear forces marked the official recognition that MAD has been relegated to the dustbin of history. The successor to Mutually Assured Destruction for our time might be called simply "Certain Destruction." What will it take to strike terror into the hearts of those who would use the physical and intellectual weapons of terrorism without fear of retaliation because of a collective failure of will on the part of their enemies? Indeed, what happens in the Fourth World War if terrorists or their national champions make use of atomic, biological, or chemical weapons that will make any conflict that has gone before barely a shadow of war.

So it behooves us to make it crystal clear that the new strategy governing the Fourth World War is Certain Destruction. Overstep the acceptable boundaries by a millimeter, and you will assuredly be destroyed—thoroughly and completely, without hesitation. This system has not worked so far. The concept of Certain Destruction in a conventionally armed world has already been repeatedly tested. And so far, with a few exceptions, it has failed each test. It has failed to assure the destruction of those who have used terrorism as a weapon. When terrorists supposedly destroyed Pan Am Flight 103 over Lockerbie, Scotland, there was no retaliatory bombing of the presidential palace of Colonel Muammar Qaddafi in Tripoli. That would have been the reaction mandated by a policy of Certain Destruction.

In some respects, the idea of Certain Destruction is almost biblical in its proportions—a return full-circle to the concept of "an eye for an eye." Effectively, the Fourth World War in many ways marks a return to our most primitive origins. The medieval mentality of an Iranian ayatollah is effectively defining the strategic concepts of the twenty-first century. We must be fully prepared to accept these new rules, to arrive at a new balance of power, or terror, to assure the peace—to make sure that Certain Destruction succeeds Mutually Assured Destruction as the strategic concept preventing the global destruction of a Fourth World War.

The conflict that will unfold as the Fourth World War may never involve mass action of any sort. Battles may involve massive movements of troops, as in Operation Desert Storm. But the fighting will undoubtedly also be waged by small, highly deadly units of terrorists who are already in place, carefully camouflaged among the immigrant populations from Southern nations who are already living in each of our Northern capitals.

This is why intelligence, and the world's premier intelligence services, will play an even more critical role in this war than in the three global conflicts that have preceded it in this century.

Those intelligence services understand the need for and value of infiltration—a key arm in the arsenal of the terrorist. They understand how to use it and how to counter it. The Allies made use of it throughout much of Europe in the Second World War. It was the cornerstone of the Resistance movement in occupied Europe. At the end of that conflict, as the Third World War quietly kicked in, Stalin moved infiltration to a higher plateau. A colonel of the KGB who defected to the West once disclosed a meeting that took place in the Kremlin with Stalin presiding. Stalin at that point had decided to get rid of some three million Jews in the Soviet Union by "allowing" them to emigrate. But among the three million, he ordered, there should be at least twenty thousand KGB agents. That policy, the defector told us, has continued ever since. They were present even today in Operation Exodus, the latest wave of Jewish immigration to Israel from the Soviet Union.

But in the Fourth World War, rather than acting as mere agents for intelligence gathering, such infiltrators will become the engines of destruction and battle as well. The Fourth World War will be a terrorist war.

There will be certain nations of the South that will use terrorism more effectively, more predictably as an instrument of war and military or state policy than other nations. Today, it is clear that Libya, Syria, Iran, and Iraq, for instance, are the principal supporters of this kind of warfare. Moreover, there are certain traditions in each, deep forces within their history, that make them more likely than others to turn to terrorism as a weapon of battle against the North.

During the caliphate, when greater Turkey ruled much of the Muslim world from Constantinople, there was a group called the Hashishim—the Assassins—members of the Nizari Ismailgah, a religiopolitical Islamic sect that considered murdering its enemies a religious duty. They were from what is now northern Iraq, and they were the first to use terrorism, albeit in a primitive form, as a weapon of war. Marco Polo brought back the first tales of the young people who had been chosen for the profession of assassination. They would be given hashish and taken to a far corner of a mountain castle. There, they would find themselves in a magic garden, surrounded by marvelous fields. It was, they were told, the garden of Allah. There would be singing birds, beautiful flowering trees, perfumed brooks, magnificent women. They would be left to wander for a time through this paradise, to taste its fruits and experience its joys and pleasures.

Then they would be taken away and told, "Now you have seen a sample of paradise." And they were each given a stiletto, the terror weapon of the seraglio and the caliphate, and told further, "You are assassins. You may have to die in the course of your duties. But if you die you will go straight to paradise. And you have had a glimpse of paradise." Their corps of devoted terrorists operating from strongholds throughout Persia and Iraq claimed countless victims among the generals and statesmen of the Abbasid caliphate, as well as some caliphs themselves. The assassins were a feared force for two centuries until the Mongol invasion. Yet even today, the sect claims followers scattered across Syria, Persia, and Central Asia. And its legacy permeates the corridors of power.

Today's terrorist weapons are merely more sophisticated versions of the assassin's dagger, yet more insidious and dangerous than before. During the Crusades, it often happened that the enemies met at banquets or feasts, before or after the battles. On one of those occasions, Saladin, one of the great leaders of the Muslim side, received some of the European chiefs. Among them was Richard the Lion-Hearted, King of England, a great, powerful man who fiercely wielded a two-handed sword.

"This is how we wage war," said the king. He took the sword, set an iron helmet on the table, and smote it with a mighty blow, denting it.

He turned to Saladin. "Now let us see how you do it!" he exclaimed.

Saladin replied, "We each have our own methods." He took a silk scarf he was wearing and dropped it on his razor-sharp scimitar. And the scarf was cut in two. "This is another method of war." Saladin smiled thinly. The kinds of battles that will be fought in the Fourth World War will be fought by the kinds of nations that have inherited the mantle of the caliphate and the Ottoman Empire. We are, effectively, embarked on the new Crusades. The North lost the last Crusades nearly a millennium ago. We must not, we cannot, lose the ones on which we are now embarking. The old Crusades were acts of conquest for the West. The next Crusades will be acts of self-defense.

We must also not allow ourselves to forget that these new Crusades we are calling the Fourth World War may take place as far from our shores as those our medieval ancestors once set forth to win. At the same time, they may be as close as the corner cinema.

We must be prepared to sacrifice our lives near and far. Our adversaries, who are all around us, are willing to sacrifice theirs, prepared to die for their beliefs. We are not. Our beliefs are too deeply based on material happiness.

The terrorist regimes of the Middle East understand these weaknesses of ours. They resort to blackmail and assassination with impunity. They seek our vulnerabilities and have found them. They are as implacable in their own way as the Soviets we cherished as foes for the past decades, but far less scrutable. We must seek to understand them. Profoundly. That is one of the main roles of intelligence today.

We have embarked on a period of enormous uncertainty in the Middle East, creating a window of great opportunity. It is a time to put pressure on our enemies—pressure that our foes will understand, pressure on their terms—while building up our friends. The ultimate objective of our intelligence will be to provide a full and unbiased picture of the world to the leaders of our countries, so that they may act with wisdom and understanding. That has always been my view. It is, alas, not fully shared by most contemporary American leaders.

The American system is very different from the European. The Americans ignore the concept of *la raison d'état,* "the affair of state," which should be used, in the world of intelligence, as an excuse only for the most critical actions. They believe that it has no place in American policy. But my most profound belief is that it must be available, and without recriminations or reprisals. I once told President Reagan how strongly I believed in *la raison d'état,* which may outweigh any conventional morality. It is something we Europeans have understood for centuries.

But if ever there was a need for *la raison d'état,* it is to fight those most pitiless enemies—the terrorist nations of the South. Because they are utterly without any of the moral scruples that have served to control our actions in civilized times, we must be prepared to drop our mantle of civility and do battle with them on their terms.

This work is an attempt, in a sense, to rewrite our collective history, or at least to reveal a corner that lingers in obscurity. Without an understanding of some of the dynamics of the first three conflicts of this century, we will be entering the fourth world conflict half blind and half deaf.

As one of the longest-standing leaders of Western intelligence, I have learned that there are two sorts of history. There is the history we see and hear, the official history; and there is the secret history— the things that happen behind the scenes, in the dark, that go bump in the night. When one has a true worldview, both become comprehensible. Both are essential. As a player in the first and a manipulator in the second, I have attempted to bring to my work the kind of understanding of both aspects of history that is vital if we are to be able to function in a world increasingly dominated by pernicious forces seeking to undermine our most fundamental values and basic institutions.

Above all, what we need is an attitude of cool appraisal. And if there is any message in this book, it is that through three world wars, there is one constant that has assured our victory—the cool appraisal of the nature of our adversary.

None of our adversaries in the Fourth World War is less worthy subjects of such dispassionate appraisal than were our adversaries in the three global conflicts that came before. In each case, it has been not only appropriate but essential that we bring to bear on it the experience of a lifetime of sifting countless tiny pieces of information and, as in a giant puzzle, assembling them into patterns that make sense. The opinions of our collective maladies that we dare to set forth in these pages are more often those of a general practitioner than of a specialist. But they should be no less worthy of consideration.

CHAPTER 2

The Man Within the Cloak

I belong to an old family that paid dearly in the first two world wars. In the First World War, my father was seriously wounded. In 1918, his brother Henri was killed. In 1945, my aunt died in the Nazi concentration camp Ravensbrück.

The arts of war, and of espionage in the national interest, run deep in this family. On my father's side, our roots reach back to the Piedmont in the thirteenth century, to the Franche-Comté in 1452. We have served the Dukes of Burgundy, the House of Austria, and, after Louis XIV conquered the Franche-Comté, France itself. My mother was of French Huguenot extraction. Her forebears left the Old World for Santo Domingo (then called Hispaniola) after Louis XIV signed the Revocation of the Edict of Nantes at Fontainebleau in 1685, putting an end to the rights enjoyed by Protestants, or Huguenots, in France, and some two hundred thousand departed. Later, at the time of the slaves' revolt under Toussaint-Louverture in 1794, her family fled again, to the United States. They came there on a Dutch ship that happened to be loading cargo in the harbor of Port-au-Prince and agreed to take them. I've seen letters from our early ancestors to their French cousins who had remained in the Périgord region of France, describing their battles for survival on the southern tip of what would later be New York City, and is now Wall Street, that were every bit as hair-raising as my own battles would be two centuries later in the global conflicts of twentieth-century Europe.

"Again, last night," read one of the letters, "we were attacked by Indians with flaming arrows from beneath the walls, and the arrows hit the wooden walls of our houses which caught fire. All night we were passing buckets of water. And with the help of the Lord and lots of passing of buckets of water, and because we took refuge behind the wall, we made it, and thank God we are safe this morning when I am writing you this letter."

One might almost say that this was my family's earliest experience with a form, albeit primitive, of terror warfare. Clearly, we had learned early how to survive in such a world.

My mother was born in New York. She came to visit France in the summer of 1917, at the start of the American involvement in the First World War. She had been very interested in her ancestors' country. There was also a great romantic feeling for France at the turn of the century in America. Moreover, she had been converted to Catholicism. Her chaperone in France was the Marquise de Salignac-Fénelon, who was from a great French family. At the time she arrived in France, General "Black Jack" Pershing had established his headquarters in eastern France at the Château de Ciney, where Voltaire had lived at one time, and which happened to be the ancestral home of the marquise. One weekend, the general, in consultation with his hostess, invited some guests from the American colony in Paris to a dinner party, and my mother, who was then a beautiful young widow, once married to Wallace Monahan, a businessman with American Standard Co., was among them. General Pershing was accompanied by Colonel George Marshall, the head of his G-4 or personal office; and his aide-de-camp, Lieutenant George Patton. Pershing had met Patton on an expedition in Mexico against the outlaw Pancho Villa in 1916. Patton was assigned to Pershing because he was a cavalryman and there was a brigade of American cavalry in the first American Expeditionary Force in Europe—the same unit that George Washington had served in. It also served as a ceremonial brigade. Patton had also studied at Saumur, the French military academy.

My mother and my father—at the time, General Pershing's French aide and liaison with the Supreme Headquarters—met at that dinner party.

My father died when I was eleven, leaving a terrible gap in my life; he was an amazing man—handsome, tall and strong, brave, cultivated, and modest. As a boy, he had been a pupil of Charles de Gaulle's father, Henri, who was head of studies at the College of the Immaculate Conception, on the Rue de Vaugirard in Paris. A few years later, my father met Charles de Gaulle at Arras when they were brother officers in the 33rd Arras Infantry commanded by Marshal Pétain. My father was badly wounded at Dinan on the Belgian frontier, and was awarded one of the first Légions d'Honneur of the First World War.

He and De Gaulle met again at the Battle of Berry-au-Bac in 1916, where Father was again wounded and De Gaulle taken prisoner. After that, since he was no longer fit for active service, my father was assigned to the staff of General Pershing, who commanded the American forces at the French front. Among the volunteers he trained were the young George Marshall, George Patton, Omar Bradley, and Douglas MacArthur. Thirty years later, "Pershing's Boys" commanded the Allied forces in the Second World War, and as son of their former brother-in-arms, I often benefited from my ties with them. Apparently, they trusted that the understanding of the art of war had managed somehow to be passed on to the son of the man who had so capably trained them.

As a child, I spoke three languages, a tribute to my French origins, my German governess, and my Irish and English nannies. We were an undemonstrative family. One of my childhood memories revolves around Nanny whispering that Mother was coming to kiss me good night. A beautiful lady swept into the nursery, wearing a triple row of pearls. She bent over me, saying, *"Au revoir!"* The door closed. The car roared away. Mother had gone out to dine.

I was educated first at Les Roches, a well-known school in Normandy, then spent a few years in Switzerland, at Fribourg. But since I went to war at eighteen, I am largely self-taught. Certainly, I am no intellectual. All my family asked was that their children be sensible, know how to express themselves, and be able to ride a horse reasonably well.

My mother and my Aunt Ethel, Mrs. Henry Downe, a very prominent figure in the American colony in Paris, had adjacent town houses.

As my mother's family ties made us one of the leading families associated with that colony in Paris in those days, we had many visitors. It was from those individuals that I learned the ways that diplomacy and intelligence, military strategy and politics, all intersect in a complex kaleidoscope that shifts as a result of the various ways nations relate to each other and their own peculiar histories and traditions.

One of our regular visitors in those early years was a wonderful young gentleman named Robert Murphy, who was then a third secretary at the American embassy. We all loved him and he became very attached to us. So whenever there were parties at Aunt Ethel's town house, William Bullitt, the American ambassador, an intimate friend of Uncle Henry and Aunt Ethel's, was always invited, and Murphy was brought along. He later became a figure of extraordinary importance to the entire Allied war effort in the Second World War as President Roosevelt's personal diplomatic emissary in Europe. He was, coincidentally, to play a key role in my life.

Family connections, not to mention the impressions that were formed in my earliest years by my meeting some of the people who have shaped the history of our times, were to play important roles in my future career. Marshal Foch held me on his knee. Marshal Pétain signed the registry at my parents' wedding. One of my earliest memories was of General Pershing when he first came to our home in Normandy for a weekend lunch. It was about eighty kilometers from Paris, and he arrived in a large black car. At one moment in the afternoon, he took me by the hand. We got into his car, drove to the village cemetery in Normandy, and stood in front of my father's tomb. On the way back, he told me at great length about my father, what a fine officer and gentleman he had been, and how much he had helped the American effort in the First World War.

I will never forget September 3, 1939. The date is etched permanently in my memory. I was hay-making at a school in Fribourg, Switzerland, when news of the declaration of war broke like a thunderclap. I returned immediately to France and military service. It was our first experience with the tactic of war called the blitzkrieg, or lightning war, a total assault by fast-moving motorized columns that surprised, then overwhelmed the defending forces and that proved to be the single tactic most distinguishing the Second World War from each of the other three world conflicts of the twentieth century. In the lightning advance of the German forces, the French Army was smashed in less than a month. That magical shield, the Maginot Line—heavy, outdated concrete fortifications strung across northern France, designed to protect the nation from all hostile invaders and deemed impenetrable—had indeed never been breached. But it was simply ignored by the fast-moving and highly mobile invaders as irrelevant. They circumnavigated it, leaving it as a sorry tribute to bad military judgment and an inability or unwillingness to understand our enemy and adapt to new strategic realities. Such fortifications were relics of a previous era of warfare; the fixed-position trench combat that had characterized the First

World War was rendered obsolete by the weaponry and tactics employed in the Second. Ill prepared, stupid, lacking organization, and crippled by political intrigue, the French High Command could not bring itself to confront the new military realities of the Second World War. Blinded by their historical perspective and unable to see past the conventional wisdom, they ignored the early warnings of intelligence as the new tactics unveiled themselves in the invasions of Czechoslovakia and Poland—those rapid strikes into central and eastern Europe that proved to be merely an hors d'oeuvre before the campaign in the West. Crippled by their blindness to reality, the French military also faced an overwhelmingly superior force, driven by better organization and with the momentum of surprise behind it.

The German blitzkrieg against France, in short, was my first experience with the utter failure of military intelligence and civilian planning. A young draftee in the French Army at the time, I saw paths choked with refugees in horse-drawn vehicles, fleeing they hardly knew where, barreling pell-mell down the road, fighting for space with the rear guard of our own troops in equally panicked disarray. In pursuit were the German advance guard in their long gray overcoats often mounted on motorcycles with Zundapp sidecars; well equipped, mobile, highly motivated.

Eventually, I made my way back to my family estate in Normandy, where the talk among my friends and neighbors was all of General de Gaulle's call to fight on. The young French general had refused to cave in to the armistice signed so quickly and cowardly by Marshal Pétain. Instead, De Gaulle had fled to London, where on June 18, 1940, he launched his celebrated call to arms and resistance. In fact, I had signed on for the duration of the war, and listening to the words of De Gaulle, I concluded that the war had by no means finished for me because of the German occupation. While the fighting continued, I was determined to participate in it. It was as simple as that.

I had an opportunity to board a Polish ship leaving for England, where I might have joined General de Gaulle and many of my countrymen. But before I could think of leaving to resume the battle, I had to put my personal affairs in order. My Normandy farms were wrecked by the German advance and had been deserted. Gradually, my farmhands and neighbors straggled back in their carts. They had nowhere else to go. Though my home had been sacked by the advancing troops, much of the livestock remained. The Germans clearly realized they'd need them in the coming years of occupation. There was no telephone, no electricity. I had more than one thousand acres of arable land, and pasture suitable for raising the best grades of beef cattle. In all, I had 120 head of cattle. That was to cause us a lot of trouble, since they were clearly prime targets for the occupying German Army.

France had been divided in two. The northern half, which included my Normandy home, was occupied and run directly by the German government and military administration based in Paris. There was no pretense that this was still France. The southern half was still, ostensibly, French territory, run by a French government based in Vichy. But it was all a sham. The Vichy government was merely a puppet of the German occupiers. It had only one advantage. It allowed the Americans to maintain an embassy in what was really German territory—and that embassy became an ideal center for anti-Nazi espionage and assistance to the French Resistance. I and hundreds of my colleagues were to make good use of this tiny window on what was left of the free world.

I did not have anything against the German people, but I did not like the idea of a nation coming into your home when they are not invited. Throughout my stay in Normandy, while I began my underground service with the Resistance in occupied territory in 1940, I tried to behave in an outwardly exemplary fashion—then as now, that was the first rule for an intelligence agent operating behind enemy lines, but a rule that can often only be learned by the most perilous trial and error. So I refused to take any part in the black market, though one way or another I managed to find bicycle tires (which were quite rare) and winter boots. I had no personal, social contact with the Germans, though since I spoke German, I was often called on to represent our little village to the occupying authorities.

I used to say to the Germans, on the rare occasions when they would pay me an official visit, "I won't ask you to sit down, because if our positions happened to be reversed, I don't think you would ask me to."

My own home was requisitioned from the outset. I moved into another, much smaller house with walls a yard thick. One Sunday morning, cars pulled up outside with a screech of tires, and my housekeeper rushed upstairs to say, "The Germans are here!"

Together with my friend, George D., who was a Jew, I had spent most of the previous night cleaning the cache of arms we were storing for the Resistance, and which we usually kept hidden under a heap of potatoes in the old pigeon loft. Thinking we would finish the job the next evening, we had left them stacked in a cupboard in my bedroom on the first floor of the little house.

The Wehrmacht officer showed me a folded sheet of paper. "According to this anonymous letter, you have arms hidden here," he said sharply.

It was a terrible moment. "Do you realize what will happen if we find these weapons?" he continued. "You will be shot."

"I would most certainly do the same in your place," I replied.

"Now, with your permission, we will make a thorough search," he continued, without the least suggestion in his voice that my permission really counted for very much at all.

I visualized my own execution. The idea was far from amusing, particularly at the age of twenty. I found it difficult not to tremble or change color, and tried to show no emotion at all—an ability that I was to find most useful many times in my career as an intelligence officer.

All day they searched the château, close to the house, and probed the lake. All day I kept saying to myself that they might come back and take my house apart. I even envisioned their finding in the château weapons I had never put there.

What would I say then? "That machine gun has nothing to do with me?"

They found nothing in the château, of course. Tired by their fruitless search, thanks to one last miracle they did not even bother to search my little house. And they never returned. Fortunately, too, they had been officers of the Wehrmacht, the regular military occupation officials; they behaved correctly. It was another matter if one's business was with the Gestapo, the feared and hated secret police.

Throughout the duration of the war, I was rarely surprised by the occupation forces. They behaved as one would expect them to behave in a strange and hostile land, seizing every opportunity offered by my fellow countrymen.

Once, not long after my brush with the Wehrmacht, an elderly laborer from my village was imprisoned for some minor offense. I went to the local commandant to protest. The German was an old cavalry officer, and we got to talking first about horses, then about his situation, which he clearly did not relish.

"They didn't send me to Russia because of my age," he complained, "but I have a nasty job here. And the worst of it is the stream of anonymous letters your compatriots send me, denouncing their friends and neighbors. Look here!"

He opened a cupboard stuffed with bundles of paper, tied in sheafs of a hundred. "Anonymous letters," he sniffed. "What do you think of that?"

Having already been a victim of one of those letters myself, I could scarcely admit total surprise. What did astonish me, though, was the flagrant hypocrisy of so many of my countrymen. Returning to France at the end of the war, I would discover that forty-two million people, virtually the entire population of France at the time, had "fought for the Resistance." In Normandy, it seemed that those ersatz Resistance heroes had been quite willing to serve as stooges for the Gestapo until some point toward the end of the war when they concluded that the Allies might indeed triumph.

Yet while I tended my own property, watched over my château, and dealt with the local German authorities, awaiting my chance for a full role in the war, I did what I could to help the Resistance in this small corner of France. Together with other friends in the occupied zone, I made sketches of military installations and delivered them to the Allies at the embassies or other offices they had installed alongside the French puppet government at Vichy. Moreover, I knew a couple of Americans in high diplomatic positions, for example, Admiral William Leahy, who later became President Roosevelt's chief of staff at the White House; and journalists like Ralph Forte, United Press bureau chief in Madrid for many years, who had also served as special adviser to Ernest Hemingway for all the bullfighting sequences in the novel *For Whom the Bell Tolls*.

With their help, I managed to undertake some exciting journeys between my base of operations in Normandy and Vichy. Basically I served as a courier. I observed and took pictures of German military airports being built in Normandy and brought those documents to the American embassy in Vichy or to my friend Ralph Heinzen, an American journalist based in Vichy. It was an interesting introduction to espionage, as those documents had to be carried across a closely guarded frontier—while traveling on foot often in difficult weather conditions—from the occupied territory into Vichy, where the Allies could pick them up at their embassies for transmission overseas. Moving in the dead of night, along country roads, being relayed by various Resistance groups along the way, I learned valuable lessons in operational maneuvers and intelligence. At the same time, I set up a network in the Eure, which continued to function until the moment I made the decision to escape across the Pyrenees.

It was during this period that I began to realize that intelligence is made up of thousands of little clues, like the pieces of a jigsaw puzzle. The intelligence functions of the Resistance consisted principally of gathering the routine information about German military operations that would be vital to tracking the position of Nazi forces if an Allied invasion was to be mounted. At the same time, that kind of intelligence was indispensable to the Resistance forces conducting the sabotage missions that kept the occupying forces constantly off guard. The more the occupation regime could be kept off balance, the more resources it would need for purely defensive work, and the less effective would be its hold over the French people. Thus it would be more likely to distrust every Frenchman, and would less readily form friendships and alliances with my countrymen. In short, I learned that intelligence and the actions that spring from such information can play as vital a role in winning a war as any frontal assault.

Finally, when I turned twenty-one years old, I made the decision to leave France and resume my active military career with a Free French or Allied unit. My intelligence network was well established and functioning in the occupied territories, with an efficient and regular means of communication with the Allies in Vichy. Using that same network, passing from farmhouse to farmhouse, I managed to cross the Pyrenees into Spain, en route to North Africa. Posing as an American, which was not difficult given my command of the English language, after a brief stay in jail in Spain, having illegally entered the country masquerading as an American citizen but without papers, I was allowed to enter Gibraltar. My first sight there was a Royal Marine, perfectly turned out in his formal military dress, guarding the border-crossing barricade. For me, he symbolized everything we were fighting for, the entire free world.

After a short trip across the Mediterranean, I arrived finally in Algeria, where I joined the 2nd Regiment of Algerian Spahis—the native Algerian Army that was fighting with the Free French in North Africa. They were professional soldiers with iron discipline, and I began to learn the military craft that was to serve me well later.

We were stationed in the Er Rif border at Tlemcen, an outpost that boasted an extraordinary blend of French panache and Hollywood glamour—brilliant sun, vivid colors, horses, beautiful women; it was a real Foreign Legion-style setting. But I quickly learned that we were not fighting a war in any classic sense. Quite simply, there was no action against the German forces within a thousand miles of the Spahi base.

So after a few months, I asked to be sent back to Algiers. The Algerian French, whom we now call the pieds noirs, were being mobilized to fight under General Alphonse Juin. Juin was to become the great French commander of the Second World War, and next to De Gaulle he was the principal liaison with the Americans and the Allied general staff. De Gaulle himself later promoted him to the rank of marshal. Juin was assembling the Free French forces in North Africa at the same time the other Allies had begun disembarking their own troops. Australians, New Zealanders, South Africans, Canadians—they came from every part of the British Empire. And of course there were the Americans. Trying to mold all these disparate elements into a unified fighting force was a formidable task.

It fell to General Juin and his British counterpart, General Sir John Anderson, to take the lead in this operation. They had hit it off from the start—when the British First Army first hurled itself against Rommel and his formidable Afrika Korps, forcing the great German marshal into a controlled withdrawal across the North African desert. At the time, Juin was in command of the Tunisian Army, which fought alongside Sir John's British forces. Juin was a fighter, first and foremost, not a political soldier. Each commander, however, had enormous respect for the other, and their working relationship carried over to laughter and shared experiences off the battlefield. It was a relationship that was to have a great influence on my own working contacts with my Allied counterparts throughout my career. I came to appreciate the need to understand and respect the mentality and sensibilities of our friends, as well as our enemies, something that even General de Gaulle was to forget from time to time in the heat of the battle for Europe, and during the postwar peace.

I recall particularly the story of one dinner at Christmastime in North Africa in 1942 as an example of how two close comrades came to understand each other so well. Juin and Sir John were dining together at British headquarters a few days before the holiday.

"Christmas is coming," said Sir John. "Let's give each other little presents. What do you suggest?"

"In the circumstances, I think we should give only useful presents," replied Juin.

"Good idea," agreed the British general.

On Christmas Eve, Sir John dispatched his present—a small convoy of vehicles. It passed a single vehicle going in the opposite direction—Juin's present to Sir John. It was an amusing, subtle, yet pointed and above all highly respectful, reminder each to the other of the relative capacities of their forces at that point in the war.

One of Juin's great qualities was the wry sense of humor he managed to maintain in even the darkest days of the war. Once, after dining in the British mess, he sent Sir John a French cook.

I remained at my post in Africa through the early days of the re-taking of Europe in 1944, as Allied forces established their beach-head in southern Italy and began moving up the peninsula. One day, knowing both my family background and my work in the French Resistance, and eager that I make contact with the great French commander, who by this time had embarked in Italy to lead French forces in the advance up the peninsula, friends of Juin asked me to deliver a letter to him in Naples.

I made the dangerous trip across the Mediterranean and presented myself at the headquarters of the Allied Expeditionary Force in Naples. I was surprised and pleased when I was told that the general wanted to see me in person. It was quite an event for a junior officer to be received by the great French hero of the First World War. I met him at his command post, a kind of trailer-truck parked just north of Naples. He was a striking man, impeccably dressed in summer uniform, who saluted left-handed since his right hand had been damaged in the First World War.

He tapped the desk with his fingers. "So you've come from Algiers, young man?" he began. "What's going on there?"

I knew his code name was Hannibal, and I had been thinking about the Punic Wars launched by Hannibal that pitted ancient Rome against Carthage, whose latter-day equivalents would be Italy and North Africa (especially Algeria and Tunisia), respectively. I was seeking a particularly apt metaphor that would sum up the complex and typically French machinations then under way in Algiers, where the occupation forces had driven the Germans out and were intent on installing their own Free French government. Juin had fortunately been absent from all of this, occupied with reconquering southern Europe.

"In a word, sir," I began, "it's a case of Hanno the Great and the Carthaginian Senate." Hanno was a Carthaginian aristocrat and pacifist thoroughly opposed to Hannibal's invasion of the Roman Empire.

Juin burst out laughing, and I knew immediately that we thought very much alike. From that moment on, Juin took an interest in my career, and my whole life changed. Suddenly, I was in the center of the military confrontation with the Axis powers.

Because of my familiarity with North African fighting techniques, as a result of my time spent with the Spahis and the French colonial forces operating in North Africa, Juin had me posted as an officer in a unit of Moroccan shock troops in the Abruzzi hills—and for the moment forgot about me completely. But in terms of my personal development, it proved to be one of the great physical challenges of the war, perhaps of my entire career. In the Apennines, in the dead of winter, the temperature falls to 10 degrees Fahrenheit, even colder. Many of our wounded froze to death. In the engagements that followed, we lost three quarters of our fighting men. With African soldiers, officers had always to be in front as examples to the troops. During the fighting, I was gravely wounded and was awarded the Bronze Star by General Mark Clark, commander of the American Fifth Army. The engagement was part of the Battle of Cassino, which was called by the Germans the Stalingrad of the West.

It was during this most critical period of the Italian campaign that I met the woman who was to be my wife. The circumstances were as romantic as they were dramatic. Lillian was then seventeen years old. Trained as a Red Cross nurse, with her parents still living in Morocco, she was entrusted to the care of an extraordinary woman, the Comtesse du Luart, who had assembled and led the Number 1 Mobile Surgical Unit—the precursor of the famed MASH units of later wars.

Madame du Luart, daughter of a Russian cavalry general, wife of a big landowner in the Sarthe valley, single-handedly set the tone and atmosphere of the front-line hospital unit she led into the most dangerous battle zones of the Italian campaign. Living under canvas so near the front, surrounded by mud, blood, and critically wounded men, Lillian followed the example of her guardian—working calmly and courageously, quite oblivious of her incredible beauty. At the end of the Italian campaign, Juin himself presented her with the Croix de Guerre.

I was instantly attracted to Lillian. She was the only woman who refused at that time to go out with me—which both attracted and shocked me. By the end of the war, though, my persistence had won out. She had fortunately changed her opinion and accepted my proposal of marriage. While other women had been delighted to spend an evening or weekend with me, she turned out to be the only woman who could stand me for more than a week. We have been together ever since.

But at the moment we first met, the Italian campaign left little time for the conquest of Lillian. It was a slow, painful, and costly series of engagements up the length of the Italian boot. The French Expeditionary Force, with four and a half divisions, served as a key element of the central column of the United States Fifth Army under the command of General Mark Clark. On our right flank was the Eighth Army, formerly commanded by Field Marshal Lord Montgomery, victor of the desert war against Rommel. Both armies were now under the joint command of Lord Alexander of Tunis, the very finest of British soldiers. There were also the gallant Canadians and the Poles under General Władysław Anders.

Still, we could not have pursued our campaign without American aid. Great Britain had been bled white. We were totally dependent on the United States for everything that was required—food, equipment, weapons, munitions—to throw ourselves against the Italians and their German allies on Europe's southern flank. So, at all times, we had to make a good impression on the Americans and their representatives. Being so dependent on another nation was enough of a blow to our pride. It was a constant goad to us to wipe out the lingering shame of our defeat in the German blitzkrieg of 1940—that was necessary not only for psychological and moral reasons, but for important long-range military and diplomatic ones as well. At that moment, we were already laying the foundation for a more equitable alliance structure in the post-Second World War era, in anticipation of the period of the Third and, ultimately, the Fourth World wars, in the latter of which France and a united Western Europe would assume a burden equal to that of the United States. But at that point, in the midst of the Italian campaign of 1944, such equality still had to be earned, on the diplomatic as well as the military front.

The man President Roosevelt had chosen to represent him in Italy, and who was to convey our position most effectively to the President and the American people, was one of the outstanding diplomats of the Second World War—a man who had the President's complete trust and who had spent considerable time in Paris—

Robert Murphy. It was the same Robert Murphy who, as a young third secretary in the American embassy, had been a frequent guest at the soirees my Aunt Ethel gave with some regularity when I was growing up.

At the height of the Italian campaign, some considerable time after my first (and until then my only) meeting with General Juin, Ambassador Murphy paid a call on the French commander. After they had discussed their business, the American representative observed, "You have a great friend of mine in your expeditionary force."

Juin was, in typically French fashion, astonished. "What?" the general wondered. "Here? A friend of Roosevelt's personal representative? Who is this important person?" More to the point, who was this important person that Juin could not recall.

Murphy pressed on. "He is Alexandre de Marenches."

Juin stared at him blankly, as did the entire room, until suddenly, the general's aide-de-camp struck his forehead. "Oh, yes, Marenches. You know him, sir."

"Bring him here at once!" Juin shot back.

I was found, God knows where, dusted off, and stuffed into a clean uniform before being hurled into a jeep that promptly sped off to the old Italian castle beside the sea that served as general headquarters for Juin's advance up the Italian peninsula. It was a far cry from his first command post in the trailer outside Naples. I remember, quite vividly, tiptoeing hesitantly into the cavernous salon where a wood fire was roaring in the fireplace. I stood at attention. I saluted. No one moved.

Suddenly, Bob Murphy saw me, for the first time since he had frequented my aunt's Paris town house. Now, he leaped from his armchair and hugged me, shouting, "How are you, my young friend? What a great pleasure to see you again!" I replied in the same familiar way.

Everyone was quite astonished. Naturally, I stayed for dinner, but very much as the junior officer at the table. And later, Juin scolded me for not telling him that I knew Roosevelt's trusted confidant.

"But, sir," I replied, "you never asked me."

Nevertheless, that evening was a turning point in my life—every bit as important as the letter that had first brought me to Juin and the Italian campaign, every bit as important as my journey across the Pyrenees and my enlistment in the Free French forces of

North Africa. That evening was the opening that allowed me access to the leading strategic thinking of the Second World War, and of all the world conflicts that have followed in this century. It was, in effect, an initiation into a unique school whose professors are those individuals who set our international priorities and fight our battles.

After that evening, General Juin kept me close to him. We were seldom apart. In some ways, he became a father figure—a man of courage and honor who taught me the nobility of war and the vitality of peace. He could be as lighthearted and amusing as he was serious and contemplative; he never took himself too seriously. Many years later, it was I who crossed his hands in his coffin.

I stayed on Juin's personal staff throughout the Italian campaign, indeed for the remainder of the war. During this phase of the war, I first met General de Gaulle. He called often on Juin—indeed Juin was the only person I ever heard speak to the great leader of the French people with the familiar pronoun, *tu*.

After the liberation of Paris, in the war room the Allies had set up to run the war in Europe out of the Trianon Palace in Versailles, I truly came to know De Gaulle. Juin and I were among the first wave of French troops to roll into the capital for the liberation. Our destination was the Hotel Continental, which during the occupation had been commandeered to serve as the headquarters of the Nazis in France. We had barely installed ourselves when we were told to prepare for the arrival of General George Marshall—after Roosevelt, unquestionably the single most important individual responsible for the defeat of the Nazi war machine. Marshall, not Eisenhower, was the one who really commanded the Allied operations. But since Marshall was so indispensable to Roosevelt, the President would not let him leave and go to Europe to take personal command. So Marshall created a Supreme Headquarters staff, including Eisenhower, that was disciplined, obeyed orders, but had never made war. All Marshall really needed was a coordinator who was unlikely to challenge Marshall's fundamental strategy. Ike filled that role to perfection—a complex role certainly, but performed no more, no less than this role he was assigned.

We all knew that the real power lay with Marshall. And at that moment, he was about to arrive in Paris. It was only at the last instant, though, that someone thought to inquire whether he could speak French.

"Not very well," came back the reply. "You will need an interpreter."

In those days, of course, we had no official interpreters; we simply made do. And this was one very important occasion where we needed someone to pitch in.

Thirty years earlier, on the First World War staff of General George Pershing, my father had trained the young American officers—Marshall, along with George Patton, Omar Bradley, and Douglas MacArthur. They became close family friends.

"I know General Marshall," I volunteered. "I'd be delighted to help out."

"You might have said so before!" Juin shot back for the second time in our relationship.

"You didn't ask me, sir," I echoed.

Almost immediately, we heard the sirens of his motorcade. Marshall arrived and entered the hotel suite that served as Juin's offices. He spotted me immediately.

"Alexandre!" he exclaimed. He turned to Juin and explained how he and Pershing had known me when I was a little boy.

I began translating their conversation. Toward the end, Marshall said, "There is a French liaison mission attached to the Supreme Headquarters, Allied Expeditionary Forces. Wouldn't it be a good idea if you had a personal liaison officer attached to General Eisenhower, so you could deal with him directly?"

"We'll find some general," Juin said. To Juin's astonishment, and even more to mine, Marshall replied, "Well, why not use Alexandre here? He has a unique understanding of world affairs. He is the son of my great friend, someone whom I truly believe we can trust implicitly."

Juin shrugged. In that typically French fashion, he had clearly found it difficult, if not impossible, to accept that anyone less than a general could perform a sensitive function. The hierarchy of age, rank, even birth, still counts for far more than competence in French society.

But the Allies' top general made an immediate decision. "On leaving here," he continued, "I am going straight to Eisenhower at Versailles. I'll take Alexandre with me and introduce him to Ike." It was the first time I had heard Eisenhower's nickname. It was certainly not the last. We left the Hotel Continental immediately in the general's staff car, heading for the Trianon Palace Hotel at Versailles. Eisenhower had decided to set up the headquarters so far from Paris to maintain a bit of distance from the excitement of the French capital, to keep some perspective. He was, after all, liberating Europe, not just France. The hotel itself is situated in a park not far from the Versailles Palace, the summer home of the French kings. The large reception room had been converted into Eisenhower's war room. It was here that Eisenhower, Churchill, Patton, Bradley, Juin, Field Marshal Montgomery, all the Allied commanders, met, as partners in the umbrella command known as SHAEF (Supreme Headquarters, Allied Expeditionary Forces), to plan the tactics and strategies of the war against Nazi Germany.

There is an ironic footnote connected with this room. Decades later, following the fall of the Shah of Iran and his death a short time later from cancer, his son, who tried to assume his mantle, also came to the Trianon Palace, to the same room that Eisenhower had once used to liberate Europe. Lining his courtiers on both sides, he sat on a slightly elevated dais behind a desk at one end and received his guests, who passed between the ranks of his followers. This ersatz throne room was a sad contrast to the triumphant war room of Eisenhower, De Gaulle, and Churchill.

The war room itself was not far from the Supreme Allied Commander's office. There was a single opening in the room—the door. All other openings had been carefully boarded up to create what for that time was the world's most secure quarters. One wall was lined with huge maps of operations in Europe and the Pacific. On another wall were the operational charts for the air force including the targets for the next raids, and another chart indicated the positions of all the great Atlantic convoys, their dates of departure and arrival, and what they were carrying. If someone had been able to photograph that room, they would have had it all—the entire conduct of the war.

Security was desperately strict. The room was swept regularly for microphones. Two officers remained on duty for several hours, then were placed in the custody of the military police for some days so that there could be no leaks. I was the only Frenchman, apart from De Gaulle and Juin, with a permanent pass. I still have it—a small, green piece of cardboard with my photograph staring out from one corner. I remember vividly one occasion when General Redman, representing the British armed forces, was forbidden to follow the Allied Chiefs into the war room, and had to pace the corridors outside while I, a poor lieutenant, brushed past with the senior generals.

When Marshall and I arrived there on that first morning, Eisenhower had been standing on the lawn for a half hour waiting for Marshall's arrival. He snapped to attention. We went immediately to Ike's private office, where I stopped in the entryway. Marshall turned and motioned me in.

"Ike," he began, introducing me, "this is Alexandre, and he is the aide-de-camp of Juin, our friend Juin, a great soldier. He will act as liaison between you and Juin. And I want you to have the same trust in Alexandre that General Pershing had in his father."

Ike smiled. And that was that.

My principal function was performed at the top-level meetings at the Trianon—I translated General de Gaulle's thoughts from French into English for the rest of the Allied commanders, who conducted their business in English; and translated their thoughts, particularly Eisenhower's, from English into French. Everyone spoke more or less at the same time, so it was impossible to translate word for word. Even more confusing, they often did not speak directly to the person they were addressing. I often found myself summarizing what had been said, selecting the most important points.

"Marenches," De Gaulle would say to me, "explain my position to the general. This is what I want . . ."

It was difficult and exacting work. Yet, though I was scarcely aware of it at the time, it turned out to be the best possible training for a career at the highest levels of intelligence—a field that must at all times combine a sense of the nuances of world politics with an attention to the finest details of human behavior. At times, I broke out in a cold sweat, thinking of the heavy responsibility on my shoulders. The course of the war, the fate of thousands of fighting men, was being decided. Sometimes, I would ask them to repeat a sentence. I could not risk a misunderstanding. It was far too dangerous.

Most difficult to convey, delicately, was Eisenhower's exasperation with De Gaulle, who never really relaxed at these meetings. De Gaulle was always rather stiff, rather supercilious, toward the others. What I understood, and I fear the Americans did not, was that it was simply his manner.

"If one is small and weak," he often used to tell me privately, "one has to be tougher than ever." That was his way of preserving his sense of honor, and that of his country, defeated ignominiously by the Germans at the beginning of the war. In his eyes, the others were "the Anglo-Saxons." Still, they were all friends and always called each other by their first names.

All, that is, except Churchill. Everyone called him "sir." Yet more than any of the other commanders, Churchill was entirely natural. In the uniform of an RAF colonel, only his shoes broke with regulations. He had no patience with laces and instead had zippers installed. The first time I set eyes on Churchill, I had walked into Ike's office, and found maps spread out on the floor. I stood silently and respectfully at the side of the room. Soon, Churchill rose from his armchair, dropped to his knees, and, to examine the maps more closely, began crawling about the carpet on all fours, the smoke from his habitual cigar blowing back into his face. Finally, becoming increasingly engrossed in the project, he turned and handed me the cigar, which I held with the respect it deserved. He never smoked a cigar to the butt, rather lit it and took a few puffs. No doubt he enjoyed it, but he knew as well that it had become an integral part of his public persona.

After a war room session, I would often drive back to Paris and report to Juin all I had heard and, because no notes could leave the secure chamber, I had to learn the dialogue by heart. The exercise certainly helped improve my memory—it proved an invaluable discipline for my later career, though professional intelligence officers call memory "the fool's intelligence," since it so often plays tricks on you. After hearing my report, Juin would take me with him, and seek out De Gaulle for an explanation of what had been decided, the nature of the discussions, the whys and wherefores. But equally often, De Gaulle, who had no patience for such details, would dismiss Juin with a simple "Well, Marenches will tell you all about it."

During these discussions, there were some serious clashes among the huge personalities, the big egos around the conference table in the Trianon Palace. It was a difficult time, and I lost much sleep worrying about what I had heard in that soundproof chamber. Once, I recall, the British refused to obey the Supreme Commander. They wanted to withdraw to Antwerp to protect British interests when Field Marshal Gerd von Rundstedt was making his last big offensive push during the winter of 1944 in the Battle of the Bulge. Antwerp, in Belgium, was the port through which the British were resupplying most of their forces on the Continent—and many of the other Allied forces as well. But Eisenhower, quite rightly, saw the need to concentrate all possible strength for the Battle of the Bulge, to prevent a major German breakthrough by Von Rundstedt that might at that point have turned, or at least substantially altered, the immediate course of the war. Eisenhower carried the day, and the Allied forces held the line against the Germans, who never again were able to assemble a major counteroffensive.

General Bedell Smith, Eisenhower's principal aide-de-camp, was the heart and soul of Eisenhower's entire operation. While he was a consummate military strategist in his own right, his main job under Ike was to get the Americans and the British to work together, especially Field Marshal Montgomery, who wanted nothing but to make certain that the British coast was protected from any Nazi incursions. Bedell Smith, who spent much of his time phoning everyone and keeping the peace among allies, truly came to detest Montgomery and his single-minded arrogance, though I had the strong sense that he had to restrain himself with respect to De Gaulle as well.

Ike viewed the French as strange, outlandish types and was always a little suspicious of Latins in general. His closest confidants were Americans, with a few British thrown in for good measure. He never confided in the French. But Eisenhower's fundamental problem was that he preferred to maintain the status quo. As primarily a clerk for Marshall, he never deviated from the strategic direction once it was established.

After a while, I discovered that the roots of the clashes in the war room—between the French on the one hand and the Americans and British on the other—went back to long before the liberation of Paris, or even D Day. De Gaulle, it seems, had never forgiven Churchill and Roosevelt for what he considered a supreme betrayal—the invasion of Morocco and Algeria in November 1942, at a time when he felt Allied resources should have been concentrated on retaking and liberating France. At each step along the way, this disagreement about priorities produced conflict and bitterness. In 1942, when the Allies wanted to put General Henri Giraud in command of the North African forces, for instance, it took all of Bob Murphy's diplomatic tact to persuade De Gaulle and Giraud even to shake hands for the photographers. De Gaulle would have preferred to see him at the head of a column landing at Marseilles.

Throughout the period when the Allies finally retook France, there was continual friction between De Gaulle's plans and those of Eisenhower. In addition to my liaison work with the Allied Supreme Command, I was deeply involved with Juin's work as head of France's defense forces. Our French effort was masterminded by Juin and implemented by General Jean-Marie de Lattre de Tassigny, who liberated France from St.-Tropez to Alsace before moving into Germany and finally formally accepted for France the surrender of the German armies in Berlin; and General Philippe Leclerc, who helped lead the French forces in the Normandy landings and played a major role in the liberation of Paris. On the American side, Eisenhower's key aide and confidant, General Walter Bedell Smith, implemented American strategy. The British ran their own game—playing off the French and the Americans in an effort to deploy their forces as they saw fit.

There were constant opportunities for shadowboxing as French forces moved out of Paris and the south to retake the heart of France. The Germans were only part of our problem. French Communist sympathizers were already giving us trouble at every turn. Large tracts south of the Loire and west of the Rhone had escaped control of our newborn, Free-French state. De Gaulle feared that the FTP (Francs-tireurs et Partisans), the Communist-dominated partisan guerrilla movement, would create an insurrection in this key region of central France and set up an independent government to challenge his Paris-based leadership. The Gaullist government had sent a half-dozen officials to Limoges, each of whom had been arrested one after another and thrown in prison by the local "soviet."

There was a complex interplay of political imperatives, military needs, and deeply felt human passions that needed constantly to be tested and resolved. In that respect, the skills we learned during this difficult period were to prove essential in evaluating the still more complex interaction of disparate forces of religion and politics, and of the use of arms, that are now in play in the opening phases of the Fourth World War.

In the case of De Gaulle and Eisenhower, however, they each failed dismally in reconciling, or even understanding, the needs and desires of the other. De Gaulle asked Eisenhower for the use of one or two French divisions to help reestablish order in France and to assert his supremacy over the FTP forces dominated by the French Communist party. But Eisenhower wanted no part of any internal political problems in the territories the Allies were recovering, a policy that was eminently sensible in terms of the short-term priority of beating the Germans, but one that ignored entirely the postwar realities that were already beginning to emerge.

"Out of the question!" he replied to De Gaulle's pleas. "These troops are under my orders and I intend to keep them. I have only one enemy—the Wehrmacht. It is a fight to the death with the

Wehrmacht and I cannot divert our attention from our primary mission."

It was useless to argue with him. The fact is that Eisenhower had no clear picture of the political nuances of the war he was fighting in any part of Europe. During the Battle of the Ardennes, on the first day there was a terrible fog that allowed the Germans to hide, so we did not know they were almost out of ammunition. It appeared that we were outnumbered and about to be overwhelmed. Eisenhower decided on a truly perilous move—to pull all Allied troops out of Alsace to go to the aid of the Allied forces in the Ardennes. At that moment, De Gaulle wrote a letter to Eisenhower, which I carried with a final command. "You must say to Eisenhower," De Gaulle ordered me, " 'If you do this, if you remove Allied forces from Alsace, you will dishonor the Allied cause.' " I carried the letter, and when Eisenhower had finished reading it, I told him this.

"How dare you speak to me that way?" he exploded. I explained some of the history of the region. Alsace was an integral part of Germany, I said, a province as German in its way as Saxony. If it was evacuated, the Germans would massacre the population as collaborationists or worse. Eisenhower did not understand that because the Alsatians had just weeks before welcomed the Allies as returning heroes, they would be placed in the most mortal jeopardy by evacuation of the Allied armies. More important, this would have been a great moral and propaganda victory for the Reich, indeed could have reversed much of the hard-won progress of the previous months. But I'm not sure that Eisenhower was convinced. He was truly a warrior, not a politician. Indeed, I believe that Alsace was saved only when the Allies' fortunes in the Ardennes suddenly turned.

It was often left to De Gaulle to compensate for Eisenhower's lack of political sophistication. The political adroitness that De Gaulle had long mastered would have to make up for his own lack of firepower. In the case of the pro-Soviet guerrilla partisans holding south-central France, De Gaulle decided to deal directly with Maurice Thorez. Thorez was the French Communist leader who had deserted the French Army on orders of the Communist International and fled France for Moscow in 1939 at the time Hitler and Stalin were working hand in hand. Two years later, in June 1941, Hitler suddenly turned and invaded Russia, hurling Stalin into the arms of the Allies, but Thorez remained in the Soviet Union.

In December 1944, De Gaulle flew to Moscow, accompanied by

General Juin, for a series of meetings with Stalin. Unfortunately, I had fallen ill and was unable to accompany them, but Juin gave me a full account on his return to Paris. His first impression of Stalin was that the great Soviet leader looked like a man with little concentration. During the talks, he doodled on scraps of paper without raising his eyes, while De Gaulle described his intention of giving Thorez a visa and full amnesty, allowing the French Communist leader to return to France.

Of course, when Stalin brought back some of his exiled or imprisoned followers from abroad, believing them either incompetent or corrupted by foreign influences, he often sent them to concentration camps—or worse. Clearly anticipating that a similar end could befall his French Communist ally, yet delighted that Thorez, this symbol of French communism that Stalin had established, would be allowed back in Paris, Stalin turned to his terrified-looking interpreter and said, "Ask the general when he will have him shot."

Thorez did indeed return to France, and De Gaulle ultimately brought him into his first government in 1945 as a minister of state in charge of the civil service. It was a brilliant gesture that had the precise result De Gaulle had envisioned—a bloodless end to what might have been a most unfortunate civil war.

By the time De Gaulle and Juin had returned to Paris from Russia, I was up and about again. And problems were multiplying for the Allies and for the French. The German Army was in its last death throes. As the Allies began to roll toward central Europe, they began to discover the horror of the concentration camps. The difficult negotiations over the future of a divided and partitioned Berlin got under way as the Russians raced to be the first to seize the German capital.

Many of the great tactical decisions in the final days of the war were made on the spot and under most bizarre conditions. There was, for instance, the timing of the leap across the Rhine. We were at dinner in the Château of Namur in Belgium the day before the Allied crossing of the Rhine on March 22, 1945. The dinner was hosted by General Bradley, who commanded the Group of the Army of the North, including American forces and the British Army under Field Marshal Montgomery. Patton was there as well, and the contrast was striking between the quiet and self-effacing Bradley and the brilliant, indeed overpowering and flamboyant, Patton. Patton spent much of the dinner telling war stories, which I was forced to translate endlessly.

"Alex," he would say, "tell the general . . ." And he would launch into a yarn.

"Yesterday morning, they brought to my headquarters a German general as prisoner. The bastard was a Nazi. So he walks into my office, clicks his heels, and shouts, *'Heil Hitler!'* Jesus. So I punch him in the nose. And he falls on his ass. I turned to my aide and said, 'Take this bastard away.' Off they took him to the POW camp. Just before lunch, they brought in another German general. Ah, this was quite different. I could see from his insignia, he was a cavalryman. He was a gentleman. Like me. I invited him to lunch. And afterward, I gave him my Cadillac. To take him to the POW camp." He burst into laughter.

Toward the end of dinner, the toasts began. Patton rose, turned to Juin and me, and raised his glass.

"With your permission, General," he said to Juin, "I would like to raise my glass to the memory of Alexandre's father."

"It was he who taught you war," Juin replied.

"Yes," said Patton.,

"And love." Juin winked.

"Oh, no. That I knew already!" shouted Patton.

Patton sat down, and Juin turned to the timing of the crossing of the Rhine. "Are you going to let the others chase the pheasants without concerning yourself?" Juin began slyly.

Patton leaped from his chair. "By God, no!" he shouted, raced to the telephone, and ordered the Third Army to attack immediately.

Back in France, it had become a time for establishing a new order, and for settling old scores as well. There had never been very many true members of the Resistance. By the end of the war, most of them were dead or had been deported. The brother of one of my fellow officers had a small textile-printing factory. Six months after the liberation of southwest France, he received an order for sixty thousand armbands bearing the letters *FFI*—the insignia of the Forces Françaises de l'Intérieur, the most heroic French Resistance fighters. Now, it had become a badge of honor, whether earned or not.

But there was a darker side to that period following the liberation—a shadowy period of denunciations and arbitrary arrests. In a few short months, I learned more about my fellow countrymen than I ever wanted to know. The sad fact is that jealousy is our national vice. And in this period, it burst into full flower. Certainly, in the darkest moments of the occupation, there had been collaborators. It was a fact of life. My father's sister, the Comtesse de Ganay, was a victim of these "collabos." She had organized an escape network from German camps to Spain and freedom. Eventually she was denounced by Frenchmen, arrested by Frenchmen, and tortured by the sinister French gestapo before being deported to Ravensbrück, where she died bravely. Certainly, those who sold out this brave woman and countless others like her probably deserved their own such fate at the end of the war. But there were also those who coveted their neighbor's wife, or got hold of bicycle tires that had been denied to others. Now was the time to get even for a broad, and tragic, range of lapses—real or imagined.

I was one of those who believed in 1944 that it was more important to achieve national reconciliation than to inquire into the past—that we needed to put an end to our bickering, and put behind us the war, with all its peculiar passions, in order to prepare ourselves to fight the next war, the Third World War, looming ahead. The great and persistent failing of the French is the lack of unity among the tribes of Gaul. But in late 1944, I could merely suggest some steps that might ease our transition back to unity in our national life.

One of the suggestions that I put to Gaston Palewski, the distinguished *chef du cabinet* of De Gaulle, was that Marshal Philippe Pétain, the man who surrendered France to the Germans and then led the puppet government in Vichy, should fall victim to an accident. That accident could easily have been arranged by some of our security forces, and would have spared him and France much further humiliation and strife—the rubbing of salt in wounds that, even today, are barely healed. We had arranged many other similar accidents in the months following the end of the war. So I put the idea to Palewski.

"It is already too late," he replied. De Gaulle had decided on a public trial, during which Pétain uttered not a single word, followed by condemnation to death, then commutation to life in prison—where he died six years later.

By then, France had begun to put the war and its horrors behind it. As had I. But the politics of war had already begun to lay the foundation for the politics of peace.

An Impossible Mission

 t the end of the Second World War, each of the Allies had its own priorities. The French needed glory and the dominant personality of General de Gaulle to expunge their collective shame. The British in 1945 were exhausted.

And the Americans, who had practically no military tradition, at least in any European sense, had only one idea in 1945—to demobilize as quickly as possible. "Bring the boys home!" became the rallying cry of the nation, and the principal aim of Eisenhower, who was ultimately to lead that nation as President. No one among the Allies, apart from a few isolated and perceptive strategic thinkers, was paying the remotest attention to the onset of the Third World War.

That atmosphere of retreat into isolationism was the clearest characteristic of the American landscape that I found when I set foot in America in May of 1945. I was accompanying General Juin to the Pentagon to work with General George C. Marshall on the future charter of the United Nations. I also met there three other important people—President Truman, Admiral Leahy, and my mother.

It was not my first trip to the other side of the Atlantic—that had come when I was five years old, in the summer of 1925. And my memories from those earliest days colored all my reactions to America and Americans for the rest of my life. In those days, the only way to arrive had been by ship. So my first image of the United States, from the harbor of New York, was of the wagons that pulled the luggage from the boats. They were drawn by mules, and while I'd seen donkeys and horses, I had never seen a mule before. Those extraordinary animals, looking as large as horses but with great ears like donkeys, seemed to me very strange. My second memory was of the removal of my tonsils, and that had been done in New York. I found it marvelous that after losing your tonsils, you had to eat a lot of ice cream. American ice cream being by far the best in the world, I quickly became addicted to it. My final recollection was of our stay in Washington with friends who had a very fine town house with a garden. The gardener, who also took care of putting coal in the furnace, was black and he came from the South. I would sit on his knee and he would tell me stories of the old South while puffing on his pipe. Some of the stories began, "When I was a slave." He was a very fine old man. I was most moved by his reminiscences.

I had not seen my mother since the summer of 1940 when she fled France in front of the advancing German forces. She passed the war in the United States, safe from all the horrors that had befallen her homeland. It was a great burden off my shoulders during all those years to know that my mother, at least, was beyond harm. She stayed at a marvelous place in Washington called the Fairfax, a residential hotel where she had an apartment, and was accompanied by her maid, Henriette. Throughout the war she was very much involved in war relief work, sending parcels to the soldiers. It was quite a moving experience to see my mother again after all those years. She had left when I was really a young man, even a boy, and when I saw her again, I was an officer with an entire war behind me and the military aide to General Juin, the future marshal of France.

It had been a long and difficult flight—from France to Scotland, thence to Iceland, and then on to Newfoundland, and finally to New York and Washington. In Newfoundland, we were caught in a snowstorm and spent nearly four days in the barracks of the Royal Canadian Air Force waiting for it to calm down.

I had dealt with many Americans during the war years and in the immediate postwar period. But little had really prepared me for my first direct taste of the United States as it embarked on the transition from the mind-set with which it had fought the world's most devastating war to a "cold war" mentality. It was, after all, the nation that had assumed the leadership of the world to defeat the mortal enemies of democracy. Yet that was not the nation, or the leadership, that I found when I finally arrived in Washington with General Juin. By then, the Americans alone possessed the atomic bomb, which gave them a unique opportunity, to use the extraordinary power that they wielded to extend the leadership of the free world they had so rightfully claimed during the Second World War.

It was a leadership acknowledged by the rest of the free world, though curiously not by the Americans themselves—not yet. Had they desired, they were in a position to impose a Pax Americana that might have lasted a century or longer—a century of prosperity and peace. By assuming a dominant role in the partitioning of Germany, installing a nuclear capability on the European continent at the first opportunity, compelling a far smaller Soviet presence in Eastern Europe, laying down the law in no uncertain terms with respect to Russian dominance of putatively free countries like Czechoslovakia (notwithstanding the agreements at Yalta partitioning Europe, east and west), the Americans might have averted or at least drastically attenuated the Third World War. Certainly, the balance of power in the world would have been shifted substantially in favor of the West. Instead, the Americans failed, through the lack of historical vision that has been their principal problem for much of the twentieth century, to seize the moment.

Part of the problem was the stories the young American soldiers were bringing back from their reconquest of Europe. Though they had saved the Continent, it remained for them a strange and wondrous place—where few had ever set foot before they arrived at the head of a mechanized column. They were torn on the one hand by profound sentimental feelings for these people they had rescued, who had become like their little children who must be guarded and protected. On the other hand, they had witnessed, firsthand, vicious acts of reprisal, approaching barbarity, not to mention the atrocities of the concentration camps. Stories of the horrors of those camps they had liberated were just beginning to filter home, along with tales of French treatment of real or imagined collaborationists. They were tales of what some Europeans had done to other Europeans, and there was an increasingly widespread feeling that these were not, perhaps, the kinds of people that the United States wanted to be sucked into defending in situ for an indeterminate future.

The other side of this coin, though, was a feeling held by a far smaller element of the American population that was to overwhelm the United States only a decade later. It was the perception that, although the war against the Nazis had ended, it had given way, immediately and without pause, to a war against an even more insidious and dangerous enemy—Soviet communists—a war that could truly be called the Third World War. Some perceptive Americans recognized the dangers here as thoroughly as did De Gaulle, Juin, or myself. Indeed, at one point shortly before the end of the war, Juin and I encountered Ike's chief of staff, General Bedell Smith, as we were going into Allied headquarters, which by then was in Rheims. Bedell Smith looked particularly grave, and Juin inquired why. Victory appeared to be in our grasp, the road was open to Berlin.

"The worst," said Bedell Smith gravely, "is yet to come." He did not elaborate.

But a short time later, after the end of the war, De Gaulle ordered me to describe for Eisenhower reports we were receiving, through French Communist party sources, of what was going on in the Russian zone.

"Millions of Russians were rounded up in the American zone and sent by special train into the Russian zone where they are being murdered one by one when they arrive," I began.

Ike cut me off. "I know," he said curtly, appearing somewhat embarrassed. "But there is nothing we can do. It is part of the agreement with our ally."

So with Ike aware of the newly emerging Soviet menace, and strategic thinking beginning to wrap its collective mind around this new military challenge, it was not surprising that much of the talk around the Pentagon during my months there no longer concerned the race against the Russians to Berlin, but the race for the most brilliant minds and talent of the Third Reich. At that time, there were few real experts on the Communist system; the most knowledgeable ones were the Nazis, who had, after all, been fighting the Russians for years. Everyone was scrambling madly to bring those experts into their fold. It was normal in a time of war to recruit agents and others who knew the enemy. And so, the secret services of America, Great Britain, France, indeed all of Western Europe, had begun to recruit former Nazis who had belonged to the Gestapo or the armed forces—men like Klaus Barbie, "the Butcher of Lyons"—as well as the most distinguished rocket scientists. Among the Nazis were the dregs of humanity. There were also some extraordinary individuals. Much later, when I became the head of French Intelligence, I had a colleague who had been adjutant to General Gerhardt Wessel, Nazi commander of the eastern front. He became one of my closest friends. He had not, however, been a member of the National Socialist party. He was a soldier—and a professional.

On the Soviet side, thousands of notorious Nazis were immediately swallowed up by the police and armed forces of the Eastern bloc who were looking for Nazis with different talents—repression and domestic intelligence. It was, after all, quite easy to move from one totalitarian system to another. The Soviets, it seemed, had fewer scruples than the Americans, not to mention the advantage of taking a long view of world politics. Even the Americans, however, were willing to overlook the former politics of those Germans who possessed exceptional expertise, especially those with all but irreplaceable technical knowledge. They were found particularly among the extraordinary German scientific community, especially at facilities like Peenemünde along the Baltic coast, where German research chemists and physicists had been working on the V1 and V2 rockets. So both sides—Allied and Russian forces—swept down on this site at virtually the same time in the final weeks of the war. That was how the Americans latched onto Wernher von Braun, who had invented the V1, was working on the V2, and later helped launch the United States into space. On the other hand, a fair number of his colleagues found their way to Russia, where they helped the Soviets become the first nation to launch an orbiting satellite in space. It was called Sputnik, and its success touched off panic throughout the West—it was a major propaganda, if not military, victory for the Soviets, one of their first in the Third World War.

But at the end of the Second World War, our principal concern with the Russians was only indirect, since even the image of a Third World War pitting East against West was still quite fuzzy around the edges. The mission we'd undertaken to Washington was really to discuss the defense of Western Europe now that the Second World War had ended and the vast bulk of American forces were returning home. Our work laid the foundation for the North Atlantic alliance. In retrospect, it was purely by chance that we managed to construct an edifice that was to enable all of us to fight the Third World War to a successful conclusion. Each day, as we arrived at the planning rooms of the Defense Department, enormous maps were spread out and we crawled over them, exploring the political and strategic situation that existed in Europe.

Much of the time we spent with General Marshall and his aides. We were allies, friends. Moreover, Juin had enormous prestige as a result of his role in the Italian campaign and his brilliant tactics against the Italians and the Nazis. But the Americans were not only concerned with our military capacity or Juin's role in the military campaigns. Marshall, it seems, was an individual of extraordinary sensitivity. So was Juin. It was vital that the two men come to see that side of each other since both, but especially Marshall, were to play broader roles in the entire postwar recovery of Europe.

During my stay at the Pentagon, I had become great friends with General Marshall's longtime aide, a certain Colonel George, who had been with Marshall for more than thirty years—he was a devoted and indispensable aide. One day he took me aside and made a suggestion that the next morning I passed along to Juin.

"You know these Americans are not only very organized as warriors, they are also very sentimental," I told Juin. "So if I may suggest, tomorrow morning, before the official day starts around eight or eight-thirty, we should sneak out of the hotel around seven-thirty and pay our respects to the tomb of General Pershing."

Pershing, it seems, had meant more to Marshall than any other man he had known. He was a warrior who understood profoundly the nature of combat—which he had learned thoroughly and which he practiced in the First World War, just as General Marshall and his colleagues were practicing it in the Second and their successors were to do in the Third and the Fourth.

So throughout the Second World War, every fortnight, General Marshall had gone to Walter Reed Hospital, bringing with him maps of the European and Pacific theaters. General Pershing had been confined to his bed, gravely ill (he was to die shortly before the end of the war). Sometimes during those visits, he didn't even know what was going on, but every now and then he would gain consciousness.

Each time, Marshall would stop at the door to the hospital room, snap to attention, and bark, "General Marshall to report on operations, General."

Then he would sit next to Pershing and explain the status of operations. Sometimes, Pershing would ask questions; sometimes the old warrior was there, following closely, sometimes he wasn't. Finally, Marshall would stand up, snap to attention, salute, turn on his heels, and leave. No one knew of these visits except Colonel George, General Marshall, and General Pershing. I told Juin this story, and he was profoundly moved. So when I suggested that we pay our visit to the grave of General Pershing, he understood why it was so important.

We did as I suggested—quietly, unannounced, slipping out of our hotel room before seven-thirty, and then after the visit returning to the hotel to begin the official day.

Three days later, there was a big lunch at the Pentagon, given by General Marshall. All the Chiefs of Staff were there, as well as the secretary of war and the secretary of the navy. General Marshall rose and began a short speech. It was very emotional.

"You know," he said, turning to Juin, "our intelligence is pretty good. We know what you did the other morning. Not only are you a great soldier, but a man of great emotions."

It was this understanding that Americans and Europeans did share some fundamental values that led to General Marshall's proposal of the Marshall Plan for the reconstruction of Europe, a key element in setting up a Continent that would be able to defend itself in the Third World War. Marshall and his colleagues helped France particularly, enabling us to sit at the table with the other great powers after we had been so ignominiously defeated in 1940. These men had a vision of a France, not of 1940, but of 1918, at our moment of triumph, when as full-fledged members of the Western alliance, we had helped defeat the Germany of the kaiser, and without ever raising the white flag of surrender. General Marshall had participated in that triumph, and it was through his efforts that France was able to rise again. Marshall and the others were setting up France and Europe as the strong front lines of the next wars that were already upon us. Closer to home, the honor of General Marshall and those around him, their integrity, became the model for my life and set the standards for how I would operate during my period of high service to my country.

Much of the history of post-World War II Europe was decided at those meetings at the Pentagon at the very end of hostilities in 1945. The meetings were relatively brief, and I spent only a short time in Washington then, returning with General Juin to Paris. I'd already made the decision to leave the army. Juin asked if I would stay on to do liaison work with the provisional government of France and the Constitutional Assembly, and I agreed. It was my first taste of the inner workings of party politics. And I found them most unpalatable.

At the end of that year of interim civilian service, I was twenty-five. For seven years, since the age of eighteen, I had been fighting. So I was prepared with an answer when General de Gaulle summoned me to his home looking out on the Bois de Boulogne. After a few scattered pleasantries, which were not really his style, De Gaulle came immediately to the point.

"What do you intend to do now, Marenches?" he began. "Will

you go into politics? This is going to be a runaway election. All you have to do is put your name down. You'll be elected. And you can become a deputy."

"No, thank you, sir," I replied. "I came here to fight. Now it's over. As for politics, no, thank you very much. Now I am going home."

What I had seen already of politics was hardly calculated to change my determined mind. Politics and war, politics and intelligence, indeed politics and relations between nations, have never mixed very well. It is difficult to maintain the detachment necessary to battle an external adversary of any stripe when you are buried deeply in the internecine quarrels and parochial issues of your homeland.

De Gaulle raised this question of politics with me again, only once, a short time later, when he asked if I would consider becoming the chairman of the finance committee of his political party. I agreed to consider the offer, but I just did not like what I found on closer examination. There was intrigue everywhere in those days. I was still a somewhat naive young man, and I decided that all these machinations were simply not my cup of tea. Ironically, that very detachment from the political process was to prove to be among my most compelling credentials when I was later asked to head a French intelligence service that had become hopelessly mired in domestic political machinations.

So I returned to my family home in Normandy. My property was a frightful mess. After setting things right, I reentered civilian life with a vengeance and, together with a few friends from the war, opened a machinery business called Général Thermique. We made industrial steam engines, most of them produced in a plant in the industrial suburbs outside Paris. The experience taught me about both business and the nature of workers—a sense of organization and a sensitivity to the needs of those who perform the vital, detailed day-to-day tasks that make a complex operation run smoothly. Both were valuable lessons for an intelligence officer. I spent the next fifteen years in private industry, which gradually allowed me the financial independence to do as I wished later on. Particularly after we were bought out by a large conglomerate, I developed the luxury of sufficient flexibility in my business affairs to travel and carry out the missions I was often given by a succession of French governments and their leaders—sometimes as a civilian, sometimes as an officer of the reserves. The duties were of a confidential and delicate nature.

They made use of my skills in English and my understanding of the American mentality and the social and political system of the United States—how its leaders reacted, how the people felt about them.

In January of 1950, when General Eisenhower had come back to the United States, President Truman asked him to return to Europe to organize the North Atlantic alliance—officially the North Atlantic Treaty Organization, or NATO. He spent a week traveling through France to determine if France, and Europe, were in fact defensible during the Third World War that both Eisenhower and Truman perceived was about to be joined. Shortly before Ike's arrival, in January 1950, Minister of Defense René Pleven called me and said, "You are a reserve officer"—after several wartime promotions, I was then a lieutenant colonel—"will you come back for a week and be General Eisenhower's aide while he is in France?" Of course, I agreed.

As I traveled throughout France with Ike, he repeatedly asked me one question during that week: "Paint me a portrait of France."

"How many political parties are there, for instance?" he asked at one point after we had left Parliament.

"Well," I replied, "about forty-two million, sir."

"I know." He smiled ruefully. "The population of France. I might have guessed that!"

I just laughed.

Ike's visit, and the impression he carried away of the competent and loyal French military officers he talked with, were essential to his concluding that France and Europe were committed to their own defense and would serve as active partners in any American military effort. This was in sharp contrast with the general perception in Washington that Europe was simply a collection of weak and lazy countries waiting for American GIs to defend them against all comers.

A year later, in January 1951, I was dispatched again to Washington and the Pentagon on an equally important mission, from the French perspective. Even at this time, France was being sucked deeply into a quagmire that was to prove for us as deadly and demoralizing as it would for the Americans twenty years later— Indochina. Moreover, our military had quickly learned a lesson that it took their American counterparts a bit longer to learn—they could not win the war against the Communist insurgents on the ground, in the jungle. We desperately needed to bring our most advanced technology to bear on the conflict. It was the only way we could hope for any advantage.

Above all, that technology was airborne. The Vietnamese Communists, who had not yet been supplied with the kinds of superior weapons they were later to receive from their Soviet allies, were still battling with primitive arms—both offensive and defensive. Above all, their ground-to-air capability was nearly nonexistent, leaving the skies open to control by our French forces. Alas, the French Air Force had been all but exhausted by the war in Europe, not to mention our small contribution to the war in the Pacific. So René Pleven, by then Prime Minister, asked if I would go to the Pentagon to plead for more advanced aircraft for use by our forces in Indochina. I was most successful, and soon American helicopters and fighters were playing a key support role for our troops in Indochina. It was the first true Euro-American cooperation in an early skirmish of the Third World War—an East-West battle fought in a remote corner of the world.

But the most challenging mission came in October 1950. Prime Minister Pleven summoned me to his office and embarked on a broad discussion of the international situation, particularly France's involvement in Indochina.

"The future of the world is in the Pacific," I ventured brashly.

"And what are the great Pacific powers?" he asked.

"To find the great Pacific powers we must begin on the west— that is to say the Russians and the Chinese, the Japanese and one day the Indonesians. But on the other side, it must not be forgotten, there are the Americans and the Canadians. They are as much Pacific powers as these others."

Pleven seized instantly on the last statement. "What will the American policies be in the Pacific?"

"That is a very good question and I think we should try to find an answer," I responded. "It should be very interesting."

"This is not an easy question to answer," Pleven replied slowly. "Could you take on a question like this? Would you perform a mission in the Pacific?"

It was, indeed, my first intelligence mission in the sense that such a mission involves a synthesis of the most detailed field and strategic intelligence and carries with it the broadest geopolitical implications. It required an insight into both the American and the Asian mentality, not to mention into the history and the culture of some very disparate societies. It was a classic exercise in the craft of intelligence consisting at once of learning, discovering, or guessing what was going to happen in American politics, and what would be the military and diplomatic strategy of the United States in the Pacific over the next decade. The kind of information developed would be critical to understanding just what kind of commitment the United States was prepared to make to bolster the North Atlantic alliance in what were, strictly speaking, non-NATO areas of the world.

My first stop, inevitably, was Washington, where I discussed the assignment with General Marshall, who, despite the fact that my mission might be considered espionage by one ally against another, nevertheless understood the value of France's knowing what were America's goals in the Pacific region.

"The best thing you can do is to spend some time posing as an American officer in the Far East," said Marshall, who understood my need to give a texture and context to official statements of policy. "If you go as a Frenchman or a European, everyone is going to look at you, treat you differently and at a distance. So how about becoming an American officer?"

He had no hesitancy in making this possible. And that's how I became Colonel David Alexander. I still have the document he gave me that must be unique—a small card with my photograph that gave me priority permission to travel on all American planes crossing the Pacific.

I left Washington promptly for points east and south—Hawaii; Wake; Guam; Tokyo, at the time the headquarters of General Douglas MacArthur. I tried to find out what American policy would be and just what role France might play. The conclusions in my report were based on months of testing the waters—the atmosphere in Asia where the United States had a presence. In some areas, the Americans had been greeted as liberating heroes; in others (especially Japan), as proconsuls of the worst sort. So my report began with a bit of history. The Romans, I pointed out, had been powerful because they made the Mediterranean their Mare Nostrum, their private lake. I came to believe, as I prepared my report and thought about my months of wandering the Pacific, that this ocean would become the Mare Nostrum of the end of the century. But whose Mare Nostrum? At the time, I believed, and I largely still hold this belief, that the Pacific is and will always be America's Mare Nostrum.

"Movement in America was always inexorably toward the Pacific," I told the Prime Minister in my report. "This fact, more than any other, is perhaps the single greatest danger for Europe. The interest of the American people is to turn less and less toward Europe and the lands where their parents and grandparents came from."

Part of my travels were through California. I discovered that, even in 1950, many of the people there who were still living actually had come over the Rocky Mountains in covered wagons in their youth. Those people, and especially their offspring, don't look back toward Europe. Europe is beyond the Atlantic, which is beyond America, which is beyond the mountains they crossed. As America's population center moved West, its people looked in front of them. And in front of them was the Pacific.

It must be remembered, though, that the line dividing the South from the North in the South-North War we are fighting today circles the globe. It crosses the Pacific as surely as it crosses the Atlantic and bisects the Mediterranean.

The Pacific has played a role, in different forms, in each of the wars fought in this century. Indeed, the only two shooting conflicts the United States engaged in during the Third World War confirmed how prescient I had been in my first intelligence report for a French leader. Those wars, the defense of the Korean peninsula against the Communist Chinese and their allies in 1950–52, and the defense of South Vietnam in the 1960s and early 1970s, were the only two shooting conflicts the United States fought in what was considered the cold war—the Third World War. Both took place in the Far East. The French wound up contributing a very substantial military force to the joint United Nations effort in Korea, a move I heartily endorsed. It was essential, I believed then and now, to support the United States wherever it feels its interests may lie—and especially in parts of the world, like Asia, where it may see an even larger interest than we do. The United States, after all, is the only world power of the North with the reach and strength to take the lead wherever skirmishes in the Third or Fourth World wars have led us in the past or might take us in the future, as we have seen most recently in Iraq. It has long been clear that the United States would honor its commitments to NATO. But officially, NATO commitments begin and end with the North Atlantic. As events in the Middle East, and certainly the Pacific, have proven, the Fourth World War is unlikely to be fought remotely near the North Atlantic.

Throughout this period, both before and after General de Gaulle's retirement to his home village of Colombey-les-Deux-Églises, I kept in contact with him and some members of his family. Though I never belonged to any political party, not even his own, the general nevertheless called on me several times to carry out a number of missions on his behalf. He carefully kept me apart from the complex portion of his life that dealt with party politics. Politics with a capital *P,* world affairs, were what concerned me. And De Gaulle recognized my aptitude for the more global sort of mission.

In July 1959, a year after his return to the presidency, De Gaulle asked me to return to Washington and visit President Eisenhower. He wanted me to talk with Eisenhower about the French atomic bomb. By that time, two nations had an A-bomb—the United States, which had used it to end the war in the Pacific at Hiroshima and Nagasaki; and, a few short years later, the Russians.

France also needed the bomb to become the major political force in Western Europe, and guarantor of independence for the free world, or at least for Western Europe, when American forces would leave the Continent (sooner rather than later, De Gaulle believed). He felt that France needed to become the third nuclear power to play a central role in the defense of the West in the Third World War. But De Gaulle also realized that French scientists could not quickly or easily produce the bomb on their own. They would be forced to go through the same tedious process of trial and error that plagued America's early stabs at nuclear development. France needed American help.

So I set off anew for the United States with this latest and most delicate mission. And, frankly, with little hope of success.

Our meeting was held in the Oval Office, where the President sat alone. He received me warmly. We began by talking about the Second World War, and the political situation in Europe and France, and then I turned to the reason for my mission.

"General, sir," I began. I always called Ike "General"—I was never able to think of him as anything else. "I am on a mission, a personal mission for General de Gaulle. He is a man you have known well for many years. We have worked closely together, and he has asked me to come to speak with you about a very delicate, a very sensitive subject."

Eisenhower nodded slowly and asked me to continue.

"General, we need your help to build a French atomic bomb."

Eisenhower shook his head immediately. "Impossible!" he said slowly. We talked briefly, but he was clearly not to be moved. There was already a growing mood of fear in the United States over the spread of Communist influence in Europe, Eisenhower explained. I knew very well his domestic situation that included the Communist witch-hunts, led by Senator Joseph McCarthy, that were just picking up steam. Moreover, with Maurice Thorez and other members of the wholeheartedly pro-Moscow French Communist party participating in the first French postwar government—the French Communist party was a legal, powerful force in French politics—many in the American government, including Eisenhower, were aware of Communist infiltration into French atomic research. Indeed, they were correct, with respect to Communist infiltration, as our domestic intelligence disclosed. After the Germans invaded Russia in 1941, French Communists, taking their direction from the Soviet Union, became powerful elements in the French Resistance movement fighting against the Nazi occupation. The party itself became a magnet at the end of the war for a large number of the French intelligentsia. Inevitably, that elite group included many of our top nuclear scientists as well. Still, since the Russians already were long since charter members of the nuclear club, having detonated their first atomic bomb in the fall of 1949 and their first thermonuclear explosion on August 12, 1953, the reasoning of the American witch-hunters who feared the theft of Western atomic secrets six years later was more than a trifle irrational.

Nonetheless, my conversations with Eisenhower and later some of his aides in those early days of his administration resulted in a polite but thoroughly firm refusal.

I returned to France and reported to De Gaulle. Though I explained carefully Eisenhower's point of view and his domestic political situation, trying to put his decision in context (a most vital component of the report of any intelligence officer), De Gaulle was predictably enraged.

We met in his offices at the Élysée Palace in Paris, where I made my full report. Pacing back and forth, De Gaulle became furious and shouted, "I will get my bomb, Marenches! Do you understand? I will get my bomb!"

De Gaulle ordered that efforts to build France's own bomb be redoubled. But it was not until 1960—eight years after the British exploded Europe's first nuclear bomb—that France joined the nuclear club. Eisenhower's refusal created a rift that never truly healed, at least as long as De Gaulle remained in power. It had an important impact on the unity of the Atlantic alliance, influencing the ultimate withdrawal of France from the military wing of NATO and weakening the ability of the European intelligence community to function in a coordinated fashion during much of the Third World War.

During the next five years following this trip, while I built my private business, De Gaulle moved into retirement and passed an increasingly anxious time in Colombey-les-Deux-Églises, watching as his successors squabbled with one another while France drifted into a state of increasingly penurious limbo. Finally, in 1958, De Gaulle succumbed to the call of his country and returned to active political life as the first president of the Fifth Republic. The nation was in a shambles. The bitter and divisive war in Algeria continued to rage. Immediately after his return to power, De Gaulle summoned me and asked if I would accept an official position. As I had many times before, I refused.

"Politics with a small *p* has never interested me," I explained to the general. "I do not feel comfortable among politicians—they are not my scene. I have arranged my life in a way I understand. I will always agree to serve my country, and the countries of liberty, to preserve them as part of the free world. But I do not want any official position."

Still, De Gaulle persisted, and asked if I would agree to resume my old role as liaison between my wartime comrades, De Gaulle and General Juin, now at tragic loggerheads over the incident in modern French history that most excruciatingly set brother against brother—the bitter civil war in Algeria. That conflict shared many of the most pernicious characteristics of America's Civil War and Vietnam War. In the case of both Algeria and Vietnam, many at home in France saw the conflicts as efforts to impose our political will on people anxious only to take control of their own destiny. Demonstrations and slogans in Paris and Washington a decade apart were equally divisive and threatening to the stability and unity of the government and the population as a whole. Over the previous century, more than a half-million Frenchmen had arrived in Algeria as colonists—pioneers, really—seeking to build a new and better life for themselves and their families. By 1954, many had been there for generations. Algeria was more real to them in most respects than the France of which they remained full-fledged citizens. Indeed, their French compatriots even referred to them differently—the pieds noirs, the "black feet," because so many were accustomed to going barefoot in the souks and the deserts of Algeria. The night of October 31, 1954, this all ended. A massive rebellion erupted among the Algerian population seeking the independence of their country from France. French military forces, stretched thin by the ongoing war in Indochina, were pressed to the wall. But with the pieds noirs rallying to the French cause, the battle was joined and a civil war broke out. Back home, in metropolitan France, people also began choosing up sides—the forces of liberalism and decolonization siding with the rebels, the forces of nationalism with the pieds noirs. Before very long, the conflict began having a clearly cancerous impact on France's domestic unity and its ability to conduct a consistent and strong foreign policy. This was where I entered the scene, reluctantly agreeing to De Gaulle's request to mediate the dispute between him and Juin.

Personally, it was truly pitiful to see the two old comrades in such bitter conflict. Juin, who was born in Algeria of a modest French family, had cast his lot with a dying cause—that of the pieds noirs for the preservation of France's North African empire. In addition to its being his birthplace, Juin's association with Africa had a long, passionate history. His first assignment after graduating from St.-Cyr, the French West Point, had been with a rifle unit in Morocco. Over the next forty years, his career took him back and forth between France and North Africa. After our return from Washington at the end of the Second World War, Juin was sent back to North Africa as "resident general" of France in North Africa. Though he held a number of other high positions in the French military and the Allied command in later years, he never lost touch with many of his former officers who were battling the insurgents in Algeria.

De Gaulle never shared Juin's attachment to Algeria. He had never been a legionnaire, a Spahi, a colonial soldier as had Juin. De Gaulle's experience in far-flung places had been limited to a very short stay in the Middle East and a couple of brief visits to Africa. His view of world affairs began and ended with France, and often with the age of Louis XIV. In De Gaulle's view, Louis XIV was the single most powerful monarch in French history, the man who ruled France for seventy-two years, expanding its power and influence; who brooked no controversy, who was both feared and worshiped by his people; who could accept only a single, Gallocentric view of the universe. De Gaulle, in so many ways, viewed himself as the inheritor of Louis XIV's mantle (though he was a sufficiently sensitive politician never to have admitted this), and often comported himself accordingly. For those who knew him well, he was, like his father, fundamentally a monarchist.

My period of shuttling between De Gaulle and Juin, two powerful men who had adopted opposite views of the historic interest of France, was not exactly a happy time. Their bitter quarrel began in 1958 when De Gaulle began counting heavily on his great friend Juin to keep the Army of the East neutral in the growing Algerian conflict. It had become apparent that De Gaulle did not trust Juin with regard to the issue of the pieds noirs in North Africa. Juin had turned into one of their greatest defenders, and was prepared to turn the Army of the East into a force that would bow to their every whim, while De Gaulle was trying to resolve the conflict by negotiation. It was clear to Juin that De Gaulle was prepared to sell out his beloved French countrymen in North Africa in the name of peace with the Algerian rebels. At De Gaulle's request, I attempted to negotiate a face-to-face meeting with the two obdurate and inflexible leaders. Finally, after repeated shuttle trips between Juin's headquarters in Algiers and De Gaulle's residence, I arranged for Marshal Juin to come to Colombey for what was to prove a watershed summit.

De Gaulle met Juin in the narrow hallway of his country house. They turned to enter De Gaulle's private office, and I stopped, preparing to stay with the colonel who was De Gaulle's aide-de-camp. But suddenly, De Gaulle returned to me and said, "Oh, no, you come with us."

It was not a constructive meeting. "You've had it," De Gaulle began, addressing Juin. "You must make your arrangements with us. It's that simple."

Juin protested and blustered, but De Gaulle dug in his heels. There was no persuading him. Algeria was lost. The pieds noirs must be prepared to leave their adoptive country or make their peace with the rebels. In short, Juin viewed the issue as simply being couched in the black-and-white terms of either capitulation or war. He stormed out. He was not prepared to break openly and publicly with De Gaulle at that moment. But it was clear to any of us who had been at Colombey that first day; there would be no accommodation, no truce.

From that moment in 1958 until 1961, when Juin broke formally with his former comrade-in-arms and was forced into retirement from his beloved military, they never again dealt on friendly terms. Indeed, rarely did they deal directly at all. I was the one forced to accept the brunt of their anger with each other, to act as the lightning rod and the interpreter of two hostile and, despite my best offices, irreconcilable positions. Ultimately, of course, De Gaulle won. Algeria gained its independence. Many of the pieds noirs came home. France was able to begin the process of healing the wounds inflicted during this conflict, and to take a more forthright position as an important, unified European power. At the same time, my personal involvement in the Algerian war proved to be yet another stage in my preparation for the most delicate role I would ever undertake—as head of French Intelligence.

All my life I have tried to keep a low profile. That is not as easy as it sounds when one is six feet one and weighs over 220 pounds. But I mean this metaphorically, of course—that is, I have always sought to be my own man. That is why I chose to avoid elective politics. I have seen many splendid friends change when they embraced that career. Party politics demands a willingness to compromise, which is one thing I will never do. All my friends know this, as do most of my closest colleagues in public life.

François Castex was one of those who knew me best. An old friend and brother officer, he was married to the sister of Claude Pompidou, the wife of Georges Pompidou, in my opinion one of the few real statesmen in contemporary France. He had the qualities every politician should have if he wishes to become a statesman— good sense, intelligence, sensitivity, humor, and modesty.

I had lost contact with Georges Pompidou when he became prime minister. But one day Castex asked me, "Have you seen my brother-in-law recently? We were talking about you the other day, and he would like to see you."

So one evening, we dined together at François Castex's home. I found that indeed Pompidou was the same man I had known and liked years before. Right after the war, he had joined De Gaulle's staff as a civilian, and I recalled the circumstances of his arrival. De

Gaulle had an enormous, biting, sometimes nasty sense of humor. He also had the rare, natural gift of being able to write in absolutely magnificent French. And he was, in a certain way, in awe, as were most Frenchmen, of the rare and extraordinary individual known as an *agrégé*. The *agrégation* is the most advanced degree in any French university—a degree that is granted only after the most terrifying, most appalling quantity and intensity of work.

So one day, De Gaulle turned to one of his aides, René Brouillet, and growled, "Brouillet!"

"Oui, mon Général," he replied, because you never said Monsieur le Président to De Gaulle.

"Brouillet, find me an *agrégé* who knows how to write proper French." Brouillet produced Georges Pompidou, a man who indeed had a real education—an *agrégé* who spoke, and wrote, French with a flair that De Gaulle could appreciate.

Our paths had crossed from time to time in the ensuing years. After the war, he had become one of the great directors of the Banque Rothschild. Now and then he would invite me to lunch at the Cercle de l'Amérique Latine on the Boulevard St.-Germain. He would call the waiter at the end of each meal and demand an enormous cigar, which he would light with a flourish, then wink at me, and observe, "You know I love to smoke a big cigar, but I don't do it outside because I'd look like a rich banker." We had many other ties that linked us. There was, first and foremost, the Castex family, who were mutual friends. There was my great friend, Anne-Marie Dupuy, the ex-mayor of Cannes. I had met her first in Italy, where she was an ambulance driver at the Battle of Cassino. Like myself and my wife, she had served under General Juin, and became one of the most famous ambulance drivers in the French Expeditionary Force in Italy. Later, she played an important role in President Pompidou's government as his *directeur du cabinet* (chief assistant in the Élysée Palace)—the first, and I believe only, woman to have held this post. My wife and I had known and loved her for forty years. It turned out that it was Anne-Marie who had first suggested to Pompidou that he find some way to make use of me in his government.

A short time after our dinner at the home of François Castex, Pompidou asked me to call on him at the Élysée Palace. As soon as I had seated myself in front of his ornate desk, he began by chiding me.

"Why haven't you come to see me for such a long time?" he said.

"I had nothing to ask of you," I replied truthfully.

After a short silence, he said rather wistfully, "You must be the only one."

We began with a broad-ranging discussion of the world situation before he turned to his immediate problem.

"After De Gaulle," he said, "we must begin to mend fences with the Americans. How would you like to become French ambassador in Washington?"

I thanked him, and told him how flattered I was by his proposal. But, I observed, "mending fences is not exactly my line of expertise."

Pompidou nodded as though he understood, but the argument was not truly convincing. So I tried another tack that he might understand.

"You know, sir," I began, "I have spent a considerable period of time in Washington on various missions. On many of these occasions I have had the good fortune to dine, or lunch, even to spend the night at the residence of the ambassador. It is, quite rightly, reputed to have the finest table and the finest cellar in the capital. I, of course, am a great lover of the good life, of good food and fine wine. If you want me to die in a year or two, you have only to give me this position in Washington."

Pompidou smiled. We chatted some more. And finally, he said, "Of course there is something else, but quite honestly, it comes under the heading of 'Mission Impossible.' I won't suggest it to you, because you're a friend."

Suddenly, I was most intrigued. "That sounds interesting. If it is a very difficult or impossible mission, then I am interested. Tell me more."

"Well," he said gravely, settling himself deeper into his armchair, "it's about the Secret Service. I need someone to take charge of it and rebuild it. What do you know about intelligence?"

"Well, I know the basics," I replied honestly. "In occupied France, I used to do some spying during the German occupation. I would travel to Vichy and see my good friend Ralph Heinzen, who then was with United Press, or the people at the American embassy, and tell them about different activities of the Germans in occupied France and Normandy. What airfields they might be building and using, that sort of thing. Then, of course, there was my time with General Juin when I dealt, from the general staff point of view, with the various Allied intelligence reports in the final years of the war.

But I'm afraid I know very little of the vast middle ground of intelligence."

I was aware, of course, that Pompidou had a very real problem with respect to his entire intelligence apparatus. The Secret Service, as he called it—its official name was the Service de Documentation Extérieure et de Contre-Espionnage (SDECE)—I knew had fallen on very hard times indeed owing to a number of cases of outrageous intervention in the internal affairs of other countries and our own, including murder and assassination. One of the most egregious was the 1965 case of Mehdi Ben Barka. A leftist university professor in Morocco, Ben Barka founded the leading Moroccan opposition movement and after a series of incidents was exiled and condemned to death in absentia in his country. He sought and was granted asylum in Paris, where he continued his activities against the Moroccan regime, whose security apparatus maintained close ties with our own—another of the legacies of our colonial rule in French North Africa. The night of October 29, 1965, Ben Barka was kidnapped in what was allegedly a joint operation between French Intelligence and Moroccan security. His disappearance was yet another deeply discrediting blow to the entire French security apparatus. Its image in the outside world and its internal morale both plunged to an all-time low. Rescuing this organization, indeed setting French Intelligence on a new professional footing, would be an enormous task indeed—and one that could certainly blow up in the face of any individual who might take it on. Yet clearly it was an essential assignment. First, the SDECE needed to be put on a professional footing—dragged out of the mire of domestic politics, where no intelligence service has any business dirtying its hands. Second, it needed to begin functioning in a manner that could support French international and strategic objectives and to play its proper role in the intelligence effort of the Western alliance that was already deeply involved in the Third World War.

Pompidou, watching my face carefully, clearly understood many of the thoughts that were racing through my mind. He also clearly perceived the nature of the risk involved in accepting the position. So he continued quickly, "If you should survive this impossible mission, I would not leave you in the lurch. I would name you a *conseiller d'état*."

I did not answer Pompidou that evening. Indeed, a year passed from the time of that conversation—a year during which I turned over in my mind again and again his extraordinary offer. In June

was elected president, elevated from prime minister
s final retirement.

r his election, we met again. "It's no use," he con-
e Secret Service just isn't working properly. My chief
re's only one thing to be done: Shut down the whole
department and start all over again from scratch."

"I really know nothing about it, Mr. President," I replied. "But
give me a few weeks and I'll do what I can to get at least a sense of
the dimensions of the problem."

Some of my wartime friends were in the SDECE. I canvassed
opinions, poked and prodded into some of the many dark interstices
of this enormous, clearly unchecked, and, for the purposes for which
it was truly intended, largely ineffectual monster. Then I returned
to the Élysée Palace and Georges Pompidou.

"I think, Mr. President, that it would be a bad idea to shut down
the department and start again," I began. "For a dangerous length
of time, your instrument panel would be missing a critical compass.
What the SDECE does need is a complete reorganization and purge
of a number of subversive elements. But it can be set straight. And
if it is done properly, you will again have a unique instrument that
will help guide you through the most difficult decisions and most
dangerous crises. But if I take this job, you must trust me one hundred percent. Ninety-nine percent is not enough."

Pompidou agreed immediately. My appointment was kept a
closely guarded secret until the last possible moment, and made
public only after the cabinet meeting that ratified it. In France the
head of intelligence is a presidential appointee. The Parliament does
not need to ratify it—only the president's own cabinet. Even the
Ministry of Defense was not warned until a few hours before the
announcement. Everyone was surprised. Many were shocked.

At 9:00 A.M. on the day of the announcement, I arrived at the
Tourelles Barracks in Paris's remote Twentieth Arrondissement. It
was a barracks like any other military barracks. But this one served
as the headquarters of the SDECE—the French CIA, later known as
the DGSE (Direction Générale de la Sécurité Extérieure). It was
also known, informally, as La Piscine, the Swimming Pool, a term
coined by journalists since there was a municipal pool just next door.
We called it simply "the Service." I never went swimming there. But
I did plunge straight into some of the deep-seated corruption and
incompetence that were paralyzing parts of the SDECE.

My government car swung through the main gates on the Boulevard Mortier, then turned up the drive past the broad green lawn with the white flagpole. An officer of the SDECE snapped to attention and greeted me with a salute. He was well aware of the fact that, though a civilian, I carried a four-star rank. We walked quickly up the steps and through the huge front doors and found ourselves facing a stark, white wall. Later, I was to hang on that wall a Carolingian épée of Homeric proportions, lit dramatically with a single spotlight. We turned sharply right and entered the great office of the director general—some fifty square yards of space.

There were many that morning awaiting my arrival who clearly did not like the idea that I was there. I could see it in their eyes, the few I saw immediately. I could feel it in the air. And they didn't even know that some of them were about to be sacked.

In my pocket on that first day, I carried a list, short but vital, of jobs held by certain people. I knew precisely where I had to strike and who must be removed without delay. Because of the many forces within the SDECE that I knew were arrayed against me, I decided I would strike first and with great brutality. So the first morning, in three hours, I chopped a half-dozen heads, belonging to people whom I knew were not the kind I wanted to have working with me. That certainly took them by surprise.

I fired a third of the directors the first day—most notably the directors of research, counterespionage, and technology. I followed a simple routine. The big ones, I called into my office one by one. Those who were military officers would stand at attention, because of my four-star rank. The others would simply stand in front of me, waiting for the invitation to sit down. For those I wanted to impress with my toughness, I would say brusquely, after they had traversed the vast expanse of office to my desk in the corner, "I'm not going to ask you to sit down because you're fired."

They were, of course, shocked. "Well, why?" one asked me, astonished.

"Because I don't trust you," I replied curtly.

"But you don't know me. This is the first time we've met."

"I haven't met you before, but I know what you are," I concluded. Simple as that. But he had not finished.

"I'm sure we can make an arrangement," he continued with a slight simper on his face.

I jumped from my chair. I am a large man, and in those days was a lot younger and strong as an ox. I grabbed him by his collar and lifted him off the ground.

"Do you see that door?" I pointed him in the direction of the closed door he'd just entered about fifty feet away. "You have five seconds to cross that doorstep under your own power, otherwise you will go through the door without my opening it for you."

My aide told me afterward that he said to this fellow as he came bolting through the door, "You know, you're lucky you're still alive. The director general, when he takes hold of you, he could break you into pieces."

Word spread quickly throughout the Tourelles Barracks that first morning. The next ones in line were all trembling. My strategy was most effective.

So it was scarcely startling that in the following days and weeks I received a number of threats, many of them mortal. "You won't last a week," read one note that had been assembled, rather crudely I thought for a French secret agent, from letters cut from magazines. "We'll get you," warned another. There were many dangerous elements in the SDECE, many in some very high and powerful positions and whom I had not yet managed to unmask. It was them or me. As you can see, I survived. And so did France's Intelligence Service.

CHAPTER 4

The Thousand Layers

y private nickname for the Secret Service is the *mille-feuille*. This is a marvelous French pastry, often known abroad as a napoleon, and carefully constructed of dozens (supposedly a million) paper-thin layers of confection. And so was the Secret Service—concocted of countless layers of confection. But instead of belonging to a luscious little sweet that is reborn each morning at the hands of a master baker, those layers had been accumulating for years, then fossilizing, so that by the time of my arrival, they had petrified. Only here, there had accumulated antiquated people and ideas—becoming at best a less than efficient way of gathering intelligence and using it in the service of international security priorities, and an embarrassment to the administration that it pretended to serve. At worst, it had become a potentially mortal liability to the president, calling into question his judgment, his control over those who wield the power of life and death, his entire ability to govern.

It is by no means an exaggeration to suggest that this worst case was the position of President Pompidou in those days immediately preceding my arrival at the Tourelles Barracks. The president was very unhappy with the performance of the Secret Service. The kidnapping and disappearance of Ben Barka was only the most visible of the terrible games the SDECE (Service de Documentation Extérieure et de Contre-Espionnage) was playing outside France. In some cases, even people of the Milieu, or French Mafia, had been recruited for certain specific missions under the cloak of national security. It was said that some agents were running drugs and guns; others were engaged in kidnapping, murder, and the settling of the most bloody scores. Some truly unsavory characters were having their police dossiers purged and being told to set up shop anew—supposedly for the French state. But most were still doing their own dirty business on the side as well.

Phony pesetas, easier to pass on the exchange market than French francs, were being counterfeited, it was said, to help finance the pro-French guerrilla movement in Algeria. Stefan Markovic, the Yugoslav bodyguard of the French film star Alain Delon, was assassinated. It was whispered in Paris, incredibly, of Mme. Pompidou's involvement in certain "parties" where this Yugoslav was often found. The obscene rumors against Mrs. Pompidou, a very fine lady who shared a deep love with her husband, were totally unfounded, but were used by a small group of disquieting political opponents of her husband.

Barely a month went by without some new scandal hitting the press, and with the name SDECE attached to it. For the Pompidou administration, it was in many respects the worst days of Watergate and Iran-Contra rolled into one.

Those who engaged in or, even by omission, looking the other way, tacitly authorized or condoned such activities in the name of state security, had to be eliminated immediately. They could only serve to undermine morale, embarrass the Republic, and ultimately prevent the president himself from ruling effectively, if at all.

I came to have a great deal of respect and affection for President Pompidou—a respect I believe was reciprocated, since from the beginning I had had one hundred percent of his trust and confidence, just as he had promised. I was about to undertake measures that could prove politically most difficult for him. So before I began, and mindful of the extraordinarily difficult position—not to mention potentially mortal danger—in which I was about to place him, I sought one final assurance that he would back me fully.

We met, as usual in those first days and most times thereafter, in his private offices in the Élysée Palace. The setting was most ornate. As befitted a palace used for celebrated state occasions, the walls were encrusted with gilt. The twenty-foot-high ceilings framed floor-to-ceiling windows that opened as doors onto the wrought-iron balconies that looked out over the acres of carefully manicured gardens. Though only late afternoon, it was already dusk, since night comes hours earlier in the French winter than it does in Washington or New York. The small, three-armed lamps called bouillottes were already lit on the president's desk as I settled into the Louis XIV armchair that sat in front of the president's gold and mahogany desk.

"You know, Mr. President," I began, "you promised me when I agreed to take this job one hundred percent of your confidence."

"Yes," he replied simply.

"I must have a free hand in taking on and dismissing whom I choose."

"Yes," he answered again.

The subject was closed. We discussed some of the events of my first two days in office. He was delighted that my purge of SDECE had begun so early, but he wanted a briefing as well about the United States, which he was about to visit, and Leonid Brezhnev, whose health had already begun to deteriorate. We talked briefly about both subjects and I promised a more detailed review after I'd discussed those subjects with our experts in research and analysis. Here, at least, SDECE retained its unequaled competence. We stood and he walked me to the door, then embraced me simply and smiled. I knew then that I had his confidence. I was never to lose it. And I vowed never to abuse it.

So I resolved, now that I was certain the head of state was behind me, to make my mark as quickly as possible. My first stop was to pay my respects to the prime minister, Jacques Chaban-Delmas; although I held him in esteem as a person, I viewed his office, the eye of the political storm in France, with deep suspicion. At the Hotel Matignon, the offices and palatial residence of the prime minister, the usher showed me up the long ceremonial staircase that spiraled from the entrance hallway. The marble corridors echoed to our footsteps as we climbed to the second-floor landing.

At the top, I met General Pierre Billotte coming through the huge double doors of the prime minister's office. Billotte, at one time briefly a minister of defense, was, quite simply, a very badly brought up millionaire, with no manners. He paused for a brief word, butting his face directly into mine, since he too was a large man and came nose to nose with me.

"Your appointment," he blustered, "is scandalous! The job is by rights mine."

I smiled sweetly, calmly thanked him for his kind words, reflecting to myself how perpetually dangerous it was to mix domestic politics and intelligence—and how such petty squabbles can get in the way of the smooth functioning of an intelligence service. My reverie was cut short by the return of the usher who promptly admitted me to Mr. Chaban-Delmas's office. Like that of the president, his was most ornate and looked out on a very beautiful garden. Most of the official buildings of France were once the *hôtels particuliers* or town houses of the French high nobility, designed to serve as quiet and lush oases in the midst of the bustle of the French capital. Today, many of them are still such havens amid the turmoil of politics and diplomacy. The prime minister rose to greet me with a broad smile and a firm grip of his hands.

"Dear friend," he began. "We are both old warriors, old Resistance veterans. I am ashamed that I didn't think of you for this job. How splendidly the president did! You have my best wishes and my total confidence. Come and see me whenever you like. My door, my private telephone line, are open to you night and day."

He paused and rummaged about his desk. "You know we can work together. This is my secret number. I will be entirely at your disposal."

Our conversation turned to the subject of the reorganization of SDECE, and I offered my thoughts about the need for speed and efficiency if the operation was to succeed and French Intelligence be restored to a useful position as an instrument of state and government. We exchanged views, as well, on some of the more difficult trouble spots in the world. As we were wrapping up, he paused for a moment; I asked him if he had any further suggestions.

"There's no need for me to teach you about international affairs," he replied. "You've been involved with them for much of your life. What should I suggest to you? Well, there is one man . . . a man you may know . . . who I see once in a while. He has a very definite taste for matters of this kind. I'm speaking of General Billotte."

I let the last sentence hang for a long moment of silence. "Mr. Prime Minister, thank you very much," I said, smiling. "I happened to meet him coming out of your office just a few minutes ago."

He reddened perceptibly. We both smiled. And changed the subject. Our conversation ended shortly. Although most of SDECE's secret funding came from the Office of the Prime Minister, I always felt more comfortable reporting directly to the president. After all, it was Pompidou, Giscard, and Mitterrand who actually appointed me (though I only worked for Mitterrand a short while). Moreover, I felt it was thoroughly imperative that the traditional ties between French politics and SDECE be severed definitively. The prime minister's office is far more in the service of French politics than is the president, who must, by the very nature of his mandate, maintain a broader worldview, dealing with the issues of war and peace, diplomacy, and strategy that are more directly and legitimately the concern of French external intelligence. Throughout history, it has always been an enormous temptation for a nation's supreme leader to use the secret intelligence services to perform certain operations dealing with internal politics. And though he wielded the power of the most powerful prince, no president of France ever asked me to perform such tasks.

Many of the individuals with impeccable connections whom I sought to purge from SDECE turned for relief to politicians they had so carefully cultivated through the years. It was a tribute to the system of constantly changing directors general that had been one of the most malevolent characteristics of SDECE until my arrival. Rarely would a director general have the political muscle or the longevity necessary to take on some of these characters. Instead, agents closely linked to powerful politicians had come to dominate the service. One characteristic of politicians, I discovered during these early days, was that however intelligent, sharp, and wily they are (the Italians would say *fourbissimi*—too clever by half—which has a rather special sense when it comes to political skulduggery), they are often totally ingenuous, and gullible enough to swallow just about anything put before them. At times what they're asked to swallow might be merely a favor for a friend or a special contract. At times the lure might be money, particularly for those who, having acquired power, would like to have wealth as well.

My target was all those, inside and outside the intelligence services, who attempted to have the state serve them. If an intelligence service becomes a political police force, then, if the presidency changes from one party to another, the next leader will destroy it. An intelligence officer is not a policeman. The policeman wants to kill the rabbit or arrest him. I don't. I want to watch the rabbit, to see where he goes. If he's destroyed, there might be another rabbit, but it will take five years for me to find him. Yet, I am certain that despite all the care I took to insulate the Service from French politics, not only some of the directors general who preceded me, but some who followed me as well, were less scrupulous—and indeed more intensely pressured—in using SDECE to settle scores or line pockets, their own or their friends'.

Some of the undesirable characters I encountered boasted that they'd been employed by my various predecessors and were closely linked to senior political figures as well as political parties representing a broad range of factions. But their ultimate aim was to exert influence that could be highly profitable in their own personal business dealings, especially with the Eastern bloc. These "jet set businessmen," as I call them, often carried on lucrative trade with, among others, the Soviet empire and its colonies.

"We must help the Russians progress further," one of these correspondents or free-lance agents explained in my office, trying to justify his role of keeping a foot in both camps, ours and theirs. "Brezhnev is moving rapidly on some very important liberal reforms."

I often heard that refrain repeated, with modifications that suited the times, all part of one disinformation campaign or another: "Gorbachev is moving the same way as Deng Xiaoping," for instance.

As I began to move on those who subverted SDECE, two sayings (though I have no taste for facile aphorisms) summarize how I conducted my affairs—both in those early days of purges and intrigue, and now. I often said to my subordinates, whether civilian or military:

"Gentlemen, be so good as to play with the cards you have, and not with those you wish you had."

"Tell me how we are going to do it, not why we can't."

Those who followed those two edicts did quite well during my term as head of French Intelligence. And, trust me, I alone determined who won and who lost. I alone made the final, often difficult decisions, sometimes of life or death. But always both my eyes were fixed firmly on one ultimate goal—the honor of the Service.

I quickly discovered that the position of director general of SDECE is one of the loneliest in the world. He has no close associates. The final decision is his. If the result is satisfactory, politicians receive the glory. But if the affair turns out badly, he will most certainly reap the acrimony that follows.

On the other hand, it is a position of all but unlimited power and considerable means. You have your shock troops to use as you please, false papers, special funds. There is little to prevent you, should you so desire, from wiping out some politician or even the head of state, because you do not happen to agree with what he says. Only the iron-willed self-discipline that clearly must accompany this amazing job keeps the director general from abusing his power.

I took orders from only one man—the president of the French Republic. It is he who bears the final responsibility, the final burden. He makes a decision, you carry it out faithfully—whether you agree with it or not. You may remonstrate, attempt to persuade, but if he is not dissuaded, you quite simply do his bidding. This power to move world events is wielded by an American president with his unquestioned finger on the nuclear trigger. This same power is wielded by the French president through his Secret Service—a power that has already proved vital in engaging our enemies in the Fourth World War that is already upon us.

There is one final trait that must distinguish a director of intelligence. He must be the most secret of men. He must have no political ambitions, no social ones either. I never met the press. I asked the two presidents whom I served faithfully to release me from all official functions—the elegant banquets at the Élysée Palace, the presidential hunting parties, the use of the box at the opera, the social pleasures so highly prized by top civil servants. For a director of intelligence, they can be quagmires. An enormous drain on his time and energy, they may also lead to the most embarrassing, even compromising, encounters. I made few exceptions—the occasional private dinner at the Élysée or Versailles, when the visiting head of a foreign government with whom I had a long personal relationship would have been deeply offended by my absence.

With these basic precepts firmly fixed in my mind, I began to burrow into the complex organization I was leading in an effort to mold it into the kind of first-rate intelligence gathering and operational organization that the French state needed as its powerful eyes, ears, and fists abroad. The French Secret Service was, and still is, organized much like any large industrial organization. There are the financial and administrative branches, the research side. But there are other branches that no industry has ever duplicated— intelligence, communications, counterespionage, and operations.

The staff is divided into career civil and military personnel. All public servants carried the same grades as those in the Civil Service. In that respect alone, they are no different from bureaucrats in the Ministries of Agriculture or Foreign Affairs, or the Post Office.

The military personnel often put in a considerable part of their careers in the Secret Service by virtue of their specialties—for example, in Arab and Muslim affairs, oil matters, or the nomadic tribes of the Sahara. There are other career military officers who are assigned to the Service for a shorter term before returning to their regular units.

There are also reserve officers employed by the Service who in their regular civilian capacities may be found in almost any job or any country. They and other intelligence agents are often given the name "honorary correspondents." They complete our organization chart of the Secret Service—filling in the last empty spaces along the borders. In terms of their intelligence role they may lie dormant or unused for years, but may suddenly become the most valuable members of the Intelligence Service overnight. You may find one who was a taxi driver, another a dignitary in the Church, or even a government minister. Some are paid for their work—on occasion, quite a lot of money—but most perform their quiet functions from a sense of patriotism, purely for the honor. They are Frenchmen and Frenchwomen who may brave unspeakable dangers to arrive in the most highly sensitive areas, where they can see and hear what may be of some use to their country.

This is not to say that we French have a patent on such activities or such individuals. Every nation follows this practice. The Americans have their informants far more broadly spread than we— their resources, both human and financial, are far grander. Our Swiss neighbors, who guard their neutrality so jealously, have a network that is especially broad. With every Swiss male a member of that country's militia, they are able to call on reserve military officers who travel widely on the complex and secret business and financial affairs that so distinguish the Swiss. They are delighted to keep the federal government in Berne informed, wherever they may be located.

In this respect, all intelligence services have much in common— they are like an immense juice-squeezer, into which countless fragments of information are fed, hundreds or thousands each day, to allow the essence to be extracted, the few drops that matter. Carefully distilled and analyzed, they will give substance to the daily report intended for the Élysée Palace. The supervision of all this information gathering and analysis represents one of the most essential, if least dramatic, tasks of the Intelligence Service. It is the most painstaking, plodding work. No James Bonds here, still fewer Mata Haris. Few of my agents have ever dropped by parachute one moment, then dined with a stunning brunette spy. Intelligence gathering requires specialists in many of the more arcane disciplines or corners of our planet—armed not with a Beretta, but with the capacity to decipher vast masses of information from books, the press, radio monitoring, and field reports.

They must be equally adept at separating fact from fiction, bluster and bluff from bona fide evidence. For among international crooks, a large number of professional con men are prepared to swap intelligence for money. Who are these individuals operating in the shadow of the giants of intelligence? Most are struggling free-lancers, the pickpockets of the espionage community, who stumble on a small fact here or there and attempt to earn a meager day's pay from their foraging in the garbage cans of the world. But there are some stellar performers as well. They have in their possession information they have obtained—or ingeniously invented—and want to sell. How is it obtained? At times by good intelligence work on the part of the free-lancers. More often, it is the result of meetings, dinners, reading the foreign press, combined with a dollop of imagination and a soupçon of their own seasoning. It is the job of professionals to determine, before money changes hands, whether it is worth the price—to be able to say with confidence, "What you've produced for me is worthless," or "Indeed we did know about this."

One such colorful character I came to know through his work had supplied SDECE with more or less fictitious information over several years before my arrival as director general. Code-named the Cardinal, he became renowned sometime later for his involvement in the "sniffer planes"—an extraordinary airborne device that was said to be endowed with the ability to "sniff" the presence of oil deposits while flying over any territory. It cost the French government many millions of dollars to learn it had been the victim of a colossal swindler. Nevertheless, it was clear to me from the first reports I saw that the Cardinal, with the help of a Belgian aristocrat, honest and gullible, was little more than an expensive con man. What the Cardinal's "intelligence reports" revealed for the money spent on him hardly came up to the standards one would expect from a junior researcher armed with a subscription to several daily newspapers. And for this he commanded some of the highest fees paid by SDECE.

Within a few days of my arrival, I put a stop to the little game of the Cardinal and ordered my principal assistant at the time, Didier, to throw him out bodily. A Free Frenchman with a brilliant war record, Didier wasted little time in carrying out this first order from me.

So it was to Didier that I turned when it was time to launch what I dubbed Operation Ferret, my plan to overhaul the agency. We launched it suddenly and without warning, though Didier was puzzled when I first disclosed the operation's code name.

"When a ferret is introduced into a colony of rabbits," I explained, "the rabbits lose their heads, panic, and make for the exits to reach the open air. All it requires then is for a marksman to be posted at each of the holes."

The first hours were the most critical. When Didier began burrowing into the organization, as I expected, it was a case of every man for himself. A number of distraught "rabbits" found their way to his office. I remained alone in my office next door, patiently waiting for him to complete his work. The bodies, figuratively, soon littered the floor of my aide's quarters.

One such individual, who had amassed a considerable fortune using the privileges of SDECE, but who had not neglected, incidentally, to take care of some leading politicians who might ultimately be of some assistance, was fired by Didier on my direct orders.

"Summon him and tell him he's finished," I ordered Didier.

Didier summoned the man in question and read him the news of his dismissal.

"You know, I am a very important man," this official blustered. "Do you mean to tell me the director general himself won't tell me I'm fired?"

As I listened on the open intercom in my inner office, Didier explained patiently, "Yes, you're lucky he doesn't. Because you walk into his office, but you come out on a stretcher."

I was tough and rigorous, but I believe fair. The Intelligence Service, when it is run properly, is a delicate blend of artistic sensitivity and military discipline. For it to function properly in an environment like that of the Third World War, or more particularly the Fourth, it must understand the finest nuances of the enemy mind and society, while at the same time stand prepared to act with split-second timing to thwart a deadly threat to national security. My goal in Operation Ferret was to weed out those who were not competent or motivated enough to accomplish this mission, and to achieve a blend of sensitivity and discipline among those agents who remained by encouraging creativity and original thinking, while insisting on the niceties of martial discipline.

One day, shortly after the start of Operation Ferret, a young captain burst through the main door of my office, breathless with a now long-forgotten bit of information. I put him in detention for two weeks. The personnel of SDECE were meant to take the smaller service door to the side. One day, returning to the Tourelles Barracks after lunch, the guard at the front gate failed to stop my car, which he had clearly recognized.

"Stop the car," I said to my chauffeur, and the large black Citroën ground to a halt. "Send for the captain."

The captain arrived and leaned into the car with some trepidation. My reputation had clearly preceded me. I described what had just happened. "Your man didn't do his job," I said. "One more time and you're fired."

I never disciplined the little guy. If some big scandal happened in SDECE, I was responsible, no matter how little the cause. I followed the same rule consistently—discipline must be assured from the top down.

The Service as a whole had to be whipped into a single fighting unit. And each individual had to be prepared to serve that unit, and the state, before himself or any other individual, organization, or political philosophy.

So it should come as no surprise that the clean-up of SDECE on which I embarked had some bad moments. There were those who tried to destroy me, as I sought to bring them down. And in one instance, they very nearly succeeded.

It became known as the Delouette affair. And it did not come without advance notice. What is not generally known is that the affair was a direct result of my moves on various elements in the Service, following this purge, and an attempt to halt its momentum. It did not, as conventional wisdom would have, touch off the purges themselves. They had been long overdue and had no need of a further challenge to push them forward.

The warning that a plan was afoot came from Sir John R., my distinguished British colleague, in one of our early meetings. We had met in the offices of MI6, the British Secret Intelligence Service. His office was filled with pictures of former chiefs of the British Service, most in civilian clothes, some in army uniforms, many in the dark blue uniform of the Royal Navy.

He began slowly and moderately, choosing his words with care and practicing his famous understatement. "The signs are that you're on the point of bringing off your bid to overhaul the French

Secret Service," he remarked offhandedly in that impassive manner of well-bred Englishmen. "Watch out. There will be an attempt to destroy you."

"Thank you for letting me know, Sir John," I replied. "When and how will it come?"

"Be on the lookout in the spring."

Precisely as he warned, in the spring, the Delouette business erupted. It began with drugs and ended in tragedy. But not my own.

It was early on the morning of April 5, 1971, when I was phoned at my home by our overnight duty officer with the news that a former journalist with French Radio and Television (ORTF as it was then known), named Roger Delouette, had been caught in Port Elizabeth, New Jersey, reclaiming a car arriving by boat from France and that the car contained 44.5 kilos of pure, uncut heroin. He was not a SDECE agent, but after several weeks of intensive interrogation, finally broke down and told the American police that he had been working for a SDECE colonel named Paul Fournier. At that point, Delouette was formally arrested and imprisoned.

There were a few Americans who tried to get considerable mileage out of this affair, among them the young United States Attorney for Newark, New Jersey, Herbert J. Stern. Clearly his goal, and that of my enemies in France, meshed very nicely indeed. The aim was to conclude that SDECE, under my leadership, was engaged in drug trafficking to finance its special operations, or at least to give the impression that the French Secret Service had gone into drugs to make money.

Franco-American relations had a very bad time of it for several months. But I had many powerful friends in my corner. Thomas Watson, son of the founder of IBM, and at the time United States ambassador to France, was both personally embarrassed by the notoriety this affair was generating in France, and deeply disturbed that the United States was apparently being used to discredit a man who was a great personal friend of America and an institution that was an equally important ally.

I learned of Watson's distress only later when we met before a visit I was about to pay to the United States long after the affair had become history. At the time the Delouette affair was unfolding, I made every effort to avoid any meetings with American officials so as not to appear to be influencing the investigation of the case either in France or in the United States.

The people behind this plot had also spread the rumor that a middle-ranking official in SDECE was indeed the mastermind of this Mafia-style drug running being conducted under the very noses and using the facilities of the Intelligence Service. I knew this civil servant. He was no more capable of running traffic in drugs than I am of being a bishop of the Church. The whole story was, of course, a total fabrication from beginning to end.

It quite quickly became an affair of state on both sides of the Atlantic, and I saw President Pompidou frequently during this difficult time. He was being attacked everywhere. But he never once asked me about it. He did not want to embarrass me. He knew that there was nothing I could tell him until I had resolved the matter to my satisfaction, and at the time I had nothing concrete whatsoever to report. Pompidou's conduct was a demonstration of his sensitivity; he was a man of outstanding quality. One morning, at the height of the furor over this terrible embarrassment, as I was at home preparing to leave for my office, a presidential messenger arrived on his large black motorcycle. He rang the bell downstairs. My housekeeper admitted him and, without a word, he opened a large black metal box he carried—the presidential dispatch case—took out a parcel that was inside, and passed it to her. I opened it and found, in a silver frame, Georges Pomidou's official photograph with the simple, but terribly significant inscription: "*Pour Alexandre de Marenches, serviteur de la France, en toute confiance*"(". . . servant of France, in whom I have complete trust"), signed, "Georges Pompidou." You can hardly imagine the effect that had on me. I was deeply touched. It was a gesture I valued more than any decorations or citations, a gesture that showed true magnanimity on his part.

Pompidou stood by me through it all. But in the end, we never really found out who was behind the attempted putsch against my rule over SDECE. To have done so would have torn apart the entire Service and quite possibly would have destroyed the Pompidou regime itself. A judicial inquiry by a French *juge d'instruction,* the equivalent of a district attorney, failed to find evidence of wrongdoing that would have justified bringing any criminal charges. In this milieu, where the waters are murky green, you sometimes see the shadows of big fish glide past, but you can't make out any details. That was the case in the Delouette affair.

Still, there was one ironic, and tragic, postscript to this strange affair. The following year, the son of Sir John, the unimpeachable British gentleman who so gallantly had warned me of my troubles on the horizon, was implicated in a drug scandal. Sir John, seeing it as a disgrace, tendered his own resignation from the British Secret Service. Perhaps that was the ultimate revenge of those who organized the Delouette affair. And we will probably never know the answer.

The principal aim of Operation Ferret, indeed of every action I took during my first weeks and months in office, was to create a new frame of mind throughout SDECE—from the very top to the very bottom. Each member of the Secret Service, above all each operational team, must function as though they are in fact at war.

On my arrival in November 1970, I found that the Operations Service, what should have been capable of functioning as the powerful strike force, the front-line troops of SDECE in our Third World War mode, had in fact been reduced virtually to nothing. Rebuilding this indispensable core of SDECE was my most difficult and time-consuming task. It required effectively constructing an army unit from the ground up. But beyond that, it required transforming the image of the career operational intelligence officer within SDECE and within the military as well.

In the past, an unfortunate tradition made service in SDECE prejudicial to a military officer's career prospects. To a large extent that was a result of the tasks he or she would be asked to perform—tasks to which a military officer was manifestly unsuited. I lobbied successfully for a change in the promotional table, so that my military personnel would be promoted at precisely the same rate they would have had they remained in the regular army. I never fully succeeded in achieving my ultimate aim—more rapid promotion for intelligence officers, who were prepared to make great personal sacrifices and live under the most dangerous conditions, which many came to accept as a regular part of their daily lives. The fact is that those officers, unlike their counterparts who remained with French Army units, were constantly at war. Battlefield promotions were a regular fact of life for officers in combat. Certainly, that should be the case for intelligence officers as well.

For some individuals, this became possible as my tenure wore on and the image of SDECE became more professional, more "serious," as we French like to call something important. There was, for instance, the case of General Jeannou Lacaze, who was loaned to me for six years as a senior officer, promoted to general, and finally finished his career as Combined Chief of Staff of the French Army.

During my tenure, I built the Operations Service into a unit of several thousand men and women on the official and unofficial rolls. Rebuilding such units required extraordinary patience. The Operations Service was a most elite unit. We traveled to each of the major parachute regiments of the French military and asked for volunteers for our Special Forces. Out of ten we would take one. Each was an expert—in the martial arts, rifles, revolvers. There were parachutists, skin divers, demolition experts. Super-soldiers. Some wound up working full time in France or scattered around the world—general officers, senior and junior officers, NCOs, and other ranks. Many boys who had completed their military service with us quite often found the Secret Service congenial and stayed on. There were those on reserve status and others on temporary loan from the military.

I carefully cultivated the head of military personnel and the various army chiefs who were able to identify those who had the specialized abilities we so often required. There were, for instance, army, naval, or air force officers able to speak some of the most obscure languages. It's clear that for a normal career in an infantry regiment, the ability of an officer to speak Khmer is scarcely of particular value. But in my Service, he is a rare find. As our needs became known, our professionalism increasingly respected, we found a widening pool of the most extraordinary talent in the barracks of French military units.

And we did not by any means exclude women. While many were information analysts, we did have a few remarkable women officers in our Operational units as well. Some were specialists in chemistry, electronics, or nuclear physics, or in military strategy or tactics. Others were specialists in finer arts of distraction or decoy work.

The next step was to train the recruits. They were first-rate soldiers. But they needed to work together as a unit, and often under the most deadly conditions, in the darkest night, in the deepest oceans. So we replicated those conditions. We held special night maneuvers in the Mediterranean and the Atlantic. So that a plane would not be heard, the parachutists would jump from several kilometers up, yet open the parachute only a few hundred yards before hitting the sea, at the very last moment. They carried with them what they needed as skin divers, their equipment, collapsible rubber boats. They were professionals.

Until my arrival, there had been a distinct lack of discipline, of esprit de corps. Our men and women must be prepared, even in training, to lay down their lives for their country, silently, facelessly, often thanklessly, at times winding up in unmarked graves, far from their homes and family. But they had to be motivated. I tried to be their motivation, their father figure, and I quickly discovered that sometimes the chief has to walk first in the minefield, has to be around. So once in a while, without warning, I would walk through the offices, stop to chat and watch our people perform their duties. Outside Paris, in the countryside and by the sea, our Special Forces, especially the combat frogmen, maintained their elite ground, naval, and air force organizations. I would go and spend a day with them, eat at the mess and in the evening, after the meal, we would sing together. Those gestures were repaid a thousandfold.

Striking a balance between civilian and military officers was perhaps the most delicate task in my early months as head of SDECE. The civilians in my organization were career servants and included departmental directors and section heads—a total complement equivalent to a small Ministry of State. A third of the personnel, ultimately, were military officers.

On my arrival at the central office, the wildest rumors began circulating immediately. Some civilians were afraid. Others reminded them, "You've got nothing to worry about. He's a civilian himself. He'll fire the military and bring civilians in everywhere." Both were wrong.

Each had their strengths and weaknesses. I have a great deal of respect for civil servants who dedicate their careers to the state. The military, on the other hand, are at everybody's beck and call, twenty-four hours a day, including Sundays and holidays; they are totally dedicated. To fire an army man poses no problem. You simply put a line through his name and return him to his unit. Dismissing a civil servant, I discovered, is a trifle more complicated. I quickly developed a small group of personal assistants, however, who became quite adept at arranging with ministries or departments to take back the undesirable Mr. or Miss So-and-so.

So what did I look for when young recruits came to see me?

"I want an interesting life," they should begin. "Whatever I am or whatever I do, I don't want to be thanked for it. If things go wrong, I'm quite willing to take the rap, but at least it won't be boring. I'll be fighting for freedom."

If the person is well-balanced and physically fit, and has a spark of ingenuity and initiative, I would reply, "Yes, by all means, come into intelligence work and serve the cause of freedom."

In matters of recruitment, we were forced to be particularly circumspect. Never would a classified advertisement appear in the newspaper, or recruiters show up publicly on college campuses as the Central Intelligence Agency has been known to do. I selected a splendid gentleman named Dr. Maurice Beccuau, who was also a brigadier general, and happened as well to be my personal physician, to be in charge of all recruiting.

"Men and women who are thoroughly at ease with themselves, buoyant and of cheerful disposition, and whose desire is to serve the cause of freedom—those are the people we want," I told him. They were my only instructions. He performed admirably. The strength of our Service is to a large extent a tribute to his perceptive application of that simple rule of thumb.

Each recruit was most carefully screened—first by the medical directorate. I wanted recruits who were well built, content, in good health, happy in life, with a good feeling about themselves. If they were married, I wanted to see the husband or wife. And when there were important individuals I was planning to send abroad, I would invite the individual and his or her spouse to lunch together. We did this frequently, generally in my offices at headquarters. After lunch, we would take a café and a cigar. And I would look at the prospects' legs. Because most people, if they are phonies, control their faces. But their legs go up and down under the table. They would, somehow, show their agitation.

Almost immediately after their recruitment, I would insist that even the most obscure analyst spend some considerable time overseas. There is a serious problem that Americans have in intelligence work. They look American and they think American. You've got to go out and live in the souk, speak the language of the Middle East, for instance, the language of the bazaars, understand their thoughts, their dreams. Then you can become an intelligence analyst—an intelligent one at that.

So, when I took such care selecting my recruits, it has always been curious to me that whenever I have had a conversation about this matter with people outside the Service, they have shown so little understanding of it. Usually, after these civilians have finally summoned the nerve to broach the subject with me, what they most wanted to know was why the French Secret Service has never attracted the intellectual or even the social elite that in Great Britain and the United States has always considered it a great honor to serve in the shadows. The reason, I believe, is simple. The national temperament of the French has little use for people who perform this sort of work. It is quite simply not very fashionable here to be in intelligence.

By contrast, in Britain, the Secret Service has been able to recruit from the cream of the top universities, an intellectual elite that is intrigued by the mystery of the profession. In Britain, until recently, it was barely known which secret services existed. People had no idea who headed the Intelligence Service. He was a cipher, carefully protected by the Official Secrets Act. Officially, there was MI6. Should a scandal such as the Greenpeace affair or the Delouette case break, the speaker of the House of Commons, or the prime minister would say simply, "Well, it's not clear to me what service you are speaking about." A special letter would be sent around to every newspaper office in Great Britain. And the case would vanish from the press and the public. In short, intelligence was a professional's ultimate profession.

Our East European counterparts found recruitment even easier. With the extraordinary privileges accorded their secret services—the right, indeed duty, to travel abroad (unlike the vast mass of their countrymen); access to the best commissaries and schools, the best apartments and clothing; in short, a quality of life unattainable by 90 percent of their fellow citizens—the East European services had no problems in recruiting the cream of their population. And, despite what to all outward appearances would seem to be the dismantling of the East European intelligence apparatuses, it is clear to us that they still are having no problems in recruiting. The KGB in particular still offers a highly attractive, secure, comfortable career for those who are fortunate enough to be chosen.

Another reason for our difficulties in recruitment over the years was financial—the restricted resources in general that were placed at the disposal of our Service. With respect to our budget, we were forced to make a little go a very long way indeed. The East European budgets, all but unlimited in their allocations for men and materials (as many high-ranking defectors have confided to me) were a ridiculous contrast to our meager resources, and indeed those of most Western intelligence services. Our French budgets, which were more or less on a par with those of the British, were in turn meager in comparison with those of West Germany or the U.S. Central Intelligence Agency.

The low pay, the solitary working conditions, the general lack of prestige for our most dangerous profession, opened temptations for any security personnel who were not totally dedicated to their careers of service to the state. So it should come as little surprise that I did not leave the personal integrity and honesty, or the operational reliability, of SDECE entirely to the good faith of our officers. Life is too complex, temptations in our profession too pervasive. Instead, I monitored their reliability.

There had always been an Internal Security Service that served just this purpose. But through the years, as other fiefdoms in French Intelligence had acquired enormous strength within, and political support outside, the watchdog function of Internal Security had atrophied. So immediately after my arrival I added a number of extra civilian and military personnel, charging them directly with the critical task of keeping an eye on those employed by SDECE—and my own actions were not excepted. My orders were that I be kept under as careful scrutiny as anyone else. More than three hundred people were directly involved with monitoring the activities of the rest of the Service. That surveillance was both technical and human—that is, electronic monitoring and a careful watch for any dubious contacts. Anyone from our Service who wanted to travel abroad, for instance, always had to request special permission.

Occasionally, I would be asked if SDECE had been infiltrated.

"Of course it's penetrated," I always replied. "If a major intelligence service is not penetrated, one can only assume it's because it is of no interest to those whose job it is to penetrate the opposition."

I did hope, however, that any infiltration remained insignificant or was caught before it became dangerous or truly compromising to the interests of the Service or the state, not to mention to any individuals. Over the years, we did discover and got rid of a certain number of people who at the very least gave rise to suspicion, and we often found bugging devices hidden in the premises we used abroad. In one inspection of our embassy in Warsaw, we found forty-four microphones or other listening devices, all installed in the two months since the previous sweep. When I learned that our top electronic counterintelligence expert had just returned from this emergency visit to Warsaw, I asked that he come to see me and the next day he showed up in my office. I sat him down, offered him a drink, and he began his report.

"Ah, monsieur, you know in the office of the ambassador alone there were four microphones," he said proudly. "And we found them all." He had used a suitcase full of debugging devices.

It was assumed that our telephone conversations were bugged and that we were followed—by our own people, or the other side. At least our charter permitted us to carry out such surveillance, and we acted accordingly. I never discouraged such speculation. We were not paranoid, but it kept us on our toes. I refused to tolerate among us the kind of paranoia that was developed in the CIA by James Jesus Angleton. Angleton had been given the mission of eradicating the cancer of Soviet penetration.

For nearly twenty years, Angleton ran the counterespionage unit of the CIA. He was a brilliant product of Yale and the OSS, a brooding, compulsive poet, whose various code names—Mother, Orchid, the Gray Ghost, the Cadaver, the Fisherman, the Fly—spoke volumes about how he viewed himself and how others viewed him. Beginning December 20, 1954, Angleton was given the brief to tunnel deep into the CIA's already formidable bureaucracy, looking for one kind of animal—moles, the intelligence shorthand for agents who were really working for the other side, in Angleton's case, the Soviet empire.

For the next twenty years, this consummate "spymaster" used every means in his monomaniacal quest for the elusive mole at the top of American intelligence. At his height, more than three hundred agents responded to his every whim. During this period, under his aegis, the CIA opened tens of thousands of letters sent through the mails from the United States to the Soviet Union and developed a computerized "watch list" of two million names. It was, of course, illegal even for government agents to open the United States mails.

But many of Angleton's friends and enemies alike thought the greatest damage he did to American intelligence came during the period of the defection and interrogation of two master Soviet spies—Anatoly Golytsin, who defected from Helsinki in December 1961, and Yuri Nosenko, who came over in Switzerland in February 1964. Each was suspected by different elements within the CIA of being a double agent, instructed to spread disinformation or to discredit the other. Angleton, however, latched on to Golytsin as the true defector, opening the personnel files of the Soviet section of the CIA to his perusal in an effort to identify Russian moles. Within months, scores of experienced Soviet specialists were being removed from action on the express orders of Angleton, and on only the flimsiest of suspicion or innuendo. The Soviet section of the CIA was crippled for years, not to mention the ability of the agency in general to evaluate defectors of any stripe in any objective sense. That was a mistake I vowed never to make.

Shortly after I assumed office, in 1971, I paid my first visit to Langley, Virginia, to meet my American counterpart, Richard Helms, and to see the spymaster, James Angleton, firsthand.

The day after my first meeting with Helms, I stopped in to see Angleton—already a legend.

Our conversation got off to a most curious start.

"Anything really secret and confidential," he said in a hushed voice, "you come to me, not to the director."

I was shocked into what for me was indeed a rare speechless condition, so he continued unchecked.

"Anyway, our man in Paris is a KGB agent!" said Angleton. "And his wife is even worse."

In my view, the CIA's station chief in Paris was a very good man.

By this time, I could hardly breathe. It was nearly 5:00 P.M., so he broke out a bottle of whiskey and we began to drink, and I finally managed to stammer out a reply.

"Mr. Angleton," I began. "If he is a KGB spy, why don't you remove him and arrest him?" He had no reply. He continued on into the bottle of whiskey, which, by the end of our evening, he had managed, largely single-handedly, to finish. I never had more than one or two drinks in an evening.

As he finally rose to accompany me to the door, I concluded that I had to respond to his opening remark once and for all.

"My dear Mr. Angleton," I said, "I am the director general of French Intelligence. I deal with your director and your director only."

Then I added, "I hope you will not arrest me before I leave your office." He smiled, and I left. Perhaps he thought I, too, was a spy, or an agent for the GRU (Glavnoye Razvedyvatelnoye Upravleniye, Chief Intelligence Directorate of the General Staff, or Soviet military intelligence—the counterpart to the civilian KGB)!

James Jesus Angleton was in my opinion not the kind of man you wanted to have as the head of your counterespionage unit. If you start by suspecting everyone, among them even your most trusted friends, then where do you go? I made only three demands on our counterintelligence agents. No paranoia. No drinking. And no stereotypes—typecasting of a certain kind of individual as clearly prone to defection or deception. We were, after all, locked in battle with an enemy prone not to paranoia, but objectivity; who treated every individual with a healthy skepticism but accepted the need to evaluate intelligence on its own merits.

But there were many stereotypes that had little to do with contemporary intelligence. I'm afraid I never did encounter the sizzling spy of fantasy, the femme fatale dressed in black with the plunging neckline, voluptuous lips, and cigarette holder a yard long. There are some powerful myths about secret services, relayed by television, novels, magazines, and films of every sort. Along with love, espionage is one of the most worked over themes. A script combining romance and espionage can hardly go wrong. It is certainly what the public appreciates—surefire thrills, larger-than-life characters, action and intrigue that are more or less secret, glamour and romance, blood and tears. Even I was not immune from this variety of cinema. I simply had to be a bit more circumspect in indulging my tastes.

So it's here that I will confess, in the hope of forgiveness. From time to time, I would take a train or plane to Geneva or Brussels, generally wearing an overcoat with a high collar that I could pull up tight around my face. By train, I would leave in the late afternoon from the Gare du Nord or the Gare de l'Est. I would take with me an ordinary thriller—a Maigret, for instance—and sit quietly by the window watching the countryside. When I arrived in Geneva or Brussels, I would walk out to the taxi queue, wait patiently for a cab, and drive to a movie theater I had carefully selected in advance. And treat myself to a James Bond film. I always kept my escapade most quiet. I would never have risked going to see such a film in Paris, since some malicious person would most certainly have spotted me and begun to circulate the vicious rumor. As he might have put it: "Dear me—see how far SDECE has fallen when its chief has to look for gimmicks in James Bond films!"

Some of this whispering might very well have come from one or more of my rivals within the French security system. For I was quickly to discover, to my chagrin, that SDECE was not the only arm of security of the state. The constant rivalries between it and the DST were often debilitating and on occasion deeply embarrassing, if not counter to the interests of the French state itself.

The DST (Direction de la Surveillance du Territoire) is charged with the single assignment of operating within French territory and is the nearest French equivalent to the FBI. My own Service, the SDECE, the external counterespionage and intelligence service, had (with a couple of exceptions) the responsibility of operating everywhere but in France. For years, SDECE had spent much of its time and energy struggling against the Ministry of the Interior, which was the overseer of the DST.

I tried, in the common interest, to establish a working relationship between the two, and for a few years that was effective. Such a seamless integration of internal and external intelligence gathering has never been more vital than in fighting the kinds of battles that have worked in the Third World War and appear inevitable in the Fourth. In both cases frontiers are pierced before the battles are ever joined.

So one of the first calls I paid after my appointment in 1970 was on the minister of the interior, Raymond Marcellin, to let him know my strong views on these matters. My next call was on Jean Rochet, a prefect, who served at the time as head of the DST, and was a great patriot. I was ushered into his ornate offices in a magnificent old building just next to the Ministry of the Interior and tucked behind the Élysée Palace in downtown Paris. As we both sank into the armchairs that formed a more relaxed corner away from the massive desk where he carried out his daily business of watching over the internal security of the French people, I decided to come directly to the point. My agenda was a simple one—an end to the rivalry that had existed really since the end of the Second World War between the two principal security organizations of the French Republic.

"I am from neither the Right nor the Left," I began. "My unique concern is to serve France and the government." Rochet listened carefully as I continued, "So, please, let us live in harmony. No more infighting between services, and let's get at the enemy!"

It would, of course, have been difficult for any director of the DST to openly disagree with a concept so clearly in the interests of the French government, though I am equally convinced that most of his predecessors would quite promptly have turned to undermining any such agreement. I believe quite sincerely that Rochet made every effort during his tenure to make certain this cooperation became as much a reality as decades of past rivalry would permit.

It was not something that came naturally or easily to any leader of the DST, or the SDECE for that matter, nor of any two services with comparable mandates such as the FBI and the CIA. It was something that we had to work at. And we did. Almost immediately after that first contact with Rochet, in an attempt to make this new era of good feeling a concrete reality, I arranged to undertake joint training exercises on Corsica under a unified command—including both DST and SDECE commandos. The young policemen of the DST operating alongside our agents as skin divers and demolition experts, using planes and helicopters. And on the last day, we had a big dinner party and barbecue in the open air. I had both Rochet and Marcellin, the minister of the interior, to whom Rochet reported, fly down with me in one of our planes to spend the day with us. It was efforts like these that truly helped to break down some of the mistrust, at least on an operational level, between our two services.

Still, at the national level, there remains a great deal of conflict between SDECE (or now, DGSE, the successor organization known as the Direction Générale de la Securité Extérieure) and the DST. The atmosphere is not as tense as it used to be, but there is still far too much competition. When dealing with the types of warfare that characterize the Fourth World War, our struggles against terrorism or drug trafficking that take no notice of frontiers, indeed capitalizes on our division between domestic and international intelligence, all services involved must take appropriate measures. And often there is little time for close consultation. The services must, quite simply, work seamlessly together all the time, each knowing almost intuitively what is happening on the other's turf.

In 1983, the DST and the DGSE identified a large number of senior Soviet intelligence agents operating out of the embassy in Paris on the Boulevard Lannes. A decision was made by the president, a political decision, I would point out, to expel them all, en masse. It was a truly dramatic gesture. Moreover, our information was that it dealt a serious blow to the Soviet intelligence apparatus in France for some years to come.

One of those agents was a member of the press section in the Soviet embassy. The son of a onetime member of the Soviet Politburo, purged in the post-Khrushchev era and sent finally to Tokyo as ambassador, he had previously served as a member of the Soviet trade mission to Algeria, where he was first identified as a senior intelligence operative. Unlike many of the other members of the Soviet press office, he was distinguished by a command of the French language as impeccable as his tailoring. And he quickly made it his business to meet and befriend many of the top French correspondents, especially in radio and television, as well as foreign, especially American, correspondents based in Paris. At the same time, he became a close confidant of Yuli Vorontsov, the powerful Soviet ambassador to Paris, a member of the Communist Party Central Committee, who was to return to Moscow as deputy foreign minister and ambassador to the strategic-arms talks with the Americans in Geneva. As a result of his connections and his position, the KGB operative was able to feed considerable disinformation to Western correspondents.

There was, for instance, his assertion at the time that neither the Soviets nor any of their friends or allies were aiding and abetting the Abul Abass wing of the Palestine Liberation Front, which had carried off the deadly hijacking of the *Achille Lauro* cruise liner. His access to the most highly placed French journalists and key Western correspondents, with whom he often "traded" information, enabled him to gauge with exquisite precision the state of public opinion in the West, especially in France and Western Europe, and the American point of view on European affairs, as well as to sense how best to manipulate it.

We kept close track of this individual. The DST monitored his activities closely in France, developed contacts among those journalists, including some Americans, with whom he was in touch. And the DGSE monitored his travels abroad—to Luxembourg, Brussels, and Geneva. We had him identified, monitored, and surrounded. Why not be delighted to have him remain in the West—a case of the rabbit we knew being carefully watched? He was completely wired. Those journalists with whom he was in regular contact were alerted about his motives and interests. But finally, the Russians got smart. They recalled him. It was a case of ideal cooperation between our two services—the DST and DGSE. It did not, unfortunately, always work so effectively. Compartmentalization was, quite simply, accepted practice among the secret services of France that serve the state.

I was determined not to let such practices affect our relations with our Western allies, and from my first days in office did my best to cooperate with the other intelligence services of the Western family. I made it an immediate point to call on my European colleagues and get to know them.

My strategy was to arrange meetings twice a year or whenever necessary, which curiously had never been done before; at the meetings, we discussed matters that interested all of us. We met in Paris, London, Munich, on a rotating basis. And it was purely the principal European intelligence chiefs—the French, the British, the Germans. That was where cooperation was most essential if we were truly to join in battling the Soviet empire in the Third World War.

The Americans were not present at these sessions. During my entire tenure as director of French Intelligence, there was never a joint meeting between the head of the CIA and the heads of the three leading Allied intelligence agencies in Europe. Instead, I arranged separate biannual talks with the Americans. George Bush was in attendance when he headed the Central Intelligence Agency.

I have been accused at times of not keeping the Americans fully informed. There is no question that did not promote the kind of unity among the principal Northern, or Western, intelligence powers that would have made execution of the Third World War easier and defending ourselves in the Fourth World War even possible. But there were reasons for this position. In fact, there was one very simple reason, as I warned William Casey during one of our earliest meetings: For most of those years, whatever you told the Americans was known by the public the next morning.

The first time I met with my European colleagues, I laid all my cards on the table. Clearly, there were many deep suspicions, some dating back to the Second World War. The director of the BND, the Bundesnachrichtendienst, the formidable German State Intelligence Service, was present, along with the rest of the Allies, except the Americans. The intense jealousies and passions that still divided Europe also divided our intelligence services (and to a certain extent still do).

Since I had requested the first meeting and convened it in our central office in Paris, I called it to order and began, "Gentlemen, I am the chief of French Intelligence. I will defend the interests of France. But I am also an Allied chief. You know who I am and where I come from. I am not hiding anything. My heart is with you, in the right place. If there are any problems or conflicts between us, let's put them on the table now and talk about them. We are all battling the same enemies, the enemies of democracy. And if our governments have problems or differences, we should put them on the table and talk about them freely."

There were murmurs of agreement around the table as I continued, "And I'd just like to say one last thing before we begin—I will never lie to you, because I don't believe in lying. As Sacha Guitry"—I turned to the British representative and smiled—"the

French Bernard Shaw, used to say, 'Never lie, because you need too much of a memory.' "

The result of this meeting was an extraordinary level of cooperation among the leading European intelligence heads that has never been duplicated. When Sir Brian Tovey, a remarkable man who headed the British Listening Service at Cheltenham (Great Britain's powerful worldwide electronic intelligence operation, known as GCHQ), sent a copy of an intercept to MI6 in London, he'd send me a copy in Paris as well. He had a special coded telex installed in my offices. There were no better intercepts than the British in many parts of the world, and we both knew it.

The philosophy of utter candor that I elaborated during that first meeting with my Allied colleagues, and that proved to be so well received, was the centerpiece of my philosophy of conducting business, a philosophy that I used with politicians with whom I had some contacts, my foreign counterparts, and of course my own colleagues in the Service.

CHAPTER **5**

The Field of
Operations . . . or Dreams

Intelligence is a kind of perpetual puzzle, composed of many shapes and colors that are constantly forming and unforming. Intelligence consists of the never-ending search for a number of separate pieces that Secret Service analysts assemble to complete the puzzle. But just when you manage to fill one gap with new pieces, the puzzle changes shape. It is endlessly evolving. In many respects, it is also like the instrument panel in an aircraft. In the cockpit is the man who makes the decisions—the pilot, the head of state. The information before him is vital. Without it, he cannot fly the plane safely. If the Service is inept, full of amateurs or people who are incompetent or stupid or worse, it will impact on the president, not to mention his "passengers"—the people he governs. Obviously, his international position will weaken too, his compass will fail, and he will not be in possession of all the tools that enable him to steer a direct course to his destination.

The world is such that even in normal circumstances, the president is flying in adverse conditions, often in zero visibility. If he is also without essential instruments that warn him what to expect, how can disaster be avoided? At no time in history has any nation worthy of the name been able to do without an intelligence service. Twenty-five centuries ago, Sun-tzu, the great Chinese philosopher and warlord, himself an intelligence agent, observed: "Good intelligence is the prelude to victory."

But "victory" today is less clear than it has ever been. Victory may involve traditional military, political, or diplomatic success. But it may also comprise moral victories, even highly tangible, at times profitable, economic victories. Economic intelligence is becoming a strategic weapon with powerful impact, especially on our new enemies of the Fourth World War—fragile third world economies that rely heavily on their oil wealth, and dictators whose power depends on economic strength and the ability to buy weapons on world markets. Today, as other parts of the intelligence apparatus begin to wind down in importance—particularly those dealing with the East European satellite nations—the economic service is very much coming into its own. Economic espionage has become a key element of our war-fighting capability. The economic weapon is often the first invoked in time of crisis and confrontation. Moreover, properly applied, it can prove to be the critical pressure-point that chokes off violent activities by irrational leaders.

In those cases, as in the case of more conventional political, diplomatic, or military intelligence, raw information may itself become a powerful weapon when used properly. At the end of November 1971, just as the Delouette affair was winding to a particularly troubling end, I obtained information that the Americans were going to devalue the dollar on December 18. The analyst who brought that information to me at headquarters was one of my most trusted directors—the head of what we called the Economic Intelligence Service, which included not only financial and economic intelligence but, as I very early on in my administration discovered, industrial espionage as well. There are occasions when this service is often more than able to pay its own way, indeed to pay the way for all the intelligence operations of the French government.

This was one such occasion. When I received the report on the imminent American devaluation, I immediately picked up the red hot-line that tied me directly with the president's office and requested an urgent audience with President Pompidou at the Élysée Palace. Our sources, it seems, had foreseen not only the date, but the level of the devaluation as well. So I entered Pompidou's office well prepared for the inevitable questions of great detail that would be posed by this once distinguished French banker. I quickly laid out the scenario to him, expressing my confidence in the accuracy of the information and the reliability of the sources.

"Will you give me the authorization to disclose this information to someone else—for instance, the minister of finance?" I asked the president.

"No," he replied. "Only to me."

Partly because of his background, partly because of his temperament, Pompidou would often work directly in such delicate matters with the Bank of France and its governor. Now was no different. Pompidou strictly adhered to a concept that I hold sacrosanct and that is basic to the functioning of intelligence operations of any type—the concept of need-to-know. Still, while from this point I was out of the information loop, I was able to follow the outlines of the action through our own monitoring services. Working quietly through a variety of what can only be described as "cut outs," or individuals whose ties to the government were deniable, the Banque de France, France's central bank and equivalent of the United States' Federal Reserve, was able to put into effect a series of operations that proved highly successful. By quietly selling dollars and buying francs in a number of markets around the world, the central bank was able to accumulate some enormous profits—by themselves, enough to have financed all the operations of the Service far beyond my tenure in office, perhaps until the end of the century. Were we not profiting from the misfortunes of a friend and ally? Perhaps. But at times, rare though these instances are, that's part of the game.

Day in, day out, there were cases that repeatedly demonstrated how effective the most basic intelligence gathering could be in the conduct of state business, even in times of calm rather than crisis. On numerous occasions, I provided the president with a file on a leading foreign statesman a few days before the man paid a visit to France. Often, the file in question was his own personnel file, compiled in his own country by his own security services. As a result, the president knew the answers he would give before his visitor posed the questions.

Such intelligence gathering also produced information that had direct personal benefits. If, for example, a foreign dignitary wanted to meet with me on a visit, he would generally begin by contacting his own embassy in Paris before his departure. I was, of course, able to read those messages. Over the intervening weeks or months, the embassy would produce a profile of me, which would also be communicated to me by our monitors.

Eventually, the foreign dignitary would cable his ambassador: "This is what I want to discuss with him. How is the count likely to react to my questions? How will things go, in your opinion?"

By the time he arrived in my office, I would know not only what my visitor was like, his every quirk and peculiarity, but what he wanted from our meeting, how far I could go with him, where to draw the line.

Spying in the proper sense is becoming increasingly focused on business and the economy, science and industry. With the technology of terrorism and terror weapons becoming all the more intricate, not to mention miniaturized and decentralized, every major intelligence organization has been compelled to focus on the high-tech environment of the Fourth World War—to determine what our enemies may be up to, and how to protect our own industrial establishment from sabotage, attack, and theft. Inevitably, this focus has led to some discoveries that could prove very profitable in nonmilitary realms. This type of intelligence enables the Service to discover a process used in another country that might have taken years and millions of francs to develop or perfect.

The Soviets put an enormous effort into this area. In New York, a half-dozen officials from the Soviet consulate turn up each morning at the United States Patent and Trademark Office. They are there, perfectly legally, simply to make copies of all patents that have been issued in the previous twenty-four hours. But other operations are less legitimate. Military devices are rarely patented. As long as they remain under classified or top-secret status, there is no need for a patent. Also, patents are rarely issued in the early developmental stage. Yet at that stage, they may be of greatest value, and industrial espionage may produce the greatest rewards.

The Japanese are experts in these matters. Japanese industry has close ties with the government. My operatives and I studied their operations abroad, trying to understand where their next target might be in France, how the technology they pirate might find its way to our potential enemies in other countries. Within France these industrial counterespionage activities fell largely to the DST—a job they performed most professionally. At times, we shared responsibility and information.

The Japanese technique was deceptively simple. When they noticed that in a particular high-technology industry they needed a certain machine or device, they examined the global situation. If they came to the conclusion that the French or the Swiss, for instance, were the world leaders in that type of product, a delegation would be dispatched.

This happened late in 1978 with a sophisticated digital telephone switching system made by a leading French telecommunications company. We had been tipped off to the Japanese interest by conversations our British colleagues at Cheltenham managed to intercept. When we contacted the French company, and their representatives in Tokyo, they were astonished. They had assumed, after the initial inquiries from the Japanese, that they were on the verge of a major sale, not a theft.

"We are customers for some of your products," a senior official of the Japanese customer had declared in one conversation with the French representatives in Tokyo. The talk had already been of a very large contract, enough to make any French or Swiss industrialist come running, throwing open the doors of his factories to the visitors.

In this case, the Japanese arrived in groups of two or three, cameras swinging carelessly on their stomachs, and asked to see certain equipment and manufacturing processes. Our intelligence indicated that they found quite a number of particularly interesting technological innovations. We were monitoring them closely throughout the day and into the night. That evening they discussed the matter among themselves at a meeting in the suite of the chief of the delegation, who was staying at the Hotel Intercontinental overlooking the Tuileries Gardens. Detailed observations were exchanged and the photographs they had taken that day were carefully analyzed. Finally, further jobs were distributed. One delegate was assigned to convince a key French designer to discuss the innovation. Another was to return for more detailed photographs.

The next day, the factory was divided into segments for what was to have been a second and final visit. The delegation had planned to fan out with a single purpose in mind—to obtain the most detailed possible information on the nature and process of manufacturing the devices. But the French corporate executives were well informed by our agents. The final visit was suddenly and unceremoniously canceled, contract talks were broken off, and the Japanese returned home in ignominious failure. This counterespionage operation was, alas, a somewhat isolated success. There were more failures, and many West European, as well as American, technological innovations have found their way to Japan as a result of similar operations.

Western industrialists have often played even more directly into Japanese hands. Dazzled by prospects of fabulous contracts, they are often prepared to go so far as to send samples of their products to Japan. Months later, to their chagrin, they come across this same product on display at a Western trade fair—better made, less expensive, with "Made in Japan" stamped on it. More dangerously— many of those products have found their way into the hands of our enemies. Toshiba was deeply embarrassed when it was discovered that advanced, American-designed technology for manufacturing submarine propellers was being used in the Soviet nuclear fleet.

Eastern bloc countries have been pirating this kind of technology directly for years—witness, for instance, the Soviet attempt to replicate the Concorde, the SST. Though it failed in its ultimate mission of flying, it was virtually identical to the Franco-British Concorde (except for its miserable workmanship, which is what caused it, ultimately, to crash repeatedly in trials). It became known as "the Concordski." This was a classic example of industrial espionage on an international scale.

How can such pirating be avoided in our open societies in the West? For years, the French and other Western powers were providing the Soviets, openly and legally, with fully operational "turnkey" factories (so-called because the buyer has only to put a key in the door to go to work). Military trucks used in the Soviet occupation of Afghanistan were manufactured in the Kama River truck plant built by a West European corporation. In that case, and many others, short-term individual or corporate greed was the principal motive—laudable, perhaps, in a corporate context, but questionable in terms of national security. And such activity is restrained only at the margins by state regulation. Only the most advanced technology with clear national security applications was barred from export to the Soviet bloc under the Cocom (Coordinating Committee on Multilateral Export Controls) agreement among Western nations which has been in force since 1950. This left open a broad field for those who sought to trade with the East—trade that was profitable for their corporations, but of great aid and comfort to the Communist powers, our enemies in the Third World War. Lenin termed individuals responsible for such deals "useful idiots." The late Armand Hammer and his father, the first such purveyors to the Soviet state, clearly fell into Lenin's category.

In some respects, our enemies in the Fourth World War have been even more aggressive in courting Western, or Northern, industrial companies and weapons producers. Arms dealers have cashed in handsomely on the sale of French armaments and fast patrol boats to Iran and warplanes to Iraq. Libya's Muammar Qaddafi has invested heavily in European automobile companies. Pakistan and others have gone on widespread shopping sprees in the West to accumulate the equipment necessary to move toward a nuclear weapons capability. Germany's Daimler-Benz was most embarrassed when it was disclosed that its trucks were being used to ferry Iraqi soldiers to the front in the 1991 Gulf war. Even more embarrassing were the Mirage 2000 jets that France sold to Iraq for use during the Iran-Iraq war. The presence of those same jets in the skies over Kuwait meant that part of the French Air Force was all but grounded during the Gulf war for fear that allied jets would mistake French Mirages for Iraqi warplanes and shoot them down.

Yet official, at times highly publicized, transactions and others that take place under wraps are often the subject of considerable self-congratulation by the officials who have arranged them and the Western industries that obtain the lucrative contracts.

Beyond these commercial operations, many more are conducted far from the glare of television lights by seasoned intelligence agents from all the Eastern bloc countries and a number of Middle Eastern and African nations that are a continuing threat to their Northern opponents. Often shielded by diplomatic cover, those agents comprise an exorbitant proportion—between 35 and 60 percent—of embassies, consulates, and import-export organizations. In dictatorial and Communist societies, all such groups are directly responsible to the government, since everyone is an official.

The privilege to travel and live abroad in the affluent surroundings of the West often carries with it the duty to perform whatever services—industrial espionage, political intelligence, even outright terrorist activities—that may be required by the motherland. This is true for Eastern bloc nations and a number of our enemies among the dictatorships of the developing world. The French authorities believed that senior Syrian security officials, posing as diplomats attached to their Paris embassy, were directly implicated in a series of terrorist bombings in the French capital in the early 1980s, including the lethal explosion in a Lebanese restaurant on the Rue Marbeuf, just off the Champs Élysées. Libyan embassies and their diplomats stationed in Paris and London were regular distribution points for arms and explosives used by terrorists in Europe.

We must reinforce our counterespionage capabilities, as our enemies have reinforced their efforts against our agents, our governments, our business and industry. We must equalize the numbers of diplomats or spies who are authorized to be posted on both sides to ease the surveillance burden. At the same time, we must refrain entirely from employing foreigners in our installations overseas, as the Americans and the French have often done in the past—and as the Soviets have never done. That practice can only lead to trouble. In each case, the Soviets have and will seize every opportunity to tilt the playing field in their favor. In Washington, they selected a site for their new embassy on a hill overlooking the nation's capital—a prime location for all their electronic intelligence activities. And in Moscow, when a new American embassy was being built at the same time in the early 1980s, the Soviets seized the opportunity to riddle it with electronic eavesdropping devices of their own.

Moreover, we must not be content to assume that our resources can be more profitably employed elsewhere with the winding down of the Soviet threat. But the KGB and the GRU continues to operate in France, as it does throughout the Soviet empire. And while we may hope its power will diminish in the future, that is not the case for the time being—we must not, sadly, lower our guard. There are still Soviet intelligence personnel on station in Paris, Marseilles, and Lyons (where the international police organization Interpol recently opened its new world headquarters) and elsewhere. We must continue to deploy the resources to keep watch over enemy agents of every stripe who are operating in our backyards, especially the agents of our new enemies.

I have always failed to understand why the Soviet bloc should have four or five times the number of "observers" in our countries that we have in theirs. Parity should be the rule. We have long-established appropriate ratios for many third world dictatorships. In their countries we are under total supervision, you cannot move two yards without being watched. None of this has changed substantially in the Soviet Union, and has even intensified in many capitals since the Persian Gulf war. Yet diplomats or spies have always been free to go nearly everywhere they like in France. KGB and GRU (military intelligence) agents have a wonderful life. They can visit whomever they choose, travel (with certain very limited restrictions) wherever they want. And all this with practically no surveillance. In a city like Paris, where at their peak in the 1970s and early 1980s, several hundred senior intelligence agents from Eastern bloc countries, not to mention the hundreds more from third world dictatorships, were functioning as diplomats, it became physically difficult to follow them. In Moscow, there are so few cars it is relatively easy to tail someone. Try it in London, Paris, or New York, where the traffic makes it all but impossible.

Our agents, as well as our diplomats, were not allowed to leave Moscow without a special permit. Militia officers were posted every twenty or thirty miles along major highways to check them. If we did not reach one such checkpoint in a reasonable period of time after leaving the last, militia officers were sent out to look for us. And they would never help change a flat tire.

One day in the summer of 1976, I met at an official function in Paris the French foreign minister, who performs the same function as the secretary of state in the United States. While we had known each other for years, we had rarely had any direct contact during my term in French Intelligence. My information passed through the hands of the president directly, while the Service's funding came through the prime minister's office. In a certain sense, the Quai d'Orsay, the equivalent of the State Department, which the foreign minister directed, was a different reporting channel. Foreign service officers, or diplomats, were often said to provide a certain reality check on the kinds of information our intelligence agents were providing separately to the government.

"I have some good news," the foreign minister began. "I have just been to see our Russian friends in Moscow, and we are going to be allowed to open a consulate general in Leningrad. They will do the same in Marseilles."

"My God," I exclaimed. "May I ask how many people they will have in Marseilles?"

"About fifty," he replied.

"And what about us in Leningrad?"

"Five," he said, "if we can find civil servants ready to go to Leningrad."

I rushed immediately to see the president and informed him about what I considered not good news, but the worst possible news. As a result, the number of authorized personnel of the Soviet consulate general in Marseilles was lowered.

Nevertheless, a few months later, as French security officials began the routine process of screening the Russians being posted to Marseilles, we discovered that half the complement of their consulate were professional spies working for one or another of the Soviet espionage organizations. Why would the Soviets be so interested in this part of France? It is, of course, our principal port and naval facility on the Mediterranean. The French nuclear submarine pens in Toulon were and remain of intense interest to the Soviet military—not only because of the arrivals and departures of the boats themselves (which these days are much more easily monitored by satellites and electronic means), but because of the need for fleet intelligence as well. Deployment plans, military intentions, states of readiness, can be uncovered only by personal contact between Soviet intelligence agents and sailors of the French Navy.

But we must also not forget that in the region near Marseilles on the Côte d'Azur in Provence, major private French research institutions have proliferated. IBM and a number of international companies also have research laboratories there. Several months after the Soviets opened their consulate in Marseilles, my worst fears were confirmed. The chairman of IBM France paid me a visit in my offices in Paris.

"I've got a problem," he began gravely, "and since I know you, I allowed myself to come to see you. One of my research engineers at La Gaude [the principal research facility for IBM in southern France] has fallen madly in love with a girl from the Russian consulate general in Marseilles—I wonder why?"

"Why doesn't this surprise me?" I replied, and explained the genesis of the "exchange" of consulates in Leningrad and Marseilles, as well as the nature of the new Soviet presence on the Côte d'Azur.

Certainly, Leningrad would have been equally interesting to us as a listening post for our Intelligence Service. So why the wide discrepancy in staffing levels? First, we did not have enough civil or military personnel. Furthermore, the French diplomatic machine is disinclined to provide board, lodging, and essential support services for intelligence personnel. A deep mutual distrust between members of the French diplomatic and intelligence corps goes far beyond any similar divisions existing in our American or British counterparts.

There is a fundamental misunderstanding of our work, even among professional diplomats, who should have a better sense of how we operate. Diplomats operate in the light of day; intelligence agents under deep cover. In the case of the French, our own colleagues often had difficulty distinguishing our functions as intelligence officers from the work of French military personnel. Without question, more of our operational personnel come from regular army units than is the case with many other intelligence organizations. For that reason, it is inevitable that there would be some misunderstanding. But too often that misunderstanding has spilled over into outright hostility, overt suspicion.

So how do our operations differ from those of soldiers or diplomats? It is the army's job to know the strength of the Warsaw Pact armies. But to learn what their officers are thinking, to take a reading of their morale, their motivations, their psychological condition—that is a far more difficult, but equally vital, task. For that matter, to discover how terrorists move toward their targets, or how they choose their objectives, points of infiltration, weapons, and allies, can prevent the most catastrophic results. Intelligence of this nature is essential in curbing the drug trade, industrial espionage, and other mortal threats to our survival, which are only intensifying as the danger from the Warsaw Pact diminishes.

During the period when I directed French Intelligence, it was clear that advance warning of a few weeks, a few days, even a few hours, of the movements of certain key Warsaw Pact military units, of their heightened state of alert, could prove to be the critical margin for the defense of Western Europe. We devoted considerable attention, for instance, to the plans of the 20th Mechanized Army of the Guards (the Russians retained in many cases the czarist names for units). That group's field of operation specifically encompassed East Berlin, and it would have been one of the shock units had there ever been an invasion by the forces of the Warsaw Pact. If given the order to move, they would probably have been the first to cross the Iron Curtain in a drive toward Brest and the Channel.

One night I had a telephone call at home. Next to my bed were two telephones. One was the conventional phone, the other was the protected direct line to the duty officer at the central office. The second phone often rang late at night.

This time the report sounded somewhat ominous. "There's something further on that funny business from this afternoon," said one of my aides cryptically.

It was in October 1973, when the forces of Egypt and Syria had launched themselves against Israel, catastrophically, it turned out, for the Arabs. That afternoon, my director of intelligence had said to me in passing, "It's odd, but the X Soviet Parachute Division is not replying. We're not getting it any longer on our monitors."

The unit was an elite Red Army division, stationed somewhere south of Moscow. We used to listen in on it intermittently. Now, suddenly, it had disappeared and seemed to be maintaining radio silence.

"Keep me informed of what is going on," I ordered after listening to the reports of all the monitors. "We'll stick to it, then ask our allies."

I took up residence in my office and was kept briefed at hourly intervals. Each time, the report was the same: "Still not replying." The entire Soviet division had vanished.

During the night, the situation became increasingly complex. Reports began arriving that heavy aircraft were flying south over

Turkey, where the United States maintained heavy-duty monitoring facilities.

Assembling all the elements, I quickly concluded that the worst was entirely possible. I turned to my top aides and said, "Well, that's it. They're going to intervene in the Middle East."

My aviation expert turned to the maps and charts we had spread out on the conference table in my office. Poring over the papers, we worked out how many flying hours it would take between the disappearance of the parachute division and its arrival over a range of possible objectives in the Middle East—in other words, when we might have concrete, and disastrous, confirmation that the Russians had arrived. There were several possible prime targets, including the Golan Heights, where Soviet-supplied Syrian armor was being decimated by Israeli air power, and the Sinai, where virtually the entire Egyptian armored force was being taken apart by the Israelis.

I was surrounded by France's most senior intelligence officers— the general who was head of intelligence and his top military and civilian specialists. Each briefed me in turn, then all eyes focused on me. At that point, as director general of the Secret Service, I asked myself the critical question—should I telephone the president of the Republic?

I decided—purely on instinct or a sixth sense—that I would not wake the president. In the end, the alert proved to have no foundation. A few hours later, the Soviet division was picked up again on the usual frequencies. It had never left home. We never had a further explanation. But this incident demonstrates the most fundamental imperative of intelligence work—the need to assemble as many elements, as much data as possible. In the final analysis, it is one's intuition, a gut feeling born of years of experience, that must make the ultimate decision. On that may hinge the fate of a nation.

There are several lessons to be drawn from this incident. First, and perhaps the most important, concerns the entire issue of the relationship between the director general of French Intelligence and the president of the Republic. There was a point during that evening when it appeared all but certain we were on the cusp of a major international crisis involving Soviet intervention in the Middle East. I had a direct line to the president that sat on the corner of my desk. But had I disturbed him and nothing happened, my credibility would have been seriously damaged. And the principal currency of a director of intelligence with his boss, the president, is credibility. Especially when there was no action that could have been ordered by the president, there is all but zero tolerance here for the little boy who cried wolf. One false alarm may be allowed, a second becomes more problematic. By the third time, when something may really be happening, the reaction has become, "Here we go again." Above all, you are alone. The people who are with you on your staff, the technicians, the professionals, can provide the most complete and detailed information available from an intelligence point of view. But they have no power of decision. Your professional judgment is the ultimate intelligence. And it is especially needed in most European nations where decisions are made not by committee, as is often the case in the United States, but by isolated, responsible officials, acting on the advice of the experts they have appointed and trust.

Which leads to the second critical lesson from the story of the X Soviet Division—concerning the issue of evaluation and interpretation of raw intelligence data, and how to use it or act on it. As our means of capturing intelligence become more refined and instantaneous, as the enemy becomes more elusive—we must become that much more accomplished in evaluation and action. That means a return to the most basic, seat-of-the-pants estimates that only a seasoned professional analyst of world events should be entrusted to make. It means a quick, often real-time, appraisal of the intelligence data, the context and background of the situation it purports to describe, then lightning evaluation of its significance, and finally the ability to act swiftly and surely on the conclusions reached by this process.

The British have a great tradition of analysis. And they have the SAS (Special Air Service) and the SBS (Special Boat Service) to carry out operations. But if they need transportation, they have to go to the Royal Air Force; if they need more people to beef up their operational units, they have to go to the regular army or the navy, hat in hand. As head of the SDECE, I was the only Western intelligence organization chief who had personal control over full-fledged special operations units that combined the men, the aircraft, and the intelligence to put it all together swiftly and surely, no matter what the nature of the operation. Most such engagements require truly seamless units. When you land on some jungle strip, and if the two little guys who arrive by motorbike in the middle of the night with flashlights to guide you in are from the same unit as you, and you eat in the same mess every day with them, you trust them completely. Because the next time, they will be in the cockpit and you will be the one with the little flashlights on the ground. This is the kind of special mission at which we excelled. The British and the Americans did not. The American national security operation has first-rate systems of intercepting electronic intelligence. That is, for gathering raw intelligence. What distinguishes the Americans from both the British and the French is that the United States intelligence services gather so much information and act on it so infrequently that they have lost the ability of the British to reflect on what it all means and to analyze its significance or the ability of the French to take swift and effective action.

Ultimately, of course, all any director of intelligence can do is to offer his best evaluation of the situation to the head of state, who alone has the authority to act. During the Second World War, in my dealings with the senior Allied officials at Versailles, I heard one extraordinary story about Churchill that illuminates how vital it is that the most deadly actions be taken on the basis of the best possible intelligence.

The British at that time, at the height of the Battle of Britain, the air war the Germans waged over England, had managed to decode the Luftwaffe messages. The cracking of the Enigma code, perhaps the most closely guarded secret of the Second World War, enabled us to read the Germans' top-secret operational messages throughout the blitz, which was an enormous advantage for Allied pilots going into aerial combat against the Nazis. One day, the head of the RAF called on Churchill with some paralyzing news.

"Mr. Prime Minister, we have heard through Enigma that they are going to make a blitz on one of our British cities," he was reported to have told Churchill.

"Air Marshal, which one?" Churchill asked.

"Prime Minister, I don't know, but I will in a few days."

In a few days, he returned. "It's Coventry," he told Churchill. "They are going to take out Coventry. Prime Minister, what should we do? If we evacuate the population of Coventry, they will know we have deciphered their messages. They will change the code. And we will be blind and deaf in the future."

Churchill had no hesitation. But those who were close to him believe it was one of the most difficult, and least known, decisions he made during the war. "We will do nothing," he said simply. The night of November 14–15, 1940, the Luftwaffe leveled the city, turning it into a living inferno. Churchill's decision represented the ultimate use of intelligence. To know definitively—and to have the power to act, or not to act at all.

For any nation to be a power to reckon with, it needs first of all to have such a national leadership confident enough in its power and decision-making ability to implement an international and a domestic policy to match its destiny. The population must be sufficiently motivated to want to remain a first-rank power that will not abdicate its responsibilities.

One of the instruments of such a power must be a counterintelligence service equal to any threat. My first meeting in Washington with J. Edgar Hoover took place in 1970, shortly after I took office, during the same trip on which I met Helms and Angleton. Though he served as head of the American equivalent of our DST, rather than of the SDECE, Hoover had the reputation of being a "sacred monster" of counterespionage. So I tried out on him a story that I later used to great effect with both Presidents Pompidou and Giscard d'Estaing.

We were sitting in Hoover's quiet, elegant offices in the huge granite FBI headquarters in downtown Washington. I had settled into a chair with a cup of coffee, and I posed to him the following hypothetical situation:

"Let us assume that you go to an isolated part of central France. There is an explosion. And when police come to see, on a thousand acres there remains alive not a blade of grass, not a chicken. So they call the atomic experts from Paris and they confirm that it was what you feared, a small nuclear device. It was not yours. It was not a Soviet bomb. But hours later, before the news even leaks out, there is a call to the president of the Republic. And the voice spells out the name of an unknown revolutionary organization.

" 'This is just a small sample of what we can do,' he says. 'Somewhere in Paris, we have hidden a device that is one million times more powerful than that one. Our conditions are these: You are going to sink the French fleet in the middle of the Atlantic. You are going to turn over all the gold in the Bank of France. And tomorrow afternoon, you are going to walk down the Champs Élysées naked with a feather in your ass.' What does the president do?" It could happen.

Hoover replied simply, "That's what he needs us for." I smiled. It was the reply of a top cop, supremely confident of the capability of the police or intelligence organization that he has built to rise to any occasion. He and his organization, he believed, were equal to any domestic threat. And Hoover was right. His was the kind of organization the French had also created, more or less. But the FBI has always needed and received more men, more equipment, and more funds.

Intelligence agencies today, whether domestic or international, need the means to respond flexibly to every threat—to gather the intelligence, interpret it, and whenever necessary to act on it. We are playing both on a field of operations and a field of dreams.

For France, even for the United States, to be a world power, it must have world reach—wherever its political, diplomatic, and military will is to be extended. Words alone will not make a first-class power. The ability to influence or effect action—even the *perception* that the United States or France is able to take such action—is necessary to support political initiatives and diplomatic resolve. This principle is doubly true in the Age of Certain Destruction and the Fourth World War, when terrorists and the governments that send them on their deadly missions understand only the concept of certain retribution carried out swiftly and unmercifully.

Sometimes, there comes a moment when the diplomatic card can no longer be played, when bluff must give way to action. Without actually declaring war, the nation must be able to mount certain operations abroad—to come to the aid of a population in danger or to rescue its own nationals stranded or held hostage against their will, or to apply swift surgery to excise a cancer that is poisoning a dependent ally. The mission of a conventional army unit is to come in at a given point, conquer territory, then hold it. Our operations, the surgical responses, must take place at night, and be a *fait accompli* by dawn. That is a surgical strike in espionage terms.

Moreover, such surgical strike teams are also the ICBMs of our most dangerous opponents in the Fourth World War. They have neither the means nor the will to maintain enormous standing armies, massive military installations on remote islands, huge fleets of heavy-lifter military transports. And they have no need for any of this. The small terrorist cells that plan and carry out the most deadly actions, inspiring mass panic and fear, have the same impact —they demoralize us and sap our will to resist. Just as the landings at Normandy and the taking of Iwo Jima encouraged us to fight on, we will need victories in the Fourth World War against this new form of enemy if we are to have the will to win. And if we are to fight them on their own terms, we must have elite teams to match, indeed exceed, their capabilities—the special forces that are the nuclear arms of the world of active intelligence.

There were times before my arrival as director general when the Service had mounted operations that were ethically wrong, even banned by law. Certainly, this failing has not been confined to

France. The CIA has been accused of turning to Mafia hit men. My own predecessors had often turned to hired killers, criminals, and thugs; to organized crime, gangsters, gunmen, and pimps. There is no worse blunder for a security service. A paid killer or hit man is extremely dangerous and often quite ineffective. His first concern is his fee, not his mission. He commits unlawful acts for profit. Furthermore, to multiply his profit, he may attempt blackmail or extortion, at which point it may become necessary to liquidate him, establishing a vicious circle that is worse than unprofessional, indeed criminal in the extreme. The edict I established, therefore, was a simple one: Employ only those who are honest, highly trained, and highly motivated. Each must act out of patriotism and service to the state because—and this needs repetition yet again—the personnel of the Secret Service are perpetually at war.

The chief of the Israeli Secret Service once paid me an enormous compliment. The Mossad is among the most professional and most committed intelligence services in the world. Its director once came to visit at my offices in the Tourelles Barracks in Paris.

"Monsieur le Directeur-Général," he began. "You, along with us, are the only ones capable of carrying out a raid of the type of Entebbe and bringing it off. Unfortunately for you, there are two things you lack—long-range aircraft and political courage and commitment on the part of your government."

I did not hesitate in replying. "In the first instance, it's not easy," I said. "In the second, there are ways and means."

In my day, we carried out a certain number of operations on the lines of the Entebbe raid that were totally successful—the proof being that the world has never heard a word about them. We mounted three or four a year—more than forty during my tenure as head of French Intelligence. Not one went wrong: forty or more operations that no one outside of Intelligence and the highest reaches of the French government has ever heard of.

There were others we mounted with somewhat greater visibility. And it is some of those that I am at liberty to discuss in this work—among them, the overthrow of Emperor Bokassa of the Central African Empire and the police operation in Zaire. Several missions, certainly, have had a tragic sequel—with personnel killed or severely wounded in the service of France. At times, those men and women died in secret with their heroism never properly acknowledged by their nation. But that is what the Secret Service is about—not Her Majesty's Secret Service of James Bond, but the one that operates in the shadows of the real world. For in the SDECE, the tradition of silence was especially strong. There was an esprit de corps and a notion of duty that for years had been outstanding. I can never praise too highly the courage, selflessness, and devotion shown by the individuals I had the honor of commanding for so long.

All this brings us back to one of the two key questions raised by the chief of the Mossad. In my view, the political courage and commitment of the French government were nearly always there when I needed them. Certainly, this was easier in an environment that called for only minimal parliamentary or public scrutiny of our operations (whether successful or unsuccessful). In such an atmosphere, the chief of state and his advisers were able to decide on a mission purely on its merits as a tool of political, diplomatic, and military policy, that is, of statecraft. But there was another, deeper reason for the willingness to act swiftly and unhesitatingly when events warranted a swift and sure justice. There has always been a rather widely held feeling in political circles in France—indeed in much of Europe—that whatever was necessary to defend the interests of the Republic was acceptable, within certain moral limits. It was the president of the Republic who was to establish those moral limits—and to answer to them, ultimately, as well. Once elected president, he was given the benefit of the doubt and an all but unquestioned mandate. In this sense, at least, he is the direct heir of the scepter and the glory of the kings of France.

We Europeans have a term for all this, as I've mentioned. We call it the *raison d'état,* or "reason of state."

It is very difficult for an American to understand that the services of a nation must occasionally do something that is immoral and even illegal. At times, such a decision could be taken only by the president of the Republic. But during my term as director of French Intelligence, it was often left to my personal discretion whether I would order an action myself or whether I needed to defer to the president. For instance, I could not make a unilateral decision to dispose of a head of state—and we always had certain ones in mind. In such a case, I would go to the president and say, "I would recommend that So-and-so be dealt with in the proper way." It was then up to the president to say, "No, not at all, I forbid this," or simply to say nothing. That was the code I established with the three heads of state with whom I dealt. Silence meant consent.

Once, discussing this issue, I told President Reagan a story about Talleyrand, Napoleon's minister of state who was perhaps the most astute and intelligent man of his time, the early nineteenth century—he was a genius, and a survivor to boot. During his rule, the secret police of that period seized, on the other side of the Belgian frontier, the Duke of Enghien, a member of the Bourbon royal house that claimed the right to the throne of France, and enemy of the crown as represented by Napoleon. The duke, a very handsome and bright young man, was seized in the dead of night and spirited off to Paris. Napoleon had been afraid of him because he was a Bourbon, a powerful one with a large following. Arriving in Paris, the secret police took the duke to Vincennes Castle on the outskirts of Paris, and executed him promptly in the dungeons in front of a firing squad. The next day, when Talleyrand learned of this action, he was furious and rushed to Napoleon's chambers.

"Sire," he began, *"c'est plus qu'un crime, c'est une faute!"*—"it is worse than a crime, it is a mistake!"

His meaning was crystal clear. At this level, that of the emperor, a political crime crosses the fine line of being justified by war and national exigency and is no longer within the meaning of a *raison d'état*—it had become a personal vendetta. This perhaps best describes the concept—by defining it in the breach.

The relationship between intelligence services and the government is much different in the United States, as I was to discover to my chagrin in my dealings with the Central Intelligence Agency and its various leaders. Every director of central intelligence was forced to look over his shoulder at every instance. The fishbowl nature of his agency meant that he must constantly be concerned about the political and diplomatic ramifications of any operation he undertook.

Certainly, the American people are more sensitive to moral issues. Perhaps this is one legacy of the pain and divisions of the Vietnam era. Most Americans do not blindly accept that whatever is truly necessary for national security is per se acceptable. Every political act, certainly every quasi-military operation, is carefully scrutinized for its moral acceptability on the most narrow grounds. Only then is it subjected to the test of national security and the public good, which Americans define more closely than do we Europeans, especially we French with a much longer history of wars fought on our own territory. From start to finish, the Americans use a technique that can only be described as definition by committee, all in all a recipe for disaster in the fast-moving world of the Fourth World War.

The governmental system of checks and balances, deeply embedded in American public life since the Constitution was drafted, continues to tie the hands of the American director of central intelligence. The formal oversight function belonging to Congress has him running constantly to Capitol Hill before, during, and after any operation, whether successful or unsuccessful.

I never went before a full-blown parliamentary commission in eleven years in power. But I am not per se opposed to contact with the political leadership of our countries. When I was asked, I have told a number of American directors of central intelligence that I saw no problem in their having a few select members of Congress with whom they could work directly. After a number of years running the intelligence operations of any major Western country, a director of intelligence runs the distinct risk of finding himself cut off from the realities of local politics and the people he is purporting to protect. Working with trusted politicians of a high caliber would become in a sense a reality check, a corrective. They would serve less an oversight than a cooperative function, the members of Congress adding their political perspectives to the intelligence and military viewpoints of the director of central intelligence.

During my term in office, I did see French parliamentarians from time to time—as friends. Later, an interministerial intelligence commission was finally established under the prime minister's office and was chaired by the prime minister or his representative. It had no veto power over what I did, because I did not have to notify it in advance of any intelligence operation. Together with most of my predecessors and my successors, I had all but unlimited power. It was we who chose what to pump into the president's ear. We had the power of betraying the president. We had control of enormous resources of secret funds—indeed of all the secret funds of the French government, we controlled more than half, which by no means gave us the financial resources of our American, Soviet, or even British or German colleagues. But we had means. As directors of intelligence, we could make false passports, false documents of all types; we knew no frontiers. We had a special paramilitary unit, our own air force. For eleven years, I never once checked in at an airline counter or stood for passport control. The power we could command was terrifying in a way, but essential. To monitor every action of a director of intelligence is to tie him in knots. And to tie in knots as well the ability of the state to respond to its most mortal threats.

6

Memory and Politics

 hen I began rummaging through the premises of the SDECE, which I had taken over in 1970, I came upon a number of annexes. One day in one of these annexes, I was shown an enormous bundle of what appeared to be documents piled up at the back of a strong room. They were all bound in uneven stacks and slung into the corner.

"What's all that?" I asked my chief of archives, who was accompanying me.

"Oh, they're German archives," he replied casually.

They were the notorious Nazi archives of the Gestapo and the Abwehr, which had been captured at the liberation of Paris, since the Germans had not managed to take them away when they withdrew from Paris.

"How much is there?" I continued.

"Ten tons, more or less," he answered.

In occupied Europe, the military intelligence, the Abwehr, and the Geheime Staatspolizei, the Gestapo, were everywhere. Moreover, this German security network created discipline with carbon paper—they did everything in six or seven copies. One copy stayed with the local office, another went to the commander in Paris, probably a copy was sent to the general command of the Wehrmacht in France, and certainly one copy was bound for Berlin. In Berlin, there was documentation on every key individual, every agent recruited from among the people, every minor event that occurred in each occupied territory. There was similar documentation in the central archives in Paris for all of France, as there was in the capital of every occupied nation.

The Soviets understood this system. It is widely believed that

Stalin wanted to be first into Berlin at the end of the war for political and psychological reasons, and was granted his request by the Allied command because of the millions of dead the Russians had suffered at the hands of the invading Nazi armies. But the real reason the Soviets wanted to enter Berlin first was to put their hands on the Nazi central archives—the principal German civil and military archives of the Gestapo and the Abwehr. Their aim was blackmail of selected collaborators throughout the territory the Nazis had occupied in Europe. The Soviets have made good use of those archives, and indeed, over the years, the Soviets have identified and contacted many of the people named in the Nazi records. Each of those archives held the unparalleled opportunity of control over people who later were to become models of respectability, pillars of society in their nations. I would, on occasion, run across some of these unfortunates. Because of their collaborationist past, because of the hold the Russians had over them, blackmail in its crudest terms, they had become trapped into performing various services for their new Soviet masters with whom they shared neither sympathy nor interests. They were simply frantic to preserve their name and their honor. The articles they published under their bylines in certain powerful newspapers; the interviews they granted on television or radio in which they expressed a particular point of view were all the result of blackmail extracted in their own private hell.

These tactics were tantamount to a direct, frontal assault on some of the most esteemed of our citizenry by an enemy power, a new tactic developed by the Russians to fight a new war; indeed they were the first skirmishes of the Third World War in Europe.

Very few people in France knew that the SDECE got most of the French archives. The Ministry of Justice got some of them; so did the Gendarmerie. And both of those agencies still guard their copies. So does the SDECE and its successor institution, the DGSE. Compared with the Russian haul, these were the leavings, but for France they were potentially explosive material indeed.

For twenty-five years, no one had dared go through them or even take a look at them. I found that hard to believe, and I asked for an estimate of how long it would take for these archives to be thoroughly examined and cataloged.

After several days of study, my director of archives returned to me.

"Monsieur le Directeur-Général, it's like this," he began. "First of all, it is going to cost a lot of money. It will take time, unless we bring in a lot of people to examine them. And finding the experts to take full advantage of these files will not be easy. We would need people who speak perfect German and have a specialized knowledge of the organization of the German Secret Service."

That certainly narrowed the field. There were very few such people, Alsatians for the most part. I assembled a small team—a remarkable officer, Colonel U.; an officer assistant; along with a team of a half-dozen NCOs, backed up by a few bilingual secretaries familiar with documents of this sort. With a small group such as this, the job would take two years and the cost would be enormous.

I decided to proceed slowly and ordered some preliminary soundings—some random picking through the archives. What emerged was unpleasant, even painful. It was easy to see that some documents would necessarily be dealing with people who were still alive and active. Names immediately emerged of well-known people, men and women of substance, who during the war claimed to have been loyal members of the Resistance—true patriots. Instead, the reality was that they had been on the payroll of the German Secret Service, the Gestapo. They had even signed receipts for wages that were the wages of treachery.

I thought at the time, and still believe, that one of the most damaging of French vices is dissension and divisiveness. Since the people identified in these extraordinary archives were still alive, we had no need to root about in garbage pails or stir up the mud, even if there might have been some generally salutary effects, or at least object lessons for the future. Moreover, I have never forgotten the settling of scores that followed the war in France. For all that was admirable about the liberation of France, there was an equal amount of abuse, torture, and worse.

I examined some of these archives personally, those that were brought to my direct attention. I know many names that have not been published—of those who were on the payroll of the Nazis, of others who claimed to be Resistants, but who were instead the most despicable of turncoats. And I have been roundly denounced for my decision to take these names with me to my grave.

But my examination of the Nazi archives merely affirmed the decision I had wanted to make all along—to concentrate on the present and future development of the SDECE without reveling in past horrors. To have done anything else would have distracted me from the essential issues—the ongoing intelligence battles around the world. Moreover, it would inevitably have embroiled me deeply in the same kind of French domestic scandal that had so enmeshed my predecessors, demoralized the entire SDECE, and all but destroyed its effectiveness as a global espionage organization.

So ten tons of explosive documents continue to lie idle in an obscure storeroom on the outskirts of Paris. I realize that in the United States or Great Britain, silence of this sort, twenty-five or forty years after an event, would be inconceivable. But I must point out that neither the United States nor Great Britain has suffered occupation. The problem is by no means the same.

The Central Intelligence Agency, like its British and French counterparts, had access to some parts of the Gestapo and Abwehr files at the end of the war. Moreover, the Americans must have seized quite a lot, because right at the end of the war they worked for a long time with General Reinhard Gehlen, who was a great head of German military intelligence. It was well known that he brought with him in forming the Bundesnachrichtendienst a large number of quite competent people as well as their archives. These individuals would have been excellent road maps through the thickets of material that had been accumulated by the Gestapo and Abwehr in the course of the war and German occupation of Western and Eastern Europe.

There is of course one very public case of an individual incriminated by his ties with the Nazi machinery during the war—Kurt Waldheim. The man who later became president of the Austrian Republic had a past which, in the opinion of his supporters, largely in Austria, was blameless; in the opinion of others, it was execrable. During his tenure as secretary-general of the United Nations, Mr. Waldheim was never criticized for his conservative principles. Rather, he was repeatedly criticized for applying policies that could only be construed as remarkably favorable to the Eastern bloc. Were the Soviets in possession of these incriminating documents all these years? Perhaps. But why, then, reveal them just as they were on the point of having in the position of president of the Austrian Republic a man over whom they might have continued to exert total control? We may never be able to answer those questions. But the French military government occupying the French sector of Berlin was said to have come into possession of a file of German origin on Waldheim. I have no recollection of having seen it, but international policing is not the function of the secret services in the West. It is up to the government to ask the security services, the Intelligence Service (SDECE) and the Counterespionage Service (DST), their opinion of a particular individual. On my watch, we were never asked that question about Kurt Waldheim. Nevertheless, the archives, the Soviets' and ours, remain intact.

Today, we have other means of inquiring into the bona fides of key individuals around the world. In the atmosphere of the Fourth World War, when the terrorists and drug runners who are the shock troops change names and identities as casually as they change their nightshirts, when the name Muhammad Ahmed or Ahmed Muhammad carries as much meaning as John Doe or Jean Dupont, and the souk can swallow an assassin like a black hole, precision personal intelligence can be more critical than precision-guided munitions. The KGB and other Eastern intelligence agencies have acquired superior capabilities in personal intelligence. One way is to make use of officials of key international organizations that maintain vast worldwide personnel files. These kinds of activities are central to the work of any international intelligence organization.

The Russian, as well as the French, services constantly sought to place its men at some key points in certain international organizations. It is also well known that a number of present and former intelligence agents have occupied key diplomatic posts. General Vernon Walters, who served as deputy director of central intelligence at the CIA, later was the United States ambassador to the United Nations and performed a number of critical, secret diplomatic missions for the President of the United States, and served as the first American ambassador to a united Germany before he left for the States. Several years ago, we were labeled "the two sacred monsters of intelligence," and it is true that we have maintained our friendship and exchanged views whenever possible in Paris, New York, or wherever we might find ourselves together.

Since personal intelligence is so vital to the mission of secret services in the Fourth World War, not to mention the wars that have gone before, it is often assumed that senior intelligence officials are all but omnipresent—that we have virtually unlimited powers to know all there is to know about any individual. And indeed, when you have been in intelligence as long as I have, you eventually collect a great deal of information about prominent people whom you would rather not shake hands with.

It's generally believed that we arrive at such information by wiretapping. And indeed electronic surveillance is one important tool. In France, we do engage in authorized telephone surveillance. The budget is controlled directly by the prime minister, but many of the operations were carried out by the various security services. For eleven years, I had the report of official wiretapping on my desk every morning. They were summaries, but for the full transcript, I had only to ask one of my aides and it was available within minutes. I made it my business never to abuse that trust.

Still, I will confess to my moments of weakness. In the first year of my service in the SDECE, before I all but withdrew from public life, I often dined in town to reestablish a large number of contacts I had let drop. It was a year when my liver was forced to undergo considerable trials, and my ears repeatedly endured the most banal, even idiotic questions. Among the most frequent was "Am I being bugged?" To which my reply invariably was "You must think rather a lot of yourself!"

For a time, though, I did have one little, and I thought somewhat harmless, trick that I was fond of playing at the rare parties I attended—a prank I perfected—which in retrospect I concede was in rather doubtful taste. Nevertheless, I confess I relished it. When I saw a well-known individual who had a high opinion of himself—and God knows Paris, along with most other major cities of the world, including New York and Washington, is full of them—I would approach him wagging my finger under his nose (which itself is rather ill-mannered, of course).

"Ah! Ah! Ah!" I would say, smiling conspiratorially.

I could see the individual turn green and think in total panic, "He must know!"

But I played this prank once too often. One of my dear friends, Pierre Messmer, a superb soldier during the Second World War, who became prime minister of France, a totally honest and decent gentleman, and a true statesman, who was in every respect irreproachable, turned on me after I had tried my little finger-wagging on him, stared at me coldly, and said slowly, "What do you mean, 'Ah! Ah! Ah!'?"

That was the end of my little joke, then and there.

It was true that among prominent political figures, those who have nothing to hide are fairly rare. No doubt they are less rare in the United States, where the standards of morality for public figures are so much higher than in our more libertine country. But those who manifestly do have something to hide are invariably convinced that the director general of French Intelligence "knows." In truth, he knows less than some people imagine. But most people's weak spot is that they don't know just what he does know. I never contradict anyone. I prefer to leave them not knowing what to think. On a broader scale, that is a classic dictum of intelligence and one that we used frequently to good advantage. It works more effectively among isolated terrorists than among the better-informed global intelligence organizations. Terrorists often assumed we had a much deeper knowledge of their activities than was possible to acquire. Their elaborate efforts to cover the tracks that we might never have found inevitably slowed them down. And a slower-moving target is better than a faster one under any circumstances.

Curiously, politicians, who really should know better, share with terrorists and drug runners the assumption of the omniscience of espionage organizations. On several occasions, I have heard politicians of the first rank call to mind some quite distasteful financial scandal in which they assured me they had no part. But by doing so, and by discussing the intimate details of those affairs, they clearly informed me of their own depravity. Yet in politics, I quickly discovered in my new job, there is often a very different concept of right versus wrong—very different moral standards indeed. This was a very compelling reason for us to stay out of the domestic political arena, with some rare and isolated exceptions involving the security or economic well-being of the state itself.

CHAPTER 7

Serving Two Masters

uring my term as head of French Intelligence I served two very different masters—Georges Pompidou and Valéry Giscard d'Estaing. For the director general, his greatest problem is that he must never try to please.

On one particularly difficult occasion, after a long and complex discussion with President Giscard d'Estaing, I stopped and turned at the door as I was about to leave his office in the Élysée Palace.

"Monsieur le Président," I said, "I am reminded of a remark by Maréchal de Villars in a letter to Louis XIV when he wrote: 'Sire, it is not an easy thing to serve and to please.' "

In truth, relations between the Élysée Palace and the SDECE were enviably smooth and extremely cordial under President Pompidou, but considerably less so during the presidency of Giscard d'Estaing that followed. Without question, both presidents had total confidence in me. Otherwise I would never have been able to serve in this capacity with the near total freedom I possessed. But their styles differed substantially according to their personalities, and especially their backgrounds. I got to know Pompidou very well. Giscard remained for me a mystery wrapped in an enigma. Their conceptions of the nature of power and of the use of intelligence differed substantially; each approached the problems of our time, and attempted to address them, in a very different fashion. Georges Pompidou was very much a child of the Second World War who came of age fighting the Third. Giscard learned his political catechism in the cauldron of the Third World War and attempted, more or less successfully, to apply it to the Fourth World War, whose first skirmishes were beginning just as he was leaving office. (François Mitterrand, Giscard's successor, whom I served for only a matter of months in a transitional capacity, was a curious amalgam of the two—a product of the Second World War who somehow managed to assimilate its teachings into a true grasp of the Fourth World War without ever having come to grips with the cold war in between.)

As a servant of Pompidou and Giscard, I came to straddle two very different eras in the history of France and French Intelligence— with a mission of turning our very considerable intelligence capabilities ninety degrees in a historical heartbeat. The break between the two, I came to believe, was a result of the vastly disparate associations each had with Charles De Gaulle and the Second World War.

Born in 1911, Pompidou was already thirty-three years old at the time of the liberation of France, when De Gaulle's aide found him during his search for that *"agrégé* who can speak French!" He lived through that stunning quadruple reversal when Stalin's Russia turned from a neutral friend of the West to an ally of Hitler's Germany to a bitter foe of Nazism and member of the Western alliance to the Evil Empire of the Third World War. He was never able to view the Soviet Union with anything but the deepest suspicion born of this series of betrayals. It colored his entire perspective of our role in pursuing the Third World War. At the same time, he lived through France's decolonization, served beside De Gaulle throughout the traumatic civil war in Algeria, and presided as prime minister over the shedding of France's final colonies on three continents. Terrorism of the sort we have come to know as the touchstone of the Fourth World War was for Pompidou less a distinct mode of outside aggression than a by-product of a civil war that he wanted to end as quickly and painlessly as possible.

Giscard, however, was fully a half generation behind Pompidou. Born in 1926, he was barely eighteen years old at the time of the liberation and did not join De Gaulle's political circle until the Algerian war was well under way. For him, the military concepts of the Second World War were a historical rather than a tangible reality, though he managed to enlist in the army in 1945 just in time to finish the war in Germany. The Third World War was where he learned his politico-military tactics, and the first skirmishes of the Fourth World War were a pressing and critical reality.

When Pompidou was president, I often went to the Élysée Palace after work. All those who made up the presidential team would be there, sitting around on the ornate sofas and chairs in the president's private offices. Among the regulars was a tall, affable young man with keen eyes and a restless manner. He was Jacques Chirac, who then served as secretary of state for the economy, but who was later to become prime minister and run repeatedly, always unsuccessfully, for president of the Republic.

But I had more to do with Pierre Juillet, the veteran counselor to the president. I had been in touch with him for some time, from the first occasion when President Pompidou broached the subject of my taking on the monumental task of rebuilding French Intelligence until the moment I finally accepted the assignment. Since I paid frequent visits to the Élysée during my earliest and most difficult years, we had plenty of opportunities to meet and discuss a broad range of subjects. The questions that needed to be brought to the attention of the president of the Republic were first discussed in some detail between us, in person when necessary or over the special, secure "interministerial line" that stood on the desk in my office at my right hand. But our discussions often ranged far beyond the immediate affairs of state or espionage.

My arrival as the head of Secret Service came not long after the enormous scandal of the Markovic affair—the apparent execution of Stefan Markovic, the bodyguard of the French film star Alain Delon. Rumors linked Markovic with wild parties where photos were taken of high government figures.

Some people believed that Pompidou appointed me expressly to get to the bottom of that scandal and the rumors that involved Pompidou's own family, and to deal with the ugly residue that remained. This is simply not true. That view shows complete ignorance of the internal workings of the system. On only one occasion can I recall the president discussing with me his deepest feelings about all these attempts to smear his good name and that of his wife and family. It was during one of our frequent solitary meetings at the end of a difficult day, and he began pouring out his heart to me. His eyes misted over with tears as he described what his enemies were doing to his wife, not to mention himself. This couple possessed one virtue that is increasingly rare these days—they loved each other and were totally devoted.

I confess I may have been a bit maladroit in this conversation. I warned the president against the "Tout Paris," the Paris of celebrities who deal in rumor, sarcasm, and invective—each trying to outdo the next in their cleverness and ability to wound public figures. They are like sharks who at the first smell of blood on the water, the first sense of vulnerability, go in for the kill.

"When provincials come up to Paris," I went on blithely, "they are often overwhelmed by all the glitter and fall victim to its seductions. And they often fail to see where society shades off into the demimonde."

Mr. Pompidou fell silent, and I realized instantly that he was reflecting on his own situation—having misjudged those around him.

There is no question in my mind that Pompidou's final, fatal illness was brought on by those, including many politicians from his own Gaullist party, who sought to destroy him in the case of Markovic and on innumerable occasions that followed. The attempts to slander and demean Mme. Claude Pompidou, the first lady, only added to her husband's burdens. All this deeply overshadowed his entire administration through its final hours.

Though he had made up his mind not to discuss it, I became aware soon after I took office of the gravity of his illness—which did not become apparent to the world until much later in his presidency. I had too much esteem, and enough affection and admiration for him not to respect his feelings on the need to remain silent on this subject. His resolve to deny the inevitable, to keep silent and behave as if nothing was wrong, resulted from his patriotism, his heartfelt belief that it was his duty to continue to lead his nation until the last possible moment.

Some would have liked him to resign, but he was confident they would never raise the subject in his presence. Throughout, he continued with his customary agenda. His regular Wednesday cabinet meetings, his public and private audiences, were held without fail. His last week, in March 1974, was no exception. On Thursday, he received Valéry Giscard d'Estaing, his minister of finance. On Friday, he gave his views on the international situation to Michel Jobert, his foreign minister.

That weekend, he left as usual for Orvilliers, his country house. There had been no advance sign that his sickness, Waldenström's syndrome, a form of lymphoid cancer, was at a terminal stage. But he was stricken suddenly that Sunday in the country. On Monday, he returned by ambulance to his apartment on the Quai de Béthune in Paris.

I had visited that apartment many times in the course of our friendship. It was not a lavish place, by the standards of high political office in France. Nor did Pompidou own it, as most of his colleagues owned theirs. He never had the means to buy such an apartment—he had never in any sense profited from the positions he held or his service to his country. It was owned by an insurance company, as are many rental buildings in Paris, and the Pompidous were simply tenants.

The next morning, Tuesday, he was still well enough to put his signature on a few documents and approve the agenda for the next day's cabinet meeting at the Élysée Palace, which his prime minister, Pierre Messmer, was to lead. That evening he went to sleep, fell into a coma, and at 9:00 P.M., he died quietly.

Pompidou's sudden and unexpected end brought all of us considerable pain and distress. The night he died, a throng of people swarmed into the Élysée Palace. The main courtyard, the *cour d'honneur,* was brilliantly lit; there were cameras and microphones everywhere. I had not yet arrived at the palace to pay my respects, but I soon discovered that the president's entourage—his political advisers and his family—were seeking me frantically. The Service notified me by the telephone in my car that the Élysée was trying to get through to me. I returned immediately to my office to reach a secure phone and called the presidential office on the interministerial circuits.

It seems that some of those closest to the president suddenly thought that Mr. Pompidou might have left a secret political testament. The idea was certainly a sound one. Such a document could hold clues to his designation of a successor. Had Pompidou mentioned someone as being "most fit for the job," or as the one he would "recommend to France," given the overwhelming tide of sympathy that was running at the time, the individual would most probably have been elected by a landslide in the forthcoming election to choose a successor.

I discovered, in my phone call to the Élysée, that there was a more immediate problem. No one could open Pompidou's private safe because no one knew where the key was. Such French safes, it seems, had a key, in addition to the combination lock, and in the confusion of Pompidou's sudden illness, it had never been determined where he'd placed the key.

Among its other abilities, the Secret Service was the single branch of the French government with the greatest knack of being able to open safes. We had the most extraordinary wizards in our locksmiths section. In the Tourelles Barracks was a room with a range of safes representing the principal manufacturers of the world. My top experts could open any of them without keys in two minutes or less. Visitors who watched them would exclaim, "My God, how terrifying," thinking, no doubt, how insecure their valuables now appeared. Opening a safe poses no obstacle whatsoever to a small number (fortunately) of specialists. Real security means preventing people from approaching the safe, whose principal value lies in protecting the contents from a casual or amateur intruder.

Before I left my headquarters for the Élysée Palace that night, I ascertained that the president's safe was a Fichet 3 with three small combination knobs that must be turned before the key could be used. By that time, it was nearly 10:00 P.M. I summoned the head of our locks section.

"Where is your expert who specializes in opening Fichets?" I asked.

"I'm afraid he is on assignment abroad."

"Is there another available?"

"Yes, he would be at his home out in the far suburbs."

We sent for him immediately and I notified the Élysée on the secure phone that I would be arriving with my locksmith and his set of keys, but that we must at all cost be kept clear of the crowd of journalists and photographers who had congregated in the main courtyard of the palace, watching all comings and goings. Our car approached the palace from the opposite end—on Avenue Gabriel closest to the Champs Élysées. As agreed, at a special signal from the car's headlights, the gendarmes opened the huge iron gates of the entrance to the garden on the corner of the Rue de l'Élysée and the Avenue Gabriel. The Rue de l'Élysée itself is a small, private thoroughfare much like the alleyway between the White House and the Executive Office Building in Washington, since the buildings opposite the Élysée Palace on that side are all occupied by offices of the presidency. We crossed the lawns quickly to the palace itself, entered the side entrance next to the huge ceremonial glass doors that opened onto the patio, and took the back staircase to the president's private apartment. We were shown immediately to the safe, and found ourselves in the middle of the president's bathroom.

My expert opened his bag of keys, rolled up his sleeves, and loosened his necktie (which he had worn in deference to the solemnity of the occasion and the location of his work, though I suspect he'd had no idea where precisely we would find ourselves). Perched on the edge of the bathtub, I turned to him as he inspected the safe.

"How long will it take you to open it?" I asked.

"Monsieur le Directeur-Général, two to three minutes."

He was squatting on the floor in front of the safe and was about to embark on his work, when I suddenly had a terrifying thought.

"There must be witnesses," I said to myself. "What will happen if there are no witnesses?" Just imagine. He opens the safe, in a matter of moments. I find an envelope inscribed, "Political Testament." I open it. (All pure fantasy, of course, since this is neither my nature nor style.) The testament designates Mr. X, whom I dislike. I put the political testament in my pocket, and the course of history is thereby changed. All this raced through my mind in a few seconds.

"Wait!" I shouted out loud to my astonished locksmith.

I opened the bathroom door, called for Dr. Alain Pompidou, the president's son, and Pierre Juillet, his *chef du cabinet,* and ordered them into the bathroom while the safe was opened. It was a bit of a tight squeeze for the four of us in the tiny room. But finally, two minutes later, the locksmith did his work. The safe door sprang open.

There was no political testament whatsoever.

The Pompidou era had ended at that moment. The reign of Giscard began.

My first meeting with Valéry Giscard d'Estaing took place when he came to lunch at the Tourelles Barracks on July 20, 1973. At the time, he was not very well versed in international affairs, apart from international finance, since he had been serving as minister of economy and finance. As a graduate of the prestigious École Nationale d'Administration, his entire professional background had been as a bureaucrat—moreover, a bureaucrat in the economic and finance branches of French government. As he astutely divined, that was where the real political power of France lay. And Giscard was from his earliest days addicted to power. International and military affairs, especially intelligence, were of use only as they might serve his ultimate political ends—as issues in a political campaign, or as a means of building alliances with others who might be concerned with such issues and might help him. Little wonder that he was not getting along very well with France's foreign minister, Michel Jobert, whom he also saw correctly as a political rival.

Pompidou then had less than a year to live, and I already knew he was quite ill. In my view there were two possible successors in

July 1973—François Mitterrand and Valéry Giscard d'Estaing. I was well aware that it would be a disaster for France to have a future head of state who was totally uninitiated in the workings of a complex instrument such as the one I controlled, that had a direct connection to the most dangerous day-to-day events facing the Republic. At times I had the impression I was playing the role of a doctor listening carefully with a stethoscope to the faint sounds in the chest of his patient—on the lookout for the first hint of danger, the violence that might otherwise erupt suddenly and with no prior warning. And since my only possible source for a second opinion on my findings was the head of state, he should be as thoroughly informed as my powers allowed. The best apprentice must possess a certain degree of personal humility and a fair dose of patience in the business of observing.

My cousin, Thérèse de Saint-Phalle, novelist and one of France's leading literary editors, who has wide acquaintances across the political spectrum, suggested one day that Giscard d'Estaing come to lunch with me. At the time, Giscard was serving as France's secretary of the treasury, but he was clearly in line for succession to the presidency.

Giscard fetched Thérèse from her office at Flammarion, the publishers at the Place de l'Odéon, where she was a director and senior editor. As their car rolled into the courtyard at headquarters and pulled up at the broad green lawn, one of my aides approached to greet Giscard and my cousin, escorting them up the stairs to the entry to the director general's office, past the huge Carolingian épée hanging on the wall, lit by a spotlight that cast a long shadow. Giscard remarked how impressive the symbol was.

As they entered my office, I rose and noticed that Giscard's eyes narrowed and focused immediately on one wall that was covered by a huge map of the world dotted with colored magnetic arrows, some of them pointed toward Israel.

"Why all those arrows, and aimed at Israel?" were the first words out of Giscard.

"All our intelligence indicates that Israel is about to be invaded by the combined Arab armies," I explained immediately. Giscard was astonished by everything, as Pompidou had effectively isolated him when he was minister of economy and finance from anything having to do with foreign affairs, military policy, or intelligence.

We began with an aperitif, settling down on a great old brown leather Chesterfield couch and two matching armchairs, beneath an enormous painting by Edouard Detaille of a knight in gold armor with a helmet topped by a white plume. In his hand the knight held a baton of command, and he rode a dark-brown palfrey with a superb harness. Giscard studied the painting carefully. We then sat down to lunch prepared by my excellent navy chef—oeufs à la fontange, scrambled eggs set in a little light panier of potatoes and truffles. This dish was followed by a fillet, then by dessert, an apricot tart.

Giscard turned continually to the map for reference throughout lunch, expressing astonishment, for instance, at the number of arrows marking Israel and Egypt. I described the strong possibility of a war breaking out between the two countries. It was ironic, though, in view of the subsequent Soviet invasion of Afghanistan, the one event that was to dominate a good portion of the last years of his presidency, that he showed such particular interest in and astonishment at the arrows pointing from the southern portions of Russia toward Afghanistan and into Baluchistan in northern Iran.

Our discussion during that first lunch ranged over most of the world's trouble spots, and I laid out for him my weltanschauung. After lunch, as Giscard was preparing to leave, I suggested sending him a few analyses that had been prepared.

In spite of this auspicious beginning, I was never as close to President Giscard as I had been to President Pompidou. Though it was never spelled out, I suspect the problem was our disparate backgrounds and our vastly different perspectives. Like Pompidou, I was a product of the Second World War and a close observer of the malignancies of the Soviet empire. Therefore, I was never able to suspend disbelief with respect to Moscow, our enemy of the Third World War. So when Giscard became president, some of his entourage often showed a preference for entrusting the most delicate intelligence or foreign policy assignments to the president's friends who shared a more benign and conciliatory attitude toward the Soviets, and toward many of our enemies of the Fourth World War as well. These amateur experts in espionage and foreign policy had little idea how tightly regulated the operating methods of the Service could be and how strict were our standards for reporting and evaluating the ongoing progress of any mission or operation.

One of these amateur advisers to whom Giscard turned frequently, particularly in dealing with the Soviets, was Jean-Baptiste Doumeng.

We had a large file on Doumeng, as did our brethren of the DST, who dealt with counterespionage. Doumeng, a specialist in agricultural trade with the Eastern bloc, had managed to amass a vast fortune by selling wheat, butter, and other foodstuffs to the Soviets in return for products that he could resell to the poverty-stricken nations of Francophone Africa with which he also maintained close ties, building investments throughout that continent. Our agents operating in Africa were to run across his trail on innumerable occasions. Doumeng's political affiliations were quite clear. A multimillionaire many times over, he was also a member of and leading contributor to the French Communist party. Over the years, Doumeng became, effectively, France's answer to Armand Hammer—a man with clear ties and sympathies to Soviet communism, who nevertheless managed to make himself indispensable to Giscard and some members of the presidential entourage. The principal problem with relying on men like this, who have one foot in one camp and one foot in another, is that you can never be truly sure from which camp they are speaking at any given time.

Nevertheless, Doumeng managed to win the trust and confidence of a number of French leaders of the past quarter century. One result of this cooperation was Giscard d'Estaing's sudden and extraordinary visit to Warsaw for a summit meeting with Soviet President Leonid Brezhnev on May 19, 1980—perhaps the single most stunning case of suspension of disbelief of any French president, or indeed any Western leader, at any time during the postwar period. Giscard d'Estaing had totally misread both the international situation and his own personal ability to influence it in any constructive fashion.

The meeting between the two leaders—Brezhnev and Giscard, East and West—took place at a particularly sensitive moment, barely five months after the Red Army had invaded Afghanistan on December 24, 1979. The invasion was designed, at least in part, to bring under control a nation that the Kremlin viewed as strategic to Soviet imperialism: another step toward access to the warm seas in the South.

Ironically, the Brezhnev-Giscard summit took place in Poland, which at that time was the only other monolithic nation on a Soviet frontier with a religion, Catholicism, capable of rousing its own people to armed resistance, a resistance that also risked being communicated to the Soviets' own Catholic republics, the Baltic States, which they had seized at the end of the Second World War. Already, the first seeds of resistance were growing in Poland in the minds of people who would ultimately form the powerful Solidarity movement under Lech Wałesa. If there was one place where the leader of a major Western power did not want to meet a Russian, it was Poland. The Russians despise the Poles and the Poles amply reciprocate by hating, as well as fearing, the Russians. None of this background static would be calculated to produce a constructive dialogue at a summit, where the atmosphere would inevitably be tense and highly charged. Moreover, the visit of the president of the French Republic to Warsaw for the sole and express purpose of a summit with the chief of the Soviet empire could send only one signal to any Pole who was harboring even the most innocuous dissident thoughts—that France, or the French president, would not offer dissidents any moral or material support. At the same time, how could a French head of state allow himself to think that he would have any chance of exerting influence over Leonid Brezhnev in the case of Afghanistan or Poland?

Poland was poised for the onslaught of Solidarity just a few months hence. The Soviet empire was holding its breath for the last death rattle of Leonid Brezhnev. It was a time to look toward the future—indeed toward the endgame of the Third World War. Instead, Giscard and his advisers were playing out a scenario of conciliation and accommodation that could only give our Soviet enemy a much needed breather, and just at the point when we had the Evil Empire with its back to the wall.

To prepare for this ill-fated summit that was so desired by Doumeng's friends in the East, the French businessman took in tow Michel Poniatowski, Giscard d'Estaing's closest personal adviser. For the secret negotiations in Warsaw, the two flew to the Polish capital in Doumeng's personal plane. As amazing as it might seem, though I was director general of the SDECE, I received no advance notice for what in any case would have been a vitally important meeting between the president of the French Republic and the general secretary of the Central Committee of the Soviet Communist party. Certainly, I would never have presumed to attempt to shape the course of such a meeting, yet I might have had some valuable insights.

But, instead, Giscard's detailed intelligence came from the somewhat biased sources of Jean-Baptiste Doumeng and his friends, all of whom had their own very particular political agenda. Though at the point Giscard went to Warsaw the polls showed him with a comfortable lead, he clearly felt the need for some other extraordinary coup de théâtre to ensure his victory. That supposed coup turned out to be a colossal mistake. At the very least, it cost France, whose large Polish and Catholic population would have made it an ideal Western partner for Solidarity, the opportunity to play a role in helping guide the emergence of a democratic system in Poland barely three months later.

During the bitter presidential election campaign of 1981, French voters came to view the Warsaw summit as a sellout to the Soviet leadership, and François Mitterrand seized on the summit as an extraordinary campaign issue. At every opportunity, he would refer to Giscard as "the little telegraph operator from Warsaw." And so, less than a year after his "triumphant" visit to Warsaw Giscard d'Estaing was turned out of office, ushering in the fourteen-year reign of François Mitterrand and his Socialists. Mitterrand's first cabinet turned out, scarcely by coincidence, to include some very close friends of Doumeng from the French Communist party.

There was considerable discussion even among Giscard's closest advisers about precisely what was said by Giscard and Brezhnev during their hours of private tête-à-têtes. To my knowledge, no one has ever completely resolved what was discussed, but as Giscard's regime ended a short time later, and Brezhnev's not long after that, these unanswered questions quickly became moot. Only a bad taste remained in the mouths of nearly every independent thinker in Eastern Europe, who had come to view France and especially Giscard with contempt. Those memories did not fade quickly.

Though the trip turned out to be the final act of a failing regime in both countries, it served as an excellent example of the way the Giscard administration pursued the Third World War—viewing the enemy camp through rose-colored glasses, rather than with the kind of healthy skepticism that supports the best sort of espionage. Unquestioning acceptance of the motives of our enemies has no real place in the kind of intelligence or policy-making that produces victories in the environments of the Third and Fourth World wars.

CHAPTER 8

Terrorists and Other Romantics

Traditionally there have been a small number of important areas of national security in France that are controlled closely by the Élysée Palace itself, with intelligence or military forces called in on an as-needed basis. One of those areas is African affairs, because of France's long presence in and affinity for Africa. Another is the French nuclear deterrent, the *force de frappe*. A third is terrorism, because it concerns the very survival of the French Republic and the safety of each of its citizens.

Despite, or perhaps because of, the firm desire of every French president I served to maintain close, hands-on control in each of the three strategic areas, I put them at the very top of my list of priorities from my first days in office. France's role in Africa and our management of the French nuclear deterrent, I quickly learned, were already well in hand. It was necessary only to make certain that the mechanisms in place functioned as they were intended to—to gather the necessary information and act on it at the president's will. The third national priority, terrorism, was for me the most difficult strategic problem I have ever encountered, and inevitably the one that called for application of our greatest skills. We had a long learning curve to ride, and a very short and deadly period to arrive at the apex.

In the course of my preparation for taking charge of the SDECE, I learned several critical lessons from our top counterterrorist operatives—both domestically in the DST and abroad in the SDECE, which I controlled.

Terrorists are the ultimate romantics—expressed through their warped belief that they help their cause by violence. In their own isolated, deformed milieu, they travel together, they live together, they eat together, they make love together. They are organized into the tiniest cells—from five to fifty people. They have their own heroes, their villains as well. We must not think they are simply bloodthirsty vampires. They are frustrated, good-for-nothing dreamers. Yet many of them are very intelligent indeed. After many years of observing them, I can explain how they function.

We used to have a saying: "The donkey is the horse of the poor. The goat is the cow of the poor. The terrorist is the warrior of the poor." It takes very little manpower to mount a terrorist operation, very little money. Yet the results of a single engagement, and I use that term deliberately, can be as deadly and dangerous as the most massive military thrust by a division of heavily armed combat troops.

The only way to fight terrorists in a tactical as opposed to a strategic sense is to descend to their level. You must quite simply become one of them—travel with them, sleep with them, and work with them, for years sometimes. Certainly, the West's leading intelligence organizations have had more success in penetrating the top ranks of Soviet communism. We understand the East European mind-set better. After all, as I've explained to each president of France and to any number of world leaders, they are Europeans like us. Terrorists, with some exceptions, are generally not Europeans. If they are Europeans—for example the Red Brigades, the Baader-Meinhof Gang, even the Irish Republican Army—they have adopted many of the tactics, indeed have often been trained in the very training camps, of their terrorist brethren in the Islamic world who invented the techniques European terrorists use. Or they apply those techniques they learned from the Communist bloc, while continuing to refine and perfect them. Although the most pernicious Middle Eastern terrorists have been trained by Soviet, East German, or other Communist-bloc experts in weapons or other techniques, they have now unfortunately surpassed even their instructors. Most of our Western or Northern politicians have not yet mastered the terrorist mentality. And they do not know or understand the places where terrorists are spawned and how they swim.

To fight terrorists, we must first of all deprive them of the physical bases where they operate and train. They need weapons. You can buy weapons anywhere. They need a very few men. But those men must be highly trained. Any peasant can make a Molotov cocktail, but not a sophisticated plastic explosive with high-altitude dual triggers. If we pressure the countries who harbor them, where will they go? Their foot soldiers can retreat to the deep desert for training. However, the deserts are far too open and vulnerable for the commanders. If you stop somewhere in the desert, within five minutes you've got five men and three spy satellites looking at you. The desert is a very bad place for terrorist leaders to hide. The best place is a large city—in the Middle East, certainly, and increasingly in Europe itself.

Curiously, we have dealt with this problem of international terrorism considerably less adeptly than we have dealt with France's homegrown terrorist problem—the Corsican separatists. The Corsicans are in constant activity on French soil, their violent, often bloody attacks directed at French government offices, institutions, even high government officials. During my stewardship of the SDECE, the separatists also conducted massive propaganda barrages, urging an expanded campaign of civil disobedience and mayhem against France. Much of that propaganda emanated from a radio station and base on Elba, the island to which Napoleon was banished in 1814, and which is now Italian territory, and therefore, the Corsicans believed, out of reach of French justice. But as Italian authorities looked the other way, we blew up the entire facility. Elba is an island with a big mountain on its shore. One night, we landed a commando group, which made its way up the mountain, carrying tourist clothes with them. The next day, they completed a reconnaissance dressed as tourists. That night, they planted explosive charges around the entire Corsican compound and detonated them simultaneously. Seven million dollars in equipment went up in twenty seconds. The following day, Corsican terrorist leaders called an emergency meeting at their mainland headquarters-in-exile in Livorno, Italy. I asked one of our Corsican noncommissioned officers to dial the phone number of the headquarters, which we had acquired.

"You see what we did to you last night," he said in Corsican with his best Corsican accent. "The next time, we'll blow you up, too, not just the equipment. And the best proof you have of our being able to do this is the fact that I'm talking to you on the telephone at the place where you are having your top-secret meeting."

For the next six months, there was nothing—not a word, not a action—from the Corsican resistance. We had removed their c critical element—a secure base of operations.

Shortly thereafter, I developed another scheme for dealing with our Corsican terrorists. We had identified and pinpointed their five top leaders. I advised President Giscard d'Estaing that we would take the first terrorist name on the list and make him disappear. Then after a while, we would take the second name on the list. And do the same thing.

I told the President, sitting in his office at the Élysée Palace, "We will never have to get to the third name on the list. These people want to live and enjoy the good life. They are not like some Middle Eastern or Japanese fanatics who are ready to give their lives for a cause they believe in. They have money. They live in luxurious palaces, with girls. They are great heroes in their own little milieu. And they love it. They love life. They don't want to die."

But the President would not authorize this illegal action.

Such a strategy would not work with Abu Nidal or Carlos or any of the Middle East or Japanese terrorists. They don't mind dying. For these there must be other means of attack. We must penetrate each of their cells to know what operations they are planning from day to day, week to week.

By political and diplomatic means, ultimately by sheer military force if necessary, we must also remove their bases of support, neutralize those nations that have become our natural enemies, and, in short, truly engage in the Fourth World War as we have done in the three that preceded it in this century.

We French have always been much more effective than the Americans in penetrating Islamic groups, and we became known for our expertise. Our century and a half as a colonial power left us with the priceless legacy of quite a number of mini-Lawrences of Arabia. I had in a number of Arab countries people who spoke Arabic and were virtually indistinguishable from Arabs. Several of them were former officers of the Camel Corps, legionnaires who rode with and looked like Arabs. One agent was a doctor who had taken more than a decade to penetrate to the heart of one Middle East terrorist organization. Yet one day, the terrorists uncovered this mole in their midst, and the doctor simply disappeared. Penetrating an operation takes ten, fifteen, or more years. You've got to start the agent as a young man, and he's got to worm his way inside and grow with this organism, grow organically; one day he may even become a leader.

Our agents in Africa have served France's national interest on innumerable occasions, alerting us to terrorist operations, preventing terrorist incidents that would have caused unimaginable death and destruction. One of those officers was assassinated in September 1989 in Abidjan. He was serving our interests and those of Felix Houphouet-Boigny, the president of the Ivory Coast, by closely monitoring the activities of some bad guys—too closely it turned out. For twenty years, I had been telling Houphouet, "Do not let people from the Middle East come to your country because they are going to bring their problems with them." But after ten years of listening to me he finally forgot my advice, blinded by his desire to make the Ivory Coast a true refuge for political refugees of all types—and, some people say, part of his elusive and futile quest for the Nobel Peace Prize. President Houphouet also hoped that by welcoming these terrorist elements openly he would insulate his country from attacks by terrorists—alas, a Pollyannaish expectation. Those whom Houphouet gave sanctuary did indeed begin operating and killing each other in Abidjan. Using the Ivory Coast as a base, they were able to travel widely. Each had a dozen or more passports, with all but identical names and indistinguishable photos, which made any individual all but impossible to track. The terrorist presence in the Ivory Coast eventually became a concern for the French government because it regarded the security of the former colony as a keystone of its African policy. Moreover, with the excellent air links between the Ivory Coast and France, it was an easy, direct flight for any terrorist or sympathizer. So one day, when Houphouet came to Paris and said, "I have no one to monitor them," I found someone for him. I had one of my superb faithful officers who had just retired, sent to Abidjan. He was very efficient. Alas, he stuck his nose into places where he should not have. Less than a year later, he was dead.

There was another very dramatic case in the late 1970s. Two leading Palestinian members of a cell just happened to meet two young French girls in a nightclub in Haifa, the resort on the Red Sea that many French youths have discovered is quite a delightful retreat. The Palestinians seduced the two innocent young ladies, slept with them, then said they had some presents that they wanted to send to their mother who was living, they told the girls, in France. So naturally, the girls put the presents—bombs that would have exploded sometime after their arrival in France—in their suitcases. We never got the two terrorists. But because we had an agent in the group that manufactured the bombs, we were able to warn our customs authorities of their anticipated arrival. The bombs were discovered and quickly disarmed. An enormous catastrophe in the center of Paris was averted.

But penetrating individual terrorist cells at the base is little more than the military equivalent of a company-level engagement—a single, isolated component of a campaign in an entire theater of war. Ultimately, it was necessary to move up the ladder of responsibility, to pull back and examine strategy on a geopolitical, as well as a tactical, scale. Many of our friends in the Middle East would recognize the paraphrase of Clausewitz's dictum, "Terrorism is war by other means." Through the 1970s and into the 1980s, terrorism became the principal strike force of our enemies in the Fourth World War. Yet it was also having an important fallout in the moderate nations of the Middle East, whose leaders were repeatedly horrified by the atrocities their more radical neighbors were committing for the purposes of power and greed. I recognized early on that our natural allies in the Fourth World War were those moderate nations of the South who recognized that their basic self-interest, indeed their security and survival, meant casting their lot with us. Those moderate nations, driven by feelings of repugnance for the actions of their barbaric neighbors, coupled with more practical concerns for the preservation of some international order, joined with some Western intelligence leaders to form what came to be known as the Safari Club.

The Safari Club, an extraordinary and virtually unknown group, was organized during the oil crisis of 1973, a most dangerous period for the West. More rarely recognized is that the period of the oil embargo was a most perilous time for the Middle East as well, when the fragile framework of the international economy on which the oil-producing world depended for its revenues was very much in jeopardy. I thought it was vital that we assemble some of the key representatives of the Muslim world and the West to form a united front against the more irresponsible elements who might seize on this economic crisis to provoke a diplomatic or military confrontation on a global scale.

My first contacts were with the Shah of Iran, the kings of Saudi Arabia and Morocco, and President Anwar Sadat of Egypt. I visited each of those individuals personally, selling him on the idea that if we joined forces, we would all emerge from this crisis stronger and with a greater understanding of how we might deal with each other in the future to avoid a repetition. At the same time, periodic gatherings could serve as a means to exchange intelligence on the operations of their more radical neighbors. I was careful in my discussions with each of these leaders to emphasize that, while the president of France was aware of my actions, I was not acting in my official capacity as the director general of the SDECE, but rather as a private facilitator whose realpolitik was well known to each of these leaders.

Our meetings took place successively in the different capitals of each of these countries on a rotating basis. The Safari Club had its own special radio channels, and its special codes and machinery. Each of the countries was generally represented either by its head of intelligence or the national security adviser to the head of state. There was, for instance, General Ahmed Dlimi, the principal adviser to King Hassan II of Morocco. From Egypt came the head of the Mukhabarat el-Aam, their intelligence and security service. From Iran came the four-star general who headed Savak and who also served as the aide-de-camp to the Shah and first vice prime minister of Iran, General Nematollah Nassiri.

One meeting of the Safari Club stands out particularly because of the curious way it unified threads of the Third and the Fourth World wars. The session took place in Morocco after the oil crisis of 1973–74 had been resolved. We were meeting in Rabat, and each of the participants came in his own private jet. I told the Moroccans to put my aircraft, a Mystère 20, at Salé, the Rabat airport, at the far end of the field. Since the aircraft bore the French tricolor flag of an official plane, I felt it should remain well out of view. I was in Rabat for two days. On the morning of the second day, Moroccan police were on patrol on the small road outside the airfield next to the strip where my plane was parked, some thirty yards away. At six o'clock in the morning, the police spotted a car with a man leaning out of the window staring in the direction of my plane.

"Monsieur, what are you doing there?" they asked the man.

"I am breathing the beautiful fresh air of Morocco in the morning," he replied snidely.

"Well, that's very fine," the police officer told me he continued, "but are you interested in this aircraft you have been staring at and watching for the past fifteen minutes?"

"Yes, I like to look at aircraft. Nothing illegal with this, is there?"

"May we ask who you are?" the officer said.

"I am the first secretary of the Bulgarian embassy to Morocco."

The Bulgarians were not known for their subtlety in matters of espionage, but for their brutality. Moreover, there was nothing illegal in what they were doing and no reason to detain this diplomat. But it was clear there was considerable interest in the operations of the Safari Club. At that time, we were deeply embroiled with the Soviet empire in the Third World War. The Soviets were active everywhere in the world, but especially in the Middle East, where they believed they might find allies capable of attacking and destabilizing their enemies in the West. The Safari Club deeply interested and disturbed not only the Soviets, but their Middle Eastern friends, whom Moscow was seeking incessantly to cultivate.

After lunch on the final day, we all left to return to our respective capitals. As I was accustomed to do after each of our sessions, I reminded all the participants to take great care where they left their briefcases and who was given access to their secret papers. In the evening, I flew back to Paris, checked in at the office, then went home and straight to bed. Around 1:00 A.M., the phone rang. The duty officer from the central office was calling.

"Monsieur le Directeur-Général, I am sorry to disturb you," he began, "but it seems that before flying to Teheran, General Nassiri stopped over for the night in Nice to have dinner with Mrs. Nassiri and some friends. While he was at dinner in Nice, his apartment was burgled. There was a lot of money and jewels, but nothing disappeared."

I knew immediately what had happened, and promptly placed a call to the general. General Nassiri, who was head of Savak and a trusted childhood friend and classmate of the Shah's, was inclined to take somewhat cavalierly many of the precautions that professional intelligence specialists took with deadly earnestness. His situation at home, at least, he felt was unassailable and offered him rights, even privileges, that were utterly out of place for his position. It was merely one indication of the corruption that was already beginning to eat away at Iran under the Shah.

I quickly had Nassiri on the phone. "My dear friend, my dear General, I do hope you didn't have any of your papers with you," I began.

"Oh, not at all, of course not," he replied. "Thank God I sent them directly from Morocco to Teheran."

I knew he was lying. But the next morning, to verify my hypothesis, I sent a message to the Moroccans, requesting a list of all private or commercial planes that had taken off from Morocco with a flight plan for Teheran the day before. The answer I expected came back—there were none.

So I knew. The Bulgarian who had been watching the planes in the morning knew when Nassiri took off. The Bulgarians alerted their Soviet counterparts, who put a close watch on Nassiri's apartment in Nice, then staged a break-in that very night—the only night he would be within striking distance, open and totally vulnerable to their operatives. I admired their organization, but needed to know for certain if they had obtained what they came for.

The next morning, two days after the Safari Club meeting had broken up and the day that Nassiri arrived back in Teheran, I told the Moroccans to send a message, in the Safari Club code, to General Nassiri in Teheran to verify the incident and request details of the burglary "for the files." But he had lost the code that was among the papers stolen from his apartment. He never answered the encrypted message because he couldn't read it. We knew then that the other side had the code—the code that was changed after each meeting and that Nassiri was himself carrying in the briefcase that was no longer in his possession.

We were forced to change the code immediately. With information on our deliberations, the Soviets could have won a lot of points indeed with many of those nations of the Middle East that we had quite intentionally excluded from the Safari Club.

One of the nations we excluded from the Safari Club was Iraq, even though since 1970, the spectacular rapprochement between France and Iraq was a cornerstone of French policy in the Middle East. That rapprochement was part of a very deliberate and conscious plan conceived at the highest levels of the French Republic to act on the second half of the antiterrorist equation—to remove high-level government support and direction from terrorist groups, effectively to isolate one renegade nation after another that was preparing to do battle against us in the Fourth World War.

At the time, we had another, equally important agenda with respect to Iraq—one that was more geopolitical than the interests of some of Iraq's neighbors, who clearly feared more than I Baghdad's expansionist tendencies. Our other agenda was linked to our immediate priority of fighting the Third World War. Our intention was to try desperately to keep Saddam Hussein and his country out of the exclusive clutches of the Russians, who were losing ground in that part of the world—forced out of country after country for political, military, or religious reasons. In effect, Iraq was one of the last

Soviet stalking-horses, and Moscow hoped to exploit Baghdad's geopolitical ambitions and use them to attack the West at every opportunity.

My pitch to the Iraqis was a simple one. I did not say, "You must rid yourselves of the Russians and fall into the arms of the West." Clearly, Baghdad would never have accepted such patently ridiculous—at least from their point of view—not to mention dangerous, advice. The Soviets were, after all, Iraq's principal supplier of arms. My argument was much simpler: "Don't you think that you should spread the risk and have some friends in the West as well."

After Egypt's President Anwar Sadat found it prudent to show the door to his Russian advisers, it became increasingly obvious to Saddam that my advice was sound. Saddam's decision was based on a complex interplay of needs and desires mixed with more traditional Middle Eastern fear. First, it was becoming clear to him, as it had to Sadat, that the Soviets were distinctly unreliable suppliers of arms and munitions. They were unreliable because of the high price they were fully prepared to exact for every substandard tank or third-rate fieldpiece, equipment that was no match for any of the Western-supplied munitions of Iraq's neighbors and potential enemies. Not lost on Saddam was the fate of the Arab armies in their battles with the Israelis in 1967 and 1973. Saddam clearly realized that a guaranteed supply of Western, particularly French, arms paid for with the petrodollars that were flowing liberally into his national war chest, was preferable to the inferior Soviet weapons paid for with the coin of ideological conformity. Nor, clearly planning for the future, was he prepared to accept any possible veto on his expansionist plans in the region. By hedging his bets on the East and the West, Saddam thought such a veto would be considerably less enforceable.

It was in the early 1970s that I first met Sadoun Chaker, the confidant and right-hand man of Saddam Hussein. At the time Chaker was serving as chief of the Department of General Intelligence, the feared Al Mukhabarat, which functioned both as Saddam's eyes and ears abroad and his enforcer within the Baath party organization. Throughout the country, Saddam ruled with an iron hand; those who formed his team were tough, having muscled their way to power, executing their enemies along the way. But Sadoun was young, personable, intelligent, and attractive, as well as tough.

One day, not long after I took office, Sadoun came to see me in

Paris. We dined in my offices at SDECE headquarters. He was accompanied by one of his aides, I by one of my Middle East experts.

As coffee was being served after dinner, I turned to Sadoun and began:

"If Your Excellency will permit, I shall speak bluntly, brutally even. My feelings about your country are rather sad. You only need to go to the Museum of Antiquities in Baghdad to recognize that your history and your past are among the richest in human experience, more ancient even than Egypt's. Today your country is alone in the Arab world in possessing both water and oil. Fate—or Allah, if you prefer, Excellency—has ordained that most countries provided with water are without oil, and vice versa. Strange, perhaps, but that's how it is. You are the exception. Thanks to the huge rivers that come down from the Caucasus and the Taurus mountains, the Tigris and the Euphrates, you have water in abundance and, so I am assured by our experts [I turned to smile at my aide], fabulous potential in minerals and oil. Some go so far as to consider you a second Saudi Arabia. You are also considered, quite justifiably, the Prussians of the Arab world—the greatest warriors. And what are you doing meanwhile?"

I let the question hang as we left the dining room table and moved to the comfortable leather armchairs in my office. Sadoun sat on the same Chesterfield where Giscard d'Estaing had sat during his first luncheon in my offices.

"So what are you up to," I resumed, "between this prodigious past and a future that may lead you to extraordinary triumphs and riches again? You're doing stupid little things in mountain villages. You are practicing elementary terrorism."

Sadoun leaped to his feet to protest. I reached out my hand silently and motioned him back to his chair.

"Hashishim," I spat out, the Arab word for assassin. "You take young people, like the Turks took the Janissaries. They put these young people in a palace—a true paradise on earth—showed them the gardens of the palace, a marvelous land where birds sing and there are beautiful women. The young people are there for only two or three days. Then they are taken out. And they become Hashishim—Assassins. This was in the Middle Ages, but you are doing the same things in your Iraq today.

"I am not asking you if you are helping terrorists, I am telling you," I continued. I pulled out a little date book from my pocket.

"Isn't it true," I began, opening it, "that on July twenty-fourth, you sent a check for one hundred thousand dollars to a person in Cairo?" I named the individual and the bank account.

Sadoun blushed and said, "Yes."

"Six months later, did you not send him another check, with this check number?" I showed it to him.

"Right," he replied quietly.

"Do I have to continue?" I asked.

"No," he said. "I've got the message."

Equally clear was the thought going through Sadoun's mind—perhaps here there really is someone with whom we can talk! Ridding Iraq of terrorists was, perhaps, the smallest price Baghdad would have to pay for the Western arms it so desperately required.

Saddam Hussein had already begun to reflect that terrorists, whether they are South Americans, Europeans, Africans, Middle Eastern, or Japanese, are distinctly unreliable allies. While he continued to give moral and financial support to certain elements of the PLO, he clearly recognized that the disparate terrorist organizations and their military wings operating within Iraq were as capable of destabilizing his country as Western democracies. It was the same kind of concern that led Jordan's King Hussein to expel the Palestine Liberation Organization. By 1978, Baghdad would close the PLO's Al Fatah offices in Iraq, stop financial assistance to the PLO itself (though not to some of its factions), seize Al Fatah arms factories, and confiscate substantial quantities of arms in Iraq that were in transit from China to PLO forces in Lebanon. Most of the principal members of the so-called Palestinian Rejection Front (named for its rejection of any PLO compromise with Israel) were evicted from Iraq. These groups included George Habash's Popular Front for the Liberation of Palestine (PFLP), the PFLP-General Command, led by the mastermind of the *Achille Lauro* attack, Abul Abbas; the special operations branch of the PFLP, under Wadei Haddad; and Fatah—the Revolutionary Council, led by the notorious Abu Nidal. All of them would ultimately wind up in Syria and Iran, countries that were Iraq's bitter enemies and rivals for regional dominance.

Baghdad's eviction of most of the terrorist groups from Iraq was a process that was to last more than a decade, but for a while at least, it transformed the terrorist map of the Middle East.

Imagine if during the operations of Desert Storm, Saddam Hussein also had been able to muster the kind of terrorist support that

Iran or Syria could summon today from these elements to whom they gave sanctuary. The world might truly have been turned into a mindless, anarchic inferno. But the terrorists were contained and restrained by the hostility to Saddam Hussein of the leaders of Syria and Iran who control and subsidize the terrorists' operations. These other national leaders who might have unleashed a wave of terrorism on the North, instead seized the opportunity to use the allied troops to do what their own military forces were never able to accomplish—neutralize Iraq, the single most powerful standing army in the Middle East.

In short, the foundations we laid more than a decade ago enabled us to harness the violent passions that divide our enemies of the Fourth World War and turn them to our advantage in the campaign of Desert Storm.

That first night that I met Sadoun Chaker in my office, there began a dialogue between the two of us that was to last for many years, a dialogue that led to my first official visit to Baghdad in 1974 to meet with Saddam Hussein himself.

I had told the Americans of my intentions—to bring over Saddam Hussein to the side of the West and deprive terrorists of their bases in that country. So I embarked on a regular shuttle to Baghdad, and a series of meetings with Saddam. On one of those visits, he asked me to accompany him to the great stadium of Baghdad.

"Sure," I said, "as long as I am in a corner somewhere where nobody sees me."

But as things worked out, I was trapped just next to him as his entourage left the motorcade and moved through the throngs of Iraqis into the stadium itself. Saddam maintains a true cult of personality in Iraq. And the stadium on that sweltering summer day was a sea of humanity with one desire—to pay homage to their ultimate leader. The occasion was the bestowing of military medals on heroes of the war against the hated enemy, Iran. The Russians were there in the stadium in force—all resplendent in dress uniform, including KGB officials with their red shoulder-boards. One general kept pointing to the large Frenchman just next to Saddam, asking, "Who is he? Who is he?" He was no doubt surprised when he learned later that the official guest was the director general of the SDECE.

Even as we cultivated Saddam Hussein, began selling him warplanes and munitions, we monitored continually the Soviets' ongoing resupply of the Iraqi military machine, particularly the powerful

Scud missiles that were perhaps the single most effective weapon against Israeli and allied forces during the Gulf war. By not severing diplomatic, military, and intelligence ties with Iraq, we were also able to keep reasonably well informed on the state of play of Iraqi military capabilities. That kind of intelligence turned out to be of inestimable value when the armed forces of Desert Storm finally went up against what conventional wisdom held to be an all but invincible Iraqi military machine.

Saddam himself was at the time quite an impressive man—virile, rather tall, strong, good face. The man was an autocrat, without question, but capable of inspiring the most extraordinary loyalty in his followers.

When I met with him, it was generally in his private offices in the ornate presidential palace. Sadoun Chaker was usually by his side, and neither was especially surprised when I hammered away on the question of Iraq's subsidizing international terrorism. Each time, Saddam took in all my assertions without comment. He was well briefed by Sadoun, and he had equally clearly made up his mind on the key issues—severing ties with terrorists and moving toward the major powers of the West and North, but at his own pace.

Certainly, there were many anxious to put an end to his rapprochement with the West, particularly with France. And they would clearly stop at nothing to torpedo any new and closer understandings. In the course of one of my series of meetings with senior Iraqi officials, I rose from the table to stretch my legs and strolled over to the window looking out on a plaza below. I parted one of the curtains for a better view and a microphone fell to the ground with a clatter. My hosts rushed over, deeply embarrassed.

"Come on." I smiled. "Don't look like that. I'm convinced that you know how to fit a microphone perfectly. A bungled job like this can mean only one thing—whoever placed it here must have intended it to fall down in the course of our meetings." And who beside the Iraqis would have access to such a room? Their Soviet "allies," for one. Certain Arab terrorist leaders as well. And above all, the Iran of Ayatollah Khomeini.

Saddam was already planning to take on Iran. And what better allies than the major and minor "Satans"—the Western governments that were the principal targets of Iranian invective and terrorist aggression Khomeini was personally sponsoring. Iraq had been the first nation of sanctuary for Khomeini after his expulsion from Iran in 1963, quite early in the reign of the Shah. It was then that Khomeini took up residence in the Shiite-dominated region of southern Iraq where he was welcomed as a prophet. The Ayatollah remained in exile in the provincial city of Najaf, totally at the expense of the Iraqis, for fifteen years. His presence was tolerated as a sop to Iraq's Shiite population and as a thorn in the side of the Shah.

Sadoun Chaker had been given full custody of Khomeini, and he briefed me in detail on Khomeini's character. The Ayatollah, he told me, had an impossible personality. He was little more than a medieval tyrant. One day, a child in the entourage that had followed him into exile had a fight with a neighboring Iraqi child. Khomeini demanded that the Iraqi child who had dared raise a fist against his spiritual "offspring" be put to death. That was only the first of many outrageous requests that the Iraqis refused out of hand.

Throughout his exile in Iraq, Khomeini did his best with inflammatory speeches to foment unrest in the Iranian empire, believing that he had a personal score to settle with the Shah, though the Shah himself had spared his life by exiling him in 1963. Ironically, General Pakravan, the former Iranian ambassador to Paris, who was the military adviser to the young Shah, had actually been the one who saved Khomeini's life. Pakravan, then serving as the head of Savak, the Shah's feared secret police, urged the ruler to exile the Ayatollah rather than execute him. Pakravan in turn was dismissed three years later by the Shah, for being ineffective in handling opposition elements. Years later, after Khomeini returned in triumph to Teheran, General Pakravan was summoned back to Iran from his diplomatic post in France. Khomeini had him arrested and shot—to prevent him from making it known that the Ayatollah owed his life to the onetime head of Savak.

Not long after my first meeting with Saddam Hussein, it became clear to me that the Iraqi leader was making serious efforts to reestablish cordial relations with the Shah. Part of those negotiations involved Iranian demands that Saddam put a damper on Khomeini's increasingly disruptive activities while in exile. The same week I learned of these talks, I dispatched my principal aide to Baghdad with a personal, verbal message for Saddam Hussein:

"Be wary of this man Khomeini. He is a firebrand. And there is nothing more dangerous than a forest fire, because fanned by strong winds, it can jump roads, and frontiers—even frontiers of the mind—and engulf the neighboring forests."

Such warnings, and certainly Sadoun Chaker's personal observations closer to home, by no means fell on deaf ears. When my
envoy returned to Paris two days later, he reported to me:

"Monsieur le Directeur-Général, you will be pleased to learn
that the decision has effectively been made by the Iraqis to expel
Khomeini."

Khomeini did not, of course, take this very gracefully. He threat-
ened to deal one day with those in power in Iraq who were authors
of his expulsion, conveniently forgetting that many of them were the
same individuals who had given him and his entire entourage sanctuary, not to mention room and board, for the previous fifteen years.
Saddam Hussein was not accustomed to such threats. His decision
stood.

In those days, however, Saddam could at times be persuaded, as
Assad can be today, that certain policy decisions were indeed in his
best interest—for example, the decision to exercise discretion in the
care and training of terrorists. I am not confident that he still maintains this flexibility.

Two years later, Saddam Hussein's Iraq and the Iran that was
by then ruled by the Ayatollah were at war. It was then that Saddam's decision of years before to accept sensible advice and seek a
rapprochement with his friends in the West bore fruit. Western
arms and munitions were the single advantage that Saddam Hussein held over the human waves of fanatics Khomeini unleashed on
Iraqi forces.

During that war, I had an opportunity to witness firsthand the
most graphic evidence of just what such fanatic Islamic militarism
really means. I was visiting Saddam Hussein in the presidential
palace in Baghdad.

"What would you like to see while you are in my country?" he
asked. "Would you like to see the front?"

"Mr. President, frankly, I've had plenty of this," I replied, refer-
ring to the repeated visits our military people had made to the
battlefields of the war with Iran. "But there is something, if you
don't mind. There has been some talk in the West of thousands of
young Iranian boys, most of them lost waifs, that you have in prisoner of war camps."

"When do you want to go?" Saddam shot back, turning immediately to an aide.

"Tomorrow morning," I said. And it was done.

I took with me one of my own interpreters. I knew the tricks interpreters can play. But I was unprepared for the sight I was to see—a most painful image of what war in the Middle East can mean, a war waged by the fanatical adherents of Allah. That image was a harbinger of the Fourth World War that we were only dimly beginning to perceive on the radar screen.

The prisoner of war camp itself was adequate; it was spartan but clean, the food plentiful. It was not the Ritz in the Place Vendôme. But what differentiated it from a POW camp anywhere else in the Western world was that the inmates were children—eight, ten, twelve, fourteen years old. I chose one of these children at random.

"How old are you?" I asked gently, bending down so that I would be eye level with him.

"I am thirteen," he replied softly.

"How long have you been a prisoner of war here?"

"Three years."

He had been captured when he was ten years old. Like hundreds of his fellow Iranian children, he had been used as a human mine detector, running through minefields to explode the mines before the infantry attacked. Those who survived, often without one or both legs, were usually captured in the wake of the battle. Unable to crawl away, they had nowhere else to go.

I noticed a small plastic key around his neck.

"It is the key to paradise," he explained, smiling for the first and only time during our little talk. It was this motivation—the religious fanaticism of a seventeenth-century mind—that was used to propel these young people into unimaginable horrors.

CHAPTER **9**

Minefields in the Middle East

or a thousand years, the battle between Sunni and Shiite has been as bitter and divisive as the battle between Catholic and Protestant in Ulster, Christian and Muslim in Beirut, Jew and Arab in Israel. It is a blood feud that dates to the seventh century over the succession to the mantle of the Prophet Muhammad himself. Was it indeed Muhammad's cousin and son-in-law, Ali, who inherited the right to succeed the Prophet and to pass that mantle on to his twelve descendants, the last of whom remains unrevealed to this day? The Shiites, followers of Ali, are still contesting this succession, still awaiting the arrival of the Twelfth Imam. Only such a descendant, according to Shiite tradition, can be the true leader of the Muslim world. The Sunnis recognize only the Prophet Muhammad himself as the basis of their religion. The Shiites, by contrast, consider any who question Ali's legitimate leadership to be no better than infidels. The Sunnis, who dominate Iraq, not to mention Saudi Arabia, Egypt, and most other Muslim nations, are just such infidels. For the Shiites, the Sunni refusal to recognize Ali as "the Saint of God" is a perfectly legitimate reason for any individual to meet an unimaginable death.

The most recent iteration of this ancient schism was the internecine conflict between Iran and Iraq, the latest outbreak dating to the return to power in Iran of Ayatollah Khomeini in 1979. In Iraq Saddam Hussein is a Sunni Muslim, as are all other members of the Iraqi leadership. Though Iraq's population is heavily Shiite, its Sunni-dominated government makes it the one remaining non-Shiite Muslim bastion in the region. If a coup d'état brought to power a Shiite government in Baghdad, then a Shiite empire would

171

emerge stretching from Pakistan across Iraq and Lebanon to the Mediterranean. It was easy to appreciate that a Shiite Iraq would pose an enormous threat to Turkey, the easternmost member of NATO, not to mention Egypt and Saudi Arabia. A Shiite Iraq would combine all the military might of the Iraqi military machine with the religious fervor, not to mention the military support of an Iran, the other major Shiite power in the region. Geographically, it would be a dagger poised to strike any of four directions—toward the Sunni-dominated Saudi Arabia and Arabian peninsula to the south and east, Turkey to the north, Israel or even Egypt to the west.

The seeds of today's South-North conflict were laid in the earliest days of Shiite power. These winds of war were swirling across the desert in Iraq and Syria a thousand years ago, when Saladin embarked on the first of his jihads. In Iran, the forces that drove the warriors of Islam were visible long before the arrival of the ayatollahs in power, before those who, in the name of the Shiite religion, seized our hostages in Beirut, challenged Saddam Hussein and fed his megalomania, and spread the seeds of religious discontent from the Soviet Empire to the gateway of the Mediterranean.

Iran today is the home of those who still await the arrival of the Twelfth Imam, and still defend the name of Ali at the most appalling cost to others.

Iran is one of the true superpowers of the South, with its huge oil reserves, its vast territory and population. The empire that was for a thousand years known as Persia once dominated the entire region, spreading at once fear and admiration, panic and envy among neighboring Arab peoples. I discovered during my earliest visits to the region how much the Arabs still fear the Persians, who, while they are Muslim, are not of Arab ethnic origin and cultural background. Their Arab neighbors feared the power and influence of Iran under the Shah, and they have feared it even more under the ayatollahs. In part, that fear is a consequence of the influence of geography; in part, of the fierce nature of the Persians themselves. They are the "tough guys" of the Middle East, doubly dangerous when pumped up with the adrenaline of religious fanaticism and the resources bought by oil. And as a people they have changed little over the centuries. Understanding them, studying them, battling them now on a variety of levels is as important as it has ever been.

For all this time, the masses of Iran have been a terrible weapon in the hands of whoever ruled them—doubly so in the hands of those with vast financial and logistical resources and organizational

skills. The Shiite clergy and their followers in Iran were well prepared for the violence that has always been an integral part of their
history, culture, and religion. The Shiites, because of their desire to
preserve the articles of faith handed down by Ali, the Saint of God,
are at once the most primitive, most violent, and most fanatically
religious of all the branches and sects of Islam. Dominant in Iran,
they maintain minority outposts in most of the other Sunni Muslim
nations of the Middle East. Everywhere, Shiites are poised to rise,
given the opportunity, but otherwise content themselves merely
with pursuing their silent and devoted rites.

The Shah recognized the danger of this religious community,
but underestimated it, or at least overestimated his ability to contain it through the viciously repressive measures of Savak. One of
the real tragedies of Iran under the Shah was that this apparently
powerful ruler never fully understood the truly vast resources he
might have commanded had he tried to harness them. The Shah
appears to have repeatedly overestimated the appeal to the Iranian
masses of his dismal attempts at modernizing his nation. The peas-
ants of the countryside, even the middle-class merchants of the souk,
never shared in the wealth being amassed by the top fraction of 1
percent of the privileged sycophants who had attached themselves to
the royal court in Teheran. Instead, these millions of followers of
Shiism saw their rewards coming from Ali and the Prophet in the
hereafter if they only adhered devotedly to their commandments,
and followed the teachings of the ayatollahs, the sacred mouthpieces
of the Prophet, in the here and now.

We had two key objectives for French Intelligence in this part of
the world: The first was to understand the forces at work in Iran and
those who were attempting, from within and without, to influence
those forces. This increase in our own awareness of and ability to
monitor events in the region was essential because of Iran's strategic location and its petroleum reserves that are so necessary to
France and the West. Our collaboration with Iran was also important to our broader intelligence agenda. Since Iran shares a 1,200-
mile border with the Soviet Union, and a 530-mile border with
Afghanistan, it is in a position to provide a truly unique perspective
on the southern reaches of the whole Soviet empire. Our joint monitoring stations around the fringe of the Soviet Union eavesdropped
for years on critical electronic exchanges, including the most detailed battlefield communications.

Our second objective was to keep Iran, which was in both a stra-

tegic and a precarious position, at worst neutral, at best firmly im-
planted on the Northern side for the Fourth World War that was then
only vaguely visible on the horizon. That was, as it developed, a vain
hope. Iran has always been and will continue to be a Southern nation,
with a collective mentality that has changed little from that of the
seventh-century caliphs who sought to assure the succession to the
Prophet. Though the Shah Shahanshah Reza Pahlavi was a leader
with decidedly Northern and Western sympathies, our friendship
and support of the Iranian monarch served merely to postpone the
inevitable.

From the earliest days of the Shah's rule, we began picking up
indications of considerable unrest. Years before I first met the Shah,
an admiral of the French Navy had been received by His Majesty to
acquaint him with a highly technical dossier. Arriving at the royal
palace, the admiral discovered a near disaster. An attempt had been
made earlier that day on the young Shah's life, one of the palace
guards having fired at the Shah, and a firefight had ensued.

As he made his way to the audience chamber, the French officer
picked his way through glass and debris that was still being removed. The wall was stained with the blood from the fighting that
had followed the unsuccessful attack. Yet the Shah maintained his
equilibrium. Such attempts, he finally explained to his visitor, were
by no means unusual. Still, these incidents even by their repetition
failed to teach the ruler the lesson of how profoundly he was detested by so many of his people.

The Shah was often compared unfavorably with his father, a
former warrant officer who became a cossack colonel, a mounted
nomadic warrior, who fought alongside the British during World
War I. He was a giant of a man, unlike his slight, finely built son.
During one of my visits, a leading courtier who had known both
men, whispered to me, "You dared not lie to the father, but to the
son you dare not tell the truth." The not so subtle implication was
that the messenger all too often paid with his job, his career, or his
life for the message that should have been delivered forcefully and
directly before it was too late. That is, unfortunately, typical of
many nations, where instability is only intensified with the succession or attempted succession of a weak or too civilized heir to a
powerful potentate.

During the 1970s, owing largely to our remarkable chief of station in Iran, Colonel L., the French became the first of the major
Western intelligence services to detect the extent of turmoil that

was seething in the Shiite community of Iran. As early as 1972, reports were arriving at my office of the ferment among key religious elements. The SDECE network provided reports to us stressing "growing dissatisfaction . . . signs of revolt in the clergy." We repeatedly passed to the Shah those reports we were receiving of the building discontent. On my periodic visits with him, he made it clear that he relied on me to tell him unpleasant facts that others kept from him. To ensure the Shah's safety, there was no question that he needed to be warned of what was going on. Whether he acted on this information was another issue entirely.

Once, as we were seated in his private study, he told me, "You are alone in telling me some of this information. The others are telling me the opposite."

"May I point out to your majesty," I replied deferentially, "what matters is not the number of voices, but the accuracy of the information."

Throughout the period of building opposition to the Shah's reign, I warned him of unrest in the bazaars, among the mullahs in the most remote villages, and in the heart of the capital. Reports from our operatives went into considerable detail about the horror produced by the small actions that were apparently taken with utter indifference or insensitivity to their impact on his devoutly religious people. Some years before, the Shah, during what was called "The White Revolution," distributed millions of acres to the poor peasantry. Part of this land belonged to the church and some of it to the Khomeini family. His Western perspective, his burning desire to drag his country instantly out of the ninth century and into the twentieth, to telescope eleven centuries into a single lifetime, led to a number of grave miscalculations that stemmed far less from malevolence than myopia.

Repeatedly, I warned him about the excesses of his courtiers and his regime—their abuses of their wealth and position, their refusal to pay even lip service to the religious beliefs of the large mass of their countrymen, their failure to deal with the deep poverty in the countryside.

"Do you think, Sire, that the riches born of the oil bonanza are being as well distributed as they might be?" I began one such conversation.

He nodded his head, accepting this criticism that he would hear from no one in his entourage—and on which he never found an appropriate time to act.

We tried to use what scraps of intelligence we found to penetrate as deeply as possible the ideas and the minds of those in Iran we were coming to view as our enemies. Throughout this period, I would stage "war games" involving Iran. Our station chief would be called back to Paris from Teheran. Our principal Middle East and Iranian intelligence and operations specialists would also gather in my office.

"Okay," I would begin, "we are going to think about the Iranian problem." I would rise and cross the room.

"Gentlemen, we are now no longer Judeo-Christians of the end of the twentieth century. We are Europeans or French of the eleventh century. We are men at a time of the Crusades. How do we react? If we are Khomeini or the mullahs, and have their mentality, how do we think?"

I turned to my principal Farsi-speaking aide. "You have no road, no helicopters. A runner has just arrived, announcing the first troops crossing into the empire from ancient Baghdad. What do you do?" We were not always successful in coming up with a satisfactory response, despite our growing intelligence network in the souks and mosques of Iran.

While we were building our intelligence capabilities, our American colleagues also were staffing the country with thousands of operatives, many of whom worked directly for the Central Intelligence Agency. Without question, some of those individuals were as perceptive, with as sound contacts in the key power centers of the country as any of their French counterparts. But their warnings never filtered high enough to impact the councils of power in Washington, where administration after administration persisted in dividing the world into two camps—friends and enemies. And where America's friends were concerned, there could be no hint that anything unpleasant was taking place. Iran was yet another instance of how profoundly the Americans failed to understand the driving forces in the Southern world—forces that were the foundation of the early debacles of the Fourth World War and the accompanying violence and death.

But the warning signals so clear, in retrospect, to all of us were ignored not only by the Americans, but by the French, indeed by all those in the West who considered Iran a reliably friendly power. We were unwilling to admit any information that would shake this geopolitical axiom.

The myth of Savak, the dreaded Iranian Secret Service, which was believed to have every situation in Iran under total control, also contributed to our collective failure of analysis when it came to Iran—among the greatest intelligence misjudgments of the twentieth century. Savak was more of a police force than an intelligence operation, as is often the case in Southern countries, where rulers are more interested in repression and intimidation than the gathering of raw information. I began to realize quite early that there was a critical missing link in the Iranian intelligence chain. No matter how accurate the information we or other sources were providing, the interpretation was fundamentally flawed. It was being filtered by Western minds, for the Shah who had been educated in Europe and looked to the West for his sense of culture, style, and above all, politics. For his closest advisers and confidants, he chose those who were educated like him and thought like him. If the Shah had the reflexes of an Oriental, when unrest first erupted in the bazaars and mosques, he would have crushed it without hesitation, or embraced it and smothered it with affection. Instead, he hesitated and was lost.

As part of our perceived mission, we provided the Shah with much more than regular information on the extent of dissatisfaction in his empire. We also made serious efforts, within the limits of our power of persuasion or demonstration, to help him correct the widespread and growing antipathy to his rule and to himself personally.

"What's wrong with me?" the Shah asked me plaintively during one of our later visits.

"Your Majesty, your image is terrible," I replied frankly. "A lot of people don't approve of you. But there are specialists in correcting that. The same kinds of people who sell cars, frozen food, and cigarettes also can build up your image." The role of image making is as critical in the Southern world as it is in the Northern. It is simply less often used and even more rarely understood.

"Who is the best in the world in that?" the Shah asked.

"David Ogilvy. An advertising genius and a very dear friend of mine."

"Well bring him to me," the Shah demanded.

I returned several weeks later with Ogilvy, and we were ushered together into the Shah's private offices. After we were presented, he turned to Ogilvy and came straight to the point.

"The count tells me you are the best in the world," he began. "Tell me something. Would you like to make a tour of Iran, then come back and see me?" Ogilvy agreed.

I gave Ogilvy our man in Teheran to accompany him, and he was able convincingly to demonstrate to Ogilvy just how deeply the worm had penetrated the apple. Ogilvy returned to his château in the Dordogne in central France and prepared a plan for the Shah that was presented to him a short time later. But the courtiers, who saw any outside attempt to shift the delicate balance of forces they had established in Iran as a fundamental challenge to their position, were very much opposed. The Ogilvy plan never went anywhere.

At every turn, I tried to protect the Shah from his enemies abroad and within. Each time some especially troubling piece of evidence arrived, I confronted the Shah, in as direct a manner as I dared. Eventually there simply became too many holes in too many dikes.

"Beware of the Carter administration," I warned the Shah at one point. "President Carter has decided to replace you."

That decision, we had learned, followed Carter's visit to Teheran during the New Year's season of 1978 when the Shah pulled out all the stops, allowing a horrified Carter to witness firsthand the extraordinary gluttony and waste at the court of the Shah.

I followed my warning with details that the monarch continued to shrug off—the names of those in the United States who had been given the responsibility of seeing to his departure and replacement, the date and place of a meeting I had attended with other senior American intelligence officials dealing with the issue of how his departure was to be managed and who was to succeed him.

The Shah was not convinced. "I believe everything you tell me, but not this."

"But Your Majesty, why don't you believe this?" I asked.

"Because it would be sheer stupidity to replace me. I am the best means of defense the West has in this part of the world. I have the best army, the best intelligence apparatus, the greatest capacity to rule a stable nation. So this is so absurd, I cannot possibly believe it."

"And what if the Americans don't understand that?" I replied softly. The Shah smiled sarcastically and shook his head.

In no case, of course, was it envisioned by the shortsighted Americans that the folly of accelerating the removal of the Shah would be followed immediately by the arrival in power of the Ayatollah Khomeini himself.

This was the period, beginning in October 1978 with Iraq's expulsion of Khomeini, when I began repeatedly urging Giscard first not to grant the Shah's archenemy asylum in France, then at least to restrict the activities of the Ayatollah that were destabilizing the Shah, and finally not to allow him to return triumphantly to his nation. My advice was ignored repeatedly as Giscard and his advisers felt strongly that France should be at liberty to grant asylum to any who suffered from political persecution, and to build bridges to an individual who they came to perceive, correctly, would be the successor to the Shah. But Giscard deeply misjudged the extent to which France's hospitality, the hospitality of infidels, would ever be repaid with friendship.

By allowing the Ayatollah and his entourage to set up shop in the Paris suburb of Neauphle-le-Château, the French unwittingly played an important role in Khomeini's eventual triumphant return to Teheran. The job of surveillance over the Ayatollah's entourage fell to the Ministry of the Interior, who considered it far from a top priority. But for us, it was a first-rank priority, particularly after we stumbled on the anti-Shah propaganda cassettes that were pouring out of the Khomeini compound and fanning the passions back home in Teheran. Those cassettes, full of exhortations, prayers, and bitter venom against the Shah and all those who were ruling and corrupting Teheran and Islam, featured the powerful, emotional voice of Khomeini. The cassettes, recorded in Paris, were transferred to the East German embassy there, then quickly shipped by diplomatic pouch to East Berlin, where Tudeh, the clandestine Iranian Communist party, maintained its headquarters-in-exile. There, Tudeh, using East German electronic equipment, duplicated the cassettes by the thousands and shipped them on to Iran, where, through the complex network of the bazaars, they went into mailboxes in Teheran or over garden walls in Isfahan, and into the smallest rural communities.

At the end of 1978, I reported these extraordinary developments to Giscard himself and implored that Khomeini be sent packing to another country, particularly one of several Middle East or North African nations which would have had a vested interest in silencing him, and where he could be dealt with appropriately, or controlled more effectively.

The next morning, one of my principal aides, Michel Roussin, bounded into my office with a broad smile.

"Monsieur le Directeur-Général, you have won," he exclaimed. "Tomorrow or the day after, Ayatollah Khomeini will be notified that he has to leave France. He will be told politely, but he will be told."

But Roussin's information was unfortunately premature. The next day, he reappeared at my door with a distinctly different attitude.

"Monsieur le Directeur-Général, today the news is not as good," he began dejectedly. "The winds blowing from the Élysée have shifted. Khomeini is staying. The Iranian ambassador conveyed to the Quai d'Orsay [the French Foreign Ministry] the Shah's personal request that Khomeini remain in France."

It was stunning that the Shah had one last time proved as short-sighted in what were to be his final hours as he had been through much of his reign. I decided to leave immediately for Teheran to hear this decision directly from the Shah himself. As I boarded my jet, we learned that Teheran was enshrouded by fires, that a general strike had paralyzed Mehrabad Airport outside the capital. No navigational aids were functioning, there was no jet fuel, so with the short range of my Mystère 20 jet, it was necessary for us to lay over in Larnaca, Cyprus. Roussin was accompanying me, together with a remarkable young captain who was a specialist on Iranian affairs.

Early the next morning, we arrived in Teheran. The control tower was not functioning, and sinister-looking armed men without uniforms patrolled the runways. I ordered the crew to remain with the plane. Since I had been in direct radio contact with one of the Shah's aides, a car met us. It took considerable time to cross the city, where the streets were swarming with screaming crowds.

The Shah received me in the palace in an office I had never seen before. It was a tiny room lit dimly by the soft light of a single lamp with a large shade that spread a gentle glow all around. My host was wearing enormous dark glasses that hid half his face. I had never seen him with glasses of that sort. He motioned me and my aides to three chairs next to the desk,.

I plunged right in, telling him I was amazed and shocked to hear he had personally vetoed my request that Giscard expel Khomeini from France, an expulsion that might have led to the Ayatollah being sent to a country where he could be dealt with more effectively or that might at least have disrupted his propaganda network.

"Your Majesty, perhaps you have been the victim of a member of your entourage?" I continued. "Or perhaps one of your signals has gone astray? Or your ambassador in France may have betrayed you?"

"Not in the least," he replied. "This is entirely according to my instructions."

I stared at him, wide-eyed in astonishment and alarm.

"Let me explain my reasons to you," he continued. "If you don't keep Khomeini in France, he will go to Damascus in Syria. Damascus is too close to Iran. I have information that tells me if he doesn't go to Damascus, he will make his way to Tripoli to Colonel

Qaddafi. That will be the worst. As my relations with France are exceptionally good, I will ask you to make it clear to the president of the Republic that I count on his friendship to tighten the screws. And all in all, I would rather Khomeini stay with you where he will be under close observation."

I thought to myself that the Shah, for all his familiarity with our society, had little real understanding of the inner workings of Northern democracies, at least in this critical respect—the meager means at our disposal for shutting up the saintly Ayatollah just at the moment when his voice was increasing in volume. Nor was the Shah aware that with the miracle of modern communications, the Ayatollah's geographical distance from Iran made little difference.

We turned to the domestic situation in Iran, and I described my ride from the airport, the angry crowds in the streets.

"Rest assured, my dear Count," said the Shah. "I shall never fire on my people."

Now, I decided, was no time to mince words, with the hordes already spreading terror throughout Teheran. "In that case, Your Majesty, you are lost," I said simply. The Shah shrugged and rose from his chair.

Our audience was finished and, with great courtesy, he accompanied me to the door, which he opened with a flourish, the harsh light of the anteroom suddenly flooding into the semidarkness of the office. The Shah had removed his glasses and was holding out his hand to me. I looked at him before making my bow, and so saw his face for the first time in the full light, a face that had become so familiar to me through the years. But it was a vastly different face than the one I had last seen just a few weeks earlier. Already it was ravaged by the cancer that was to carry him off.

We went immediately to our car for the trip back to the airport, passing through a dozen or more roadblocks manned by jittery soldiers with automatic weapons. Our plane was miraculously intact.

The next morning, I went immediately to the office of the president of the Republic. Valéry Giscard d'Estaing rose briskly and strode across the room to meet me.

"Well?" he asked quickly.

"It is Louis Seize," I replied.

"In that case, it is the end," he said simply.

That was the last contact between the Shah of Iran and the French Republic. Since the Shah was clearly unprepared to help himself, and believing that he would soon have to deal with the Ayatollah as the driving force in Iran, the French government made no further effort to restrain Khomeini. We continued our surveillance and let history take its course. Within weeks, the Shah was in exile. Khomeini was the ruler of the millions of his screaming followers.

Once firmly ensconced in power, Khomeini embarked on a series of international adventures designed to spread maximum terror throughout much of the Middle East and the Northern world in the ensuing years. His jihad, his holy war, had begun.

Although our intelligence operatives and our analysts have studied this extensively, and I have pondered this riddle for years, it is still by no means clear to me at what moment or under what motivation the Ayatollah began underwriting terrorist activities directed against France or French targets, repeatedly seizing French hostages in Beirut through his proxy Shiite fanatics, including the feared Hezbollah. Clearly, it was part of a broader plot—directly linked to the will of the mullahs to carry this battle against the North to the heart of our civilization. The strategy was clear, yet the tactics, to one schooled in the tactics of the first three global conflicts of this century, often remained opaque.

The first target of the Ayatollah's Iran was not France or the French. It was the Shah, whom the mullahs and their followers hounded to his final hours. Having left Iran in the most wretched circumstances, this once princely man wandered like the Flying Dutchman—to Egypt, where his friend President Anwar Sadat gave him shelter, thence to Morocco and his other best friend among Arab leaders, King Hassan II.

Hassan welcomed him and the imperial family and turned an old palace over to the Iranian exiles. Since King Hassan II was a great friend of France, and Morocco a nation of strategic importance in North Africa, we monitored the Shah's visit very closely. Hassan is an extraordinary leader of the Southern world—one who combines a profound religious belief with an understanding of the need to build bridges of all sorts to the North if some international equilibrium is to become in any sense attainable. He is a man remarkably sensitive to the deepest feelings and desires of his people.

Within days of the arrival of the Shah's entourage, our agents in Morocco began uncovering disturbing reports. Opposition circles were beginning to foment unrest, whispering about the "disgrace of welcoming this tyrant into our country." Graffiti began appearing on walls in Casablanca. For a Muslim, the pig is the most shameful animal, followed by the dog. The Western insult, "son of a bitch," is even more vicious when rendered in Arabic, "son of a dog." The grafitti scrawled in Casablanca read, "The king is the dog of the Shah."*

I had known King Hassan II for nearly forty years, since he was a young prince. My wife had grown up in Morocco, the daughter of French civil servants posted there. Shortly after the Second World War, Colonel Felix Edon, a former cavalry officer who had served for many years in the Camel Corps, knowing how fond I was of Morocco and Moroccans, suggested I meet the young Prince Hassan. We had lunch and began a lifelong friendship.

So as soon as I learned the extent of the danger, I flew to Rabat to warn Hassan of the threat the Shah's presence posed to his kingdom.

"You must understand," King Hassan explained after I had laid out the dimensions of his problem, "that I cannot refuse hospitality to a man who is living through a tragic phase of his existence. Moreover, the man in question is a Muslim monarch and, as you know, we Moroccans consider hospitality to be a sacred duty. The Shah is here, and he may stay here as long as he wishes."

"Your Majesty, this is the answer I expected to hear," I replied. "But I now have to tell you something extremely painful. The new masters of Iran, the ayatollahs, have signed a contract with a number of assassins and paid killers from the Middle East to kidnap members of Your Majesty's family—the queen or the young princes—to trade them for the imperial family of Iran."

The king gripped the arms of his chair, his hands clenched white, his features taut.

"Odious as this is, it won't alter my decision," he finally managed to stammer.

I still did my best to convince him. I pointed out that not only was he the valued ruler of Morocco, but that he had important religious duties in the Muslim world, that he and the King of Spain were the guardians of the strategic Strait of Gibraltar, keys to the Mediterranean. Yet I knew that it would be impossible for the king of Morocco personally to ask the Shah and his family to leave. I volunteered to do the dirty deed. Hassan reluctantly agreed.

The next morning, the Shah received me in the small palace that had been put at his disposal. The Shabanoo was with him. The children had been sent away. It was one of the most tragic conversations of my life, as much for its brevity as its contents.

* Phonetically, Shah means "cat" in French (hence the pun).

I described to him the terrifying threats hanging over the family of his royal host; my fears for the safety of the Moroccan kingdom itself; the power his presence gave to the weak, but growing, opposition to Hassan II. Throughout, the Shah remained silent, solemn, hidden by his dark glasses he wore whenever he appeared now before an outsider.

At the end, he responded softly and simply, "I will do as you suggest."

Two weeks later, he was gone, continuing his odyssey to the Bahamas, to New York, and finally to Egypt, where he died.

It was clear from these earliest indications that the ayatollahs would stop at nothing to achieve what they perceived as their mission from Allah. The jihad, the holy war, was uncompromising. Their allies became the most unsavory elements in the Arab world, those prepared to perform, generally for money, at times for the promised reward hereafter, the most heinous crimes against God or man.

By the time the Shah had arrived at Memorial Sloan-Kettering Cancer Center in New York, the ayatollahs were already moving to their next target—the American embassy and its diplomats in Teheran.

On November 4, 1979, a large group of Iranian "students," all fanatic Muslims and fully prepared to die in the service of Allah, occupied the embassy compound in Teheran, taking hostage fifty-two American diplomats and touching off a year-long confrontation that was the most difficult diplomatic and military problem in the early period of the South-North War. The announced demand of the students quickly became the rallying cry of the mullahs themselves who controlled the Iranian government—that the United States turn over the Shah of Iran and his entire family, who had taken up residence in New York as the dethroned monarch sought treatment for the cancer that was to kill him eight months later.

Two days after the American hostages were seized, three senior officials of the Central Intelligence Agency called on me at my Paris headquarters. We were known for our operational abilities in Teheran and our profound understanding of Iran and its new leaders, as distasteful as they might be. The leader of the CIA contingent came straight to the point.

"What can we do?" he asked.

"I'm not sure what you can do now," I replied. "If you had asked me within the first five minutes, even the first five hours, I might have suggested mounting an operation involving troops airlifted into the embassy compound by helicopter. Even supposing the rescue party managed now to reach the teeming city of three million people, then land in the embassy grounds or on the rooftops, the religious extremists, the guardians of the revolution, would then have more than enough time to execute every last one of the hostages. Perhaps some of the revolutionaries would be killed, but that would be your only scant satisfaction. The hostages would never be brought out alive."

The Americans rose to leave. "Still, please think this over," one said. I agreed.

We did more than that. I dispatched some of my most experienced operatives to Iran, at great personal danger to each of them. It was clear to us that the Americans were holding an empty hand. They had no cards, no bluff, no possible pressure they might exert.

As we learned through years of bitter experience, the first rule of terrorism is never to play with an empty hand. Terrorists and dictators understand and respect only power and dominance. They will seek advantage wherever they can find, or seize, it—be it in the form of funds, hostages, or the kinds of threats that can be conveyed vividly only through the international media. So our aim was to find the Americans a card to play.

We first discovered what the world later came to know well— that the Ayatollah had the habit of returning frequently to his home in the sacred city of Qom. He lived in a quiet area close to a piece of wasteland where helicopters could set down easily. The plan we began to formulate called for interception of His Eminence as he arrived in Qom, escorting him firmly to waiting helicopters, thence to a waiting ship in the northern Indian Ocean, in the Sea of Oman. We mapped the operation in exquisite detail—with house-by-house maps of Qom, floor plans of the Ayatollah's residence, second-by-second movements for each element. The operation was, in many respects, not dissimilar to one carried out with extraordinary success by Louis XI against Cardinal de La Balue. This eminent prelate, having been uncovered engaged in traitorous negotiations with the Duke of Bourgogne, was seized in the dead of night in a meticulously prepared operation and spirited away to the Château de Loches, where he remained imprisoned for eleven years.

The Americans had never heard of the good cardinal. But that made no difference. This plan was workable. It was discussed at the highest levels in Washington, and finally presented to President Carter himself. Carter studied the maps, the plan, fascinated as he was by exquisite detail. But his final rejection was typical.

"You just can't do that to a bishop, and most definitely not to a man of his age."

The plan ended in the Oval Office.

Instead, nearly five months later, the United States attempted its own ill-conceived and misguided rescue operation under the leadership of Colonel Charles A. Beckwith. It was the mission that my first CIA visitors had discussed with me two days after the taking of the hostages and that I and my colleagues had warned was misguided and all but impossible to carry out. Fortunately, it never got as far as the compound of the American embassy itself in Teheran, where its failure would inevitably have led to the death of some, if not all, of the hostages and most of the raiding party as well. Instead, it foundered in the Iranian desert, its helicopters crippled by swirling sand, Beckwith himself hog-tied by commanders who were directing his every move from a "situation room" in Washington thousands of miles away.

This fiasco, the extraordinary bumbling of the negotiations, the fits and starts, the threats and missed opportunities, prolonged the ordeal of the American hostages for 444 painful days and only confirmed the suspicions of every terrorist chieftain and renegade head of state in the Southern world that the United States was unwilling to take the steps needed to implement the concept of Certain Destruction. Retaliation was simply not part of the strategic equation at that time in the battles of the Fourth World War. And so the rulers of Iran, not to mention of Syria, Libya, and Iraq, found themselves with wide latitude to support random international bloodshed. And they embraced this freedom of operation wholeheartedly.

There are many in the Middle East, and indeed elsewhere in the world, who have taken comfort from this failure of response by the West. For instance, Qaddafi's support of terrorism knows no bounds—his only motivation appears to be destabilization of the Northern democracies and the extension of his sphere of direct influence. As a result, the terrorists he directs and finances range throughout Europe. His military and intelligence forces focus from Chad to the Central African Republic, where Qaddafi's expansionist plans have been barely concealed.

Qaddafi maintains terrorist training camps in a number of locations in Libya. When those terrorists need money, he furnishes it.

He also furnished, some time ago, the means for the Czechoslovak, East German, and Palestinian instructors to function in those camps as specialists in the kinds of skills needed by today's modern, high-tech terrorists. This has been clear from all our sources and our monitoring. Though the East German state police machine has been disbanded, enough such instructors have been converted to a mercenary status and a sufficiently large, skilled cadre of homegrown terrorists has been turned out that training has been able to continue unabated. The terrorist elite in Qaddafi's Libya has become self-perpetuating.

In the first half of 1990, the opening of the archives of some of the East European secret police operations confirmed many of these activities. Former Czechoslovak secret police officials who have been debriefed by our services have even acknowledged carrying out tests to see how much Semtex plastic explosive would be needed to blow up an airliner in the air. These experiments, conducted in November 1984, disclosed that as little as two hundred grams, less than half a pound, of Semtex-H, the most powerful grade, could blow a hole in the side of an airplane. Five years earlier, the Czechs had sold one thousand tons of this explosive to Qaddafi, who promptly became a key middleman. The explosives were passed on to the Irish Republican Army, which operates against the British in Northern Ireland and elsewhere, and to a number of Middle East terrorist groups based in Libyan territory, including the violent Popular Front for the Liberation of Palestine–General Command (PFLP-GC). Substantial intelligence exists that the PFLP-GC used the Semtex explosive to bring down Pan American World Airways Flight 103 over Lockerbie, Scotland, in December 1988. While this particular cell operated out of West Germany, intelligence shows that at least some of its members were trained in Libyan commando camps. However, in November 1991, a United States grand jury indicted two Libyan intelligence officers on 193 counts of murder and conspiracy for the explosion on board Pan Am 103.

Territory, weapons, money, and passports—all supplied by Qaddafi's Libya—are critical ingredients allowing these terrorists to operate throughout the West. Illych Ramirez Sanchez, the terrorist known as Carlos, and as many as thirty-five of his men have used Libyan diplomatic passports to move through Hungary and East Germany and into Western Europe. Employees of Libyan embassies in places like Berlin help terrorists function and even help plan terrorist attacks.

A Libyan-Palestinian terrorist group that bombed a West Berlin discotheque in April 1986, killing 2 American servicemen and a Turkish woman and wounding 229 other people, was directed by Yasir Chraidi, a Palestinian employee of the Libyan embassy in East Berlin, and by another Libyan, Musbah Abulgasem.

We monitored Qaddafi and his international network closely, since so many of its members passed through or near France, our territories, or those of our closest allies. Because Qaddafi-sponsored terrorist operations are integral components of the terrorist international, knowledge of activities in Libya was essential to prevent or neutralize terrorist threats. There was also no question that throughout the 1970s and into the 1980s, at least as long as it served his purposes, Qaddafi was an important agent of Soviet operations in the southern Mediterranean region. In other words, Libya directly straddled the time warp between the Third and Fourth World wars. So we devoted considerable energy to watching the comings and goings of the denizens of the camps, the flow of the funds that supported their operations, the materiel that they used in their dirty tricks.

Qaddafi's principal source of power was his wealth, and the source of his wealth was his oil reserves. Oil by itself, however, has never been a guarantee of political or economic power in the Southern world, or indeed anywhere else. It has to be transformed into some other currency. The currencies favored by Qaddafi, like many of his fellow Southern autocrats, were weapons and gold. The Soviet Union was happy to supply both in exchange for oil—at a healthy discount, of course.

Huge stockpiles of weapons were transferred to the more remote reaches of the Libyan desert, and then dispersed in various caches to render them less vulnerable to surprise attack from any of Qaddafi's numerous enemies. At the same time, of course, this also considerably shortened their life span since desert sands are as corrosive as ocean salt to weapons that are not specifically constructed to withstand such elements. Libya, bordered on the north by the Mediterannean, on the south by the most hostile of desert environments, has both salt and sand in spades. After six months in the desert, nothing functions. The Libyans are not very good at maintenance. A combination of salt, air, and sand makes a very hostile environment for sophisticated weaponry. The Soviets, of course, were delighted to continue routine replacement of these arms and materiel in return for oil. The battalion of Czech engineers that was finally supplied to care for these weapons was too little, too late.

The Soviets were equally happy to provide the gold that Qaddafi used to finance his operations and those of his closest friends. We first stumbled on the gold route in Brittany in the mid-1970s. It turned out to be the last stop on a lengthy and peculiar odyssey. Tracing backward, we discovered that the gold that originated in Soviet mines found its way to Libya, thence to Quebec, where portions of it were used to finance the Free Quebec movement. From Quebec, what remained passed on to the Irish Republican Army. From there, the remaining gold found its way to Brittany, which was where we discovered the cache in the hands of Breton separatist groups who were staging violent attacks on French targets. It was still a large quantity, enough to buy automatic weapons and explosives—all of them of Czechoslovak origin. The gold consisted of one-kilo bars and Libyan gold coins.

The hand of the Russians was apparent on innumerable occasions when the Libyans were the front men. The deep-water port of Tripoli—the most sophisticated such facility on the southern Mediterranean—was constructed by Qaddafi but used extensively by the Soviets.

The Libyans, backed by the Soviets and more often than not, we discovered, doing their bidding directly, wandered far from home. Perhaps the most curious such adventure was their foray into the Tonga islands. Each year, I received a visit from the head of the New Zealand Secret Service, who was generally en route to or from a top-level briefing with his British colleagues in London. One time in the early 1970s, he came to spend a weekend at my apartment in Paris. He was a veteran of the Second World War, and we shared many memories of that era.

After dinner on Saturday, he turned to me and began, "I have to tell you that for years I have been fascinated by the stories you have told me about how the world at large functions in our profession. Alas, living as I do in the Antipodes, I have rarely been able to reciprocate. But for once I have something that you might find useful."

"That's fine," I said. "Tell me more."

"Just before I left Auckland," he plunged ahead, "we had some information that the king of Tonga had received two messages from Qaddafi."

The kingdom of Tonga is a small island group in the South

Pacific, the southernmost inhabited islands before reaching the mainland of Antarctica. The king of Tonga is a ruler of immense power—and immense size as well. Indeed, the king is chosen because he is the largest man among a people who are themselves of enormous height and girth. They are originally a warrior people of the South Pacific. And they are totally fearless. They owe no man, no nation, anything.

My friend from New Zealand continued. "These two messengers, we discovered, were bringing heavily loaded Samsonite suitcases, filled with money. But just what Qaddafi wants with Tonga remains a total mystery to us."

The next morning, I called in one of my general officers, who was also an admiral in the French Navy, and charged him to investigate.

Three days later, he returned. "Well, the navy was as flabbergasted as I was," the admiral reported smugly. "We have concluded, however, that there is a real strategic significance in this intelligence. In a time of war, that part of the Pacific Ocean could be very interesting as a refuge for certain Russian submarines. A place for these submarines or their tenders to put in would be quite useful indeed."

Russian submarines never began calling Tonga home port as far as we could determine. Nor was it clear that the Soviets had truly put Qaddafi up to this particular adventure. Yet there is no question that this was Qaddafi at his best, juggling multiple agendas—protecting what he perceived as the flanks, or polishing the apple, of his Soviet supplier of munitions and technical expertise. At the same time, he would be serving his own interests—looking to forge a new, strategically important alliance in a critical part of the world for the coming global conflict of South versus North.

Qaddafi was not then and is not now a Russian agent in the classic sense. A Russian agent is an expensive individual. He must be paid at the end of every month, and paid handsomely. Qaddafi, by contrast, pays the Russians, for his weapons and his logistical support, though admittedly at discount prices. He uses the Russians, as they have used him. But Qaddafi, by contrast with many captive leaders, is also inclined to act entirely on his own, reacting only to his personal megalomaniacal fantasies against enemies—real or imagined. So he has not hesitated to go after political opponents, allies of and sympathizers with Libya's deposed King Idris, wherever they might be found and whatever might be the consequences for innocent bystanders.

Qaddafi is no madman. He is a very cunning desert fox. He is a man with a uniquely warped vision, but a vision nonetheless. Part of that vision is to divide, then dominate, a large part of the African continent, which he surveys from his perch in the northernmost reaches of the Mediterannean. That would involve seizing a large swath of territory—Chad and the Central African Republic, a dagger pointed straight at the mineral-rich nation of Zaire and dividing neatly East from West Africa. The Libyans could exploit a victory of this sort by focusing their political, if not military, attention either on the Gulf of Guinea to the west, or the Red Sea and the Horn of Africa toward the east and south, and at one time could have provided support for the Communist rulers of Ethiopia. A large part of Africa would be forced, on its knees, to pay tribute to Colonel Muammar Qaddafi. That part of Africa has supplies of strategic minerals that are vital for the North and contains vast populations and nations with long and deep cultural, social, political, and economic ties with European nations.

The Central African Republic has long been one of the most deprived, backward nations on earth. Its only real resource is industrial-quality diamonds, of which nearly a quarter-million carats are mined each year. On December 31, 1965, it came under the sway of a true megalomaniac, Jean-Bédel Bokassa, who overthrew the president, David Dacko, and seized power in a coup d'état. Naming himself "President for Life" in 1972, he took the title of Emperor Bokassa I in 1976 and a year later crowned himself emperor in a ceremony that could only be called a boulevard comedy, complete with a gold-encrusted carriage. The cost of that ceremony alone could have fed his entire nation for a year. Nevertheless, since his nation was the keystone of former French Africa, France lavished its attention on Bokassa. The country was also handy for big-game hunting, and Bokassa became a kind of private gamekeeper to the French Republic and those who ruled its government and industry. It was also a key staging area for French air and ground forces that guaranteed the security of much of central Africa.

Because of France's considerable interest in African affairs—along with terrorism and the nuclear threat, it was one of France's three main security concerns—we kept a close watch on Bokassa and his despotic rule.

Early in my tenure in office, shortly after Bokassa declared himself President for Life, I began to alert Giscard d'Estaing to the menace that the ruler represented. His behavior left much to be desired. By the time Bokassa had himself crowned emperor, he had become a dangerous alcoholic. And the most bizarre rumors began to surface. At one point, following the spread of a particularly pernicious tale, we had one of our operatives check the refrigerator in the presidential palace. There was no human flesh in it. There were also the frequent stories about his diamonds. Early in 1979, the celebrated French satirical weekly *Canard Enchaîné* delighted in revealing stories of gifts of expensive Central African diamonds lavished on Giscard during his various hunting trips to the "empire." Even the mass of the French people—who are generally most tolerant of the excesses of their rulers, and indeed expect them to live lives of luxury as befits the effective heirs to the French throne— found this excess in the company of a petty African tyrant too much. While Bokassa's gifts to Giscard d'Estaing became celebrated and nearly caused the fall of the French government, in fact the "emperor" spread the largesse of his nation's mines far more widely. The Central African Republic does produce industrial diamonds, as do many other nations. But it turns out that these are little diamond chips—a far cry from blue-white solitaires or the crown jewels of England. Still, Bokassa delighted in putting his tiny diamonds on lavish mountings, giving them to guests who passed through. Giscard and his party were the unfortunate recipients of what could scarcely be called largesse. Bokassa's gifts were of no value and the whole affair was a nasty blow at the president of France.

But what concerned us the most—and for which we were most closely vigilant—was any foreign entanglements of Bokassa's that might prove inimical to French interests. In the spring of 1979, we developed hard evidence of just such an entanglement. I requested an audience with Giscard. I laid out for him the arrival of Libyan special forces in the capital of what had been renamed the Central African Empire. Giscard was reluctant to proceed. Bokassa, beyond the diamonds, had become his private gamekeeper and he enjoyed hunting elephants and lions.

"How do you know all this?" he shot back after I detailed Bokassa's Libyan connection.

"Usually, Monsieur le Président, I don't have to tell you all the details of our trade. But I'll tell you this time."

I pulled some photographs out of my pocket. "Our evidence comes from several sources," I began, "agents working in French organizations, local residents who cooperated with us. Our operatives were very adept at purloining these photos while the wallets' owners were exercising or at a swimming pool." The Libyans were not exactly Prussian in their discipline. Although while in the Central African Empire the Libyans were dressed in civilian clothes, the photographs in their wallets with their mothers, fathers, or girlfriends revealed them dressed in uniforms, complete with medals and insignias, of the Libyan Secret Service. They were clearly not the civilian advisers they claimed to be.

"The Libyans are one thing," I continued. "But what happens next, when we discover as well that they are accompanied by East German or Cuban advisers, and we are suddenly involved in an all-out confrontation? Monsieur le Président, I am going to write this down when I return to my office. If something happens there, it will be in the files."

Giscard thought for a moment. "Well, all right, do what you want," he said.

In late summer of 1979, we discovered that Bokassa was planning a visit to his friend, Colonel Qaddafi. Clearly it was now time to get rid of Bokassa, and so Operation Barracuda was born. Our aim was to depose Bokassa without firing a shot and to locate and install a successor who would move toward restoration of democratic, Western-allied rule. The man Bokassa deposed fourteen years before fit the bill perfectly. David Dacko was a political refugee in France. It was not easy to convince him to undertake what would inevitably be a dangerous and difficult operation. Dacko was no longer a young man, but he was finally persuaded that this maneuver was essential to rescue his nation from total ruin.

We sent several emissaries to talk with him at his home outside Paris.

"We are launching this operation," he was told, "with the understanding that you will make your own independent declaration on arrival. We are not colonialists trying to recover a colony, but people who wish to forestall the disaster that would follow should the Libyans establish a position in the center of Africa."

"Who will be there to receive me when I arrive?" he replied.

We did our best to reassure him that there would be an entire infrastructure installed to welcome him to Bangui by the time his plane landed. Above all, we convinced him that we wanted nothing beyond his reinstallation at the head of the government.

Over the next two weeks, Dacko, with some help from our speechwriters, prepared his arrival message, and we prepared our operation. Such operations must be precise—undertaken in total secrecy, under cover of darkness, employing a maximum of 100 to 150 men. In every case, we arrive with the night and are out by first light the next morning.

Our field intelligence was a model for any such operation, anywhere in the world. I had been laying my plans for three years. Throughout that time, whenever I had an officer who went on vacation, I gave him or her a plane ticket to—instead of the Côte d'Azur or Italy—the Central African Empire. Each went with a girlfriend or boyfriend, or with wife or husband and children. And when they arrived, they began taking pictures everywhere—just like tourists. Only the pictures were posed in front of the post office, television station, army barracks, telephone switching center. We located other officers who had been stationed in the Central African Republic in colonial times, still others who spoke the tribal language of the guard company at the Bangui airport.

Two of SDECE's own aircraft were used to ferry our troops to Bangui. A small number were sent in advance, to make certain just how the airport operated, when it opened and closed, where the lights were located, who manned the control tower, and so on. The field also had two machine-gun posts to protect it, manned by the airport guard company, who we also learned had not been paid for a month. Moreover, the last time they were paid, it was in local currency, which galloping inflation had rendered all but worthless.

So by the night of the operation, September 21, 1979, we were well prepared. Two of our own airmen were in place on the darkened runway, equipped with battery-powered lamps to guide our planes. The French planes were already in the air from France when a hitch developed. An Egyptian plane, on the ground in the neighboring Congo, asked that the airport be reopened for a late-night landing. That would have blown the entire, carefully planned and scripted operation. But we had some good people of our own in the Congo. Some last-minute engine trouble delayed that plane's takeoff for a day.

My command post was underground in our headquarters command center in Paris. There, I was surrounded by my charts and staff—my chief of staff, the general commanding the Special Forces, our specialists on black Africa and the Central African Empire. Just as the operation was getting under way, Colonel M., who was leading our forces in the field, radioed a last-minute question:

"Monsieur le Directeur-Général, we think he [Bokassa] is in

Tripoli now, but suppose he arrives by chance back in Bangui during the night? Suppose he comes charging into town in a jeep with a saber in his hand?"

I only hesitated a moment. "Take him prisoner. And turn him over to President Dacko in the morning."

"And suppose he starts killing some of our people?"

"Then shoot him."

I had already given very explicit orders before the force set off. "We have marvelous communications. But I will never call you. Never. Because you are busy and I am not. I am sitting on my ass in my bunker in Paris. Anytime you need advice, you call me. I have no intention of stepping in. You are the one in charge. If you have any questions, by all means ask them, but we are not going to get in your way." I was determined that this was not to be an operation like Carter's abortive attempt to rescue the American hostages in Iran when poor Colonel Charles Beckwith had twelve people all giving him orders from thousands of miles away throughout the operation.

The first plane landed without incident, guided in by our two men on the ground. The airport was closed and the staff had already left for town. Our agents were in full battle dress and their jeeps were off the transport in minutes, the assault group speeding toward the building where the airport guard detachment was in position with submachine guns at the doors and windows. The officer who spoke their tribal dialect immediately addressed them through a loudspeaker:

"We have not come here to take over your country, but simply to help you rid yourselves of a tyrant, and if possible bring back democratic government. Now, we know you have not been paid in a month. Please form a line along the wall and you will be paid immediately."

When the guards emerged with a table and chair for the paymaster, we knew we were home free. He settled down and took out a stack of bills from a metal box. They were CFA (Communauté Financière Africaine) francs—fifty to the French franc but a solid currency backed by the central banks of the other, solvent Francophone African countries.

The payment began as the officer in charge of our detail announced to the guard detachment, "Officers, you may remain armed. We trust you to do what you have to do." We wanted a local, armed constabulary on our side.

Our commander turned to the soldiers who formed the local guard regiment and said, "Please lay down your arms next to the building."

Not a single shot was fired. The officers of the guards offered to take our men with them to town and serve as guides. We occupied a few strategic points, but in a small village that is at the same time a capital, the strategic points are not difficult to locate, and we knew them all intimately—the presidential palace, the telephone exchange, the television headquarters, a few military barracks.

By that time, the second plane, carrying Dacko and his presidential car, had landed at the Bangui airport. At that moment, a press agency, which we had created expressly for this operation, and which disappeared by the next day, put out a report saying that there appeared to be a coup under way in the Central African Empire.

No one, not even the Quai d'Orsay, had been informed. So the French Foreign Ministry telephoned its ambassador in Bangui who, awakened, checked briefly and reported back that he could find nothing out of the ordinary.

The next morning, President Dacko, installed in the presidential palace, made his official statement to the nation. Our Special Forces had packed up their equipment and departed, as planned, with first light. They were replaced, quite officially, by regular French Army units stationed in neighboring Chad.

As for Bokassa himself, now stateless, his friend Colonel Qaddafi offered him asylum in Libya. He chose, instead, a far more comfortable exile in the Ivory Coast. Qaddafi's own special forces left Bangui within days, the Libyans' ambitions thoroughly thwarted.

This is not to say that Qaddafi has by any means abandoned his designs on a greater African empire for Libya—his territorial ambitions have long been clear and intense. He has at least twice mounted outright assaults on Chad from the north, columns of armored troops moving on the oasis of Faya Largeau deep in the desert north of the capital, N'Djamena. A force of French paratroops was dispatched during one such maneuver to provide support for Chadian government forces arrayed against the Libyans. At the time, I urged a French air attack to destroy the Libyan column completely—under the concept of Certain Destruction that should by then have become the guarantor of Northern security against the Qaddafis of the Southern world. Instead, the Libyan troops were ultimately allowed to retreat untouched back to their own frontiers. Without any doubt, a decisive French action destroying the invasion column would simultaneously have provoked some decisive action inside Libya's army and perhaps the nation as a whole that would have removed Qaddafi permanently as a threat to the North.

Indeed, during the 1970s, there were several attempts on Qaddafi's life and several plans that never came to fruition—any one of which, alas, would have served to send a message of Certain Destruction.

On March 1, 1978, President Anwar Sadat of Egypt conveyed a message to me that he was interested in disposing of Qaddafi. It was never clear to me whether Sadat, whose country had been repeatedly menaced by Libya and its military forces, wanted our advice or technical assistance. The fact is, I was not in charge of a team of hired assassins. So my answer to Sadat was that I did not run an organization that carried out that sort of work. But I did point out that at the time there were 250,000 Egyptians—roughly 10 percent of the population—living and working in Libya. Surely little would stand in the way of infiltrating a team of his own Egyptian nationals who could be easily camouflaged to take whatever action he felt appropriate. But Sadat changed his mind. A short time later, the Egyptian leader himself died at the hands of killers from his own country who were intoxicated by their religious fanaticism.

There is no evidence that Qaddafi or his supporters were behind the assassination of Sadat. But destabilization of the Northern democracies has long been as crucial a political tactic of Qaddafi as attempts to divide and conquer Africa have been. And in this respect, he has had many allies—leaders of what might be called the international terrorist cartel.

But removing a Qaddafi or a Khomeini is no answer to the problem of international terrorism. Quite clearly, the passage of Khomeini has had little real impact on the intentions of the Iranian government and the mullahs to subsidize terrorist activities—or any real impact on their effectiveness. Even the return of democracy to Libya would have little real impact. There is always another refuge that can be found for this type of activity, another patron prepared to supply support and assistance.

There are scores of potential sanctuaries, some better than others, for those such as Abu Nidal, Abu Daoud, or the famed international terrorist Carlos who now call Libya their home base. None has ever hesitated to attack any target that appears appropriate at a given moment, and often without any direct suggestion from his godfather.

From 1970 to 1981, transactions took place between the French government and certain terrorist groups, particularly the cells controlled by Abu Daoud, in largely successful attempts to spare French territory and citizens from attack—and this during a period of considerable tension between Paris and Tripoli. Throughout those years, there was a tacit understanding that terrorists operating out of French territory, even targeting our European allies, would not be disturbed, provided no operation took place in France. I never approved of this decision, but the arrangement with these groups was a domestic political decision that French Intelligence was powerless to influence. The truce was violated with the bloody attack on the synagogue in the Rue Copernic in Paris, and finally destroyed with the arrival in power of the Socialist government of President François Mitterrand in 1981. Thereafter, French territory became a battleground of various terrorist groups—in many respects, the front line of what has developed into the Fourth World War.

CHAPTER **10**

Minefields of the Mind

errorism has often been described as the weapon of the poor. It is a weapon that affects our entire system of political organization not only in the North, but in those parts of the Southern world as well that depend on us for their very survival. The often bloody skirmishes in which it is used overshadow all our lives. The Fourth World War itself, of course, is one with no clear victor as yet, indeed no talisman of victory. But what already live on in memory, in our nightmares, are the defeats.

And, unless we change our strategy for fighting this global conflict—understanding that it is by no means like any other we have ever engaged in—we will continue to suffer defeats. Few of those who lead our nations, indeed few who are on the front lines every day, have fully grasped that we are embroiled in a series of battles for which we are totally unprepared. We have many weaknesses that terrorist organizations, through their flexibility, are repeatedly able to exploit.

One key weakness is that we continue to think of defense fundamentally in national terms, whereas terrorism operates in an international or global context, moving at will across frontiers, choosing targets carefully where opportunity presents itself rather than for any specifically nationalist end.

Basque terrorism is a subject that concerned us deeply through much of the 1970s, into the 1980s, and continuing today. Since before the time of Julius Caesar, the Basques, a unique and passionately nationalistic people, have clung to their mountainside villages that straddle the often treacherous Pyrenees on the border of what is now France and Spain. They fought alongside the Arab armies that in-

199

vaded Europe and did battle with the forces of Charlemagne during the jihads of the eighth century. The French medieval poet Roland perished in one of the Basques' most famous ambushes at Roncevaux. In modern times, since the boundaries of Spain and France were drawn, they have yearned for a Basque homeland that would unite them in fact as they are so deeply united in spirit, but that dream has eluded them. The Basques, as much as any people on earth, are divided between two countries, with barely 250,000 in France, nearly 2 million across the frontier in Spain. The violent struggle to unite them has been going on since the 1950s when groups of students, seeking to radicalize the conventional Basque National party, formed the paramilitary organization called the ETA. Gradually, through the 1960s, and intensifying into the 1970s and 1980s, Basque terrorists plunged deeply into the most violent activities and began looking for allies wherever they might be found. Training in terrorist camps in places as far-flung as Libya and Cuba, they returned armed with the latest automatic weapons and plastic explosives.

From Biarritz to Bilbao throughout this period, violence—unexpected and often lethal—became a way of life. In 1979 alone, ETA commandos machine-gunned the Paris–Madrid express, assassinated a young police officer and his girlfriend out for an evening of dancing and fun in a remote Basque village, and in apparently random violence killed taxi drivers and even a city bus inspector. After each lethal incident, the terrorists melted back across whichever border offered shelter—a murder in France meant flight to Spain, a bombing in Spain meant refuge in France. And with the lack of on-the-ground coordination by police and intelligence forces in both countries, it was open season on both sides of the frontier.

But Basque terrorism is by no means unique in its exploitation of pannational activities to further narrow nationalistic or ideological ends. In Japan, for instance, there had always been indigenous secret societies, but the Japanese Red Army was a violent, even anarchic splinter organization with international aspirations, born out of the fragmentation in September 1969 of the Trotskyist League of Revolutionary Communists in Tokyo. Its student members saw themselves as part of a world revolutionary struggle that they would ignite through extensive urban guerrilla warfare, taking their inspiration directly from the Paris student demonstrators of May 1968. The Japanese Red Army's first impact was in Asia with the hijacking of a Japan Airlines plane in April 1970. Throughout the 1970s, its field of action expanded. In August 1975, members wearing black hoods and carrying submachine guns invaded the modern office building in Kuala Lumpur that held the offices of the United States consulate, seized fifty-two hostages, and won the release of five of their colleagues held in Japanese jails. The terrorists were then flown to Libya—their first visible connection with Qaddafi's terrorist international.

In September 1974, the French ambassador to the Hague was kidnapped and held hostage for five days by a commando group of the Japanese Red Army. We were deeply involved in the ultimately successful efforts to rescue the French ambassador, who, throughout his captivity, showed enormous courage. We quickly realized to our chagrin that some weeks before, French authorities had inadvertently released the leader of this terrorist group, whom we had considered a most dangerous individual. He had been detained at the Prison de la Santé in Paris for a relatively minor infraction, then due to bad coordination and bureaucratic bungling, the terrorist was suddenly released without the SDECE being given any warning. Had we even been apprised of his release, we would promptly have notified the heads of security of each of our neighbors, including our Dutch counterparts, and would have saved France from a most lamentable humiliation. This Japanese terrorist, it seems, was able to make his way unhindered to the Hague, where he promptly set about plotting a direct act of revenge for the indignities he believed France had inflicted on him. Moreover, by kidnapping the ambassador, the terrorist also hoped to effect the release of one of his own colleagues who remained in prison in France.

Since professional terrorists change their identities at will and usually carry impeccable false documents and passports, frontiers and the barriers they impose are far less key to uncovering or preventing terrorist activity than the kinds of intelligence work that proceeds, day in, day out, on all sides of those frontiers. The first group of Libyan-backed terrorists who were plotting to place an altitude-detonated bomb on Pan Am Flight 103—the same type that finally destroyed the plane as it passed over Lockerbie, Scotland, late in the evening of December 21, 1988—manufactured the device in a bomb factory in a small apartment on the fringes of Munich. This bomb factory, it later developed, had been raided by West German police. By the time this critical information worked its way through the international intelligence network it was tragically too late. The government-to-government intelligence networks were, and in most respects still are, simply inadequate to their tasks.

There is no more central component in the success of an operation, or defusing a terrorist activity, than information—its gathering, its analysis, its dissemination, and its use. On the other side, professional terrorists analyze every action meticulously, searching for the weakest link in any chain. Once they select their targets or victims, they carry out a detailed study of their victims' lives and habits, closely scrutinizing, tailing, and photographing them without their knowledge; and determine their daily, weekly, and monthly schedules. A doctor might be found to monitor the targets for an evening up close at a cocktail party or dinner, examining their nails and complexion, and draw up a diagnosis that could be of use to the terrorist leadership. The weak link might be a physical ailment; or it might be a place or time where the victims are less well protected than unusual.

One such operation touched me deeply and personally. It was the assassination by the IRA of Admiral of the Fleet Earl Mountbatten of Burma in 1979. I had known Mountbatten since the Second World War. In June 1946, I had gone to China on a mission for General Juin to meet with Chiang Kai-shek, the Chinese leader. Mountbatten at the time was commander in chief of the Allied forces in Southeast Asia. As I was returning via Indochina, my plane had made a crash landing in Burma. We came down in the jungle, and as far as I know the plane is still there. We managed to survive because Mountbatten's people heard our distress signal and sent in small aircraft, which flew us out one by one.

It was not until thirty-five years later in Paris that I was truly able to thank him—at a lunch arranged in the fall of 1978 at the home of my cousin, the writer and editor, Thérèse de Saint Phalle. I had been head of the French Secret Service for some time. Mountbatten, the handsome and accomplished cousin of Queen Elizabeth II, godfather of Prince Charles, had become the great symbol of the British monarchy, epitomizing its power and glory. If the IRA could destroy him, it would be a strike at the very heart of the British system and its presence in Northern Ireland, though Mountbatten's superb castle was located in the Republic of Ireland at Classibawn, County Sligo.

After thanking him for extricating me and the others from the jungle, I turned to him as we were finishing our lunch.

"Our intelligence service has discovered that there is a serious threat to you from the IRA and from Qaddafi, who is funding many of their operations," I said. "I implore you to take extra precautions, beyond any you are already taking."

I explained that it could be dangerous for him to continue his habit of staying with his children and grandchildren for an entire month during the summer in Ireland without protection.

Admiral Lord Mountbatten laughed out loud and said, "People around me at Sligo are very fond of me, as I am of them. I've heard it all before, and I have nothing to fear." Later, he suggested that we continue our conversation on a return visit to his stately home, Broadlands, in Hampshire, England. It has been a source of great regret to me that I was never able to take him up on that invitation. Before I could accept, less than a year later, he was dead.

There was, as I feared, a chink in Mountbatten's armor—the small boat he used to take to sea during his summers at his Irish retreat. The boat was not under constant surveillance, as it most certainly should have been. And during the night of August 26–27, 1979, terrorists were able to plant explosives in it with the greatest of ease. The bombs blew him and one of his grandchildren to pieces and seriously injured other members of his family, particularly his daughter, Lady Brabourne.

Intelligence can and should work effectively for both sides. Certainly, terrorists, not to mention those leaders of the Southern world who finance and target them, understand how to make intelligence work for them. There is no reason why the Western democracies cannot. But often we are too blinded by the power of our military muscle to appreciate just how important it is to understand a situation deeply. Instead, we continue to stumble repeatedly into hidden quagmires or play directly into the hands of those who are prepared to exploit our weaknesses or just plain sloppiness.

Shortly after the American invasion of the island of Grenada in the Caribbean, which had been developing dangerously close ties with Castro's Cuba, I saw Bill Casey, the director of central intelligence. At the time, it was little known that victory had only barely been snatched from the jaws of a most ignominious defeat.

"Bill, you did a good job," I said expansively.

"Yeah, but we nearly had trouble."

"What kind of trouble?" I asked.

"Look, we discovered a battalion of Cuban combat engineers when we arrived on the island," he confessed, "and we didn't even know they were there, certainly that they were combat-ready. We simply didn't have the proper intelligence on the island."

Incredible, I thought, to undertake with so little intelligence preparation the invasion of an island known to be developing close ties with Castro's Cuba, a nation that has scarcely shown its reluctance to place its military muscle at the service of any potential friend or ally. My service knew for some time that the Cubans were building landing facilities on Grenada.

Casey looked at me carefully, clearly able to read my thoughts. "What would you have done?"

"I'd put a man on each island, have him blend into the landscape for a week, and voilà. Or I'd get a guy with a little local boat, and send him around the island, landing here and there. You know, in places like the Caribbean, a little boat is like a taxi. It blends into the background. You never see it. It transports, it has a radio and what more do you need?"

The first time I met William Webster, long before President Reagan had named him director of central intelligence in March 1987, he was the boss of the F.B.I. I told him about my travels in Washington. "You know, I took thirteen cabs over the past several days. Out of those thirteen taxi drivers, there was only one American. All the others were Ukrainian, Pakistani, Arabs, even one from the French Ivory Coast of all places. Don't you think this is a great danger to allow all these people to drive cabs in the capital without monitoring or identifying them more closely?" In Paris, more than eighty percent of all taxi drivers are French.

"Why is this a security threat?" he asked, startled I would even bring up something as trivial as this.

"A cab is quite simply an automobile with a big trunk that can transport people, papers, ideas, explosives, weapons, plus it has a radio. It's perfect. If I had to organize terrorists in Washington, I'd recruit a couple of cabbies. They're terrific. They're everywhere. And totally invisible."

He had never thought of that before, although in those days, taxis could even enter the compound in Langley, Virginia, housing the CIA, as long as the passenger had valid identification.

Indeed, it was clear to me from my earliest visits to the United States that there is a major incident that might one day happen if we are not careful. This is a nation with no national identity card, with enormous frontiers both to the north and to the south, enormous coastlines to the east and to the west, foreigners and minorities of every persuasion and paranoia, some of them nursing every bitterness known to man.

I went one day to the White House to meet with President Reagan again. I plunged straight in with the President:

"You have a major security problem in your country, Mr. President. You have between ten and fifteen million people who are not accounted for and may never be accounted for until it is too late."

"My dear Count, don't you think this is a little high?" the President asked.

"No, Mr. President, I think these numbers are conservative. You don't know where these unregistered aliens are from, what they are doing, why they are doing it. Mr. President, can you imagine the fifth column you could organize among all those people. You don't even have identity cards. Every country has that."

"Well, those figures are very bad." The President frowned. "Let's ask Judge Clark." He picked up the phone to summon him.

He was told that William Clark, the secretary of the interior, was at the White House. "Then send him to my office."

In walked the judge, as he had been referred to since his days on the California bench; and Mr. Reagan filled him in on our conversation. "These illegals in America are between ten and fifteen million people, says our French friend. Don't you think these figures are a little high?"

"Mr. President, he's right," said Judge Clark. "But the figure is nearer fifteen than ten million."

In a nation like the United States, where it takes only five years to become a citizen, our information indicates that huge numbers of Russians, but also Middle Eastern and North African immigrants, have taken advantage of the law. Some are agents in waiting. When followed, they turn on their pursuers and charge harassment. Lawsuits follow. Even the FBI is not equipped to deal with people like this.

Throughout my time in office, and as a private citizen in recent years, I have made efforts to consult with foreign governments concerning the aspects of our political, administrative, and intelligence systems that pose security lapses that terrorists are able to exploit. Formal mechanisms are still needed. But we must make a start.

Throughout my tenure as head of French Intelligence, the

French were often consulted—at times even before the Americans, probably because of our more intimate, firsthand acquaintance with terrorist operations—for advice in dealing with crises as they arose in different parts of the world.

One such occasion was the Shiite assault on the sacred Kaaba of Mecca in November 1979. It is a small, square cube of a building with a single room located near the center of the Great Mosque in the city of Mecca, which in turn is located in the center of Saudi Arabia. While all Muslims are supposed to turn toward Mecca when they pray, they are actually turning toward the Kaaba, and more specifically toward the Black Stone, a meteoric rock enclosed by a silver ring, which sits in the eastern corner of the Kaaba itself. Muslim tradition says that the Black Stone was given to Abraham by the angel Gabriel and that Abraham and Ishmael built the Kaaba to house it. By the time of Muhammad, infidels had invaded the shrine, and the Prophet purged the idols that had contaminated it. It became the holy of holies of the Islamic religion. The hajj, the pilgrimage to Mecca, is to be made at least once in a Muslim life. Before airplanes, when the faithful were crossing the desert and seas with great difficulty, it was quite a dangerous accomplishment. Those who successfully completed it were entitled to add the honorific "Hajji" to their names for the rest of their lives.

When they arrive in Mecca, the faithful participating in the hajj walk or run around the Kaaba seven times, chanting portions of the Koran, the ceremony ending with each pilgrim kissing the sacred Black Stone. The truly faithful, when they die, are placed on stretchers that are carried seven times around the sacred Kaaba by their relatives before they are buried.

The Great Mosque and the ground where the Kaaba rests are like a Gruyère cheese, laced with caves and passages. Although the mosque is out of bounds to all but devout Muslims, we knew quite a lot about the locale and the surrounding area. Saudi Arabia had become as important to us, and indeed to most Western nations, as Iran. Our senior intelligence officer in Saudi Arabia, Colonel C., a magnificent camel corps officer, was a consummate Arabist who had spent years in the Sahara and had grown to know and love many of the Saudi leaders who had themselves been nomadic bedouins. A profound understanding of these lords of the desert is not acquired on a school or university bench, but on a *rahla*—the saddle of a dromedary—and through long evenings spent sipping tea in a tent around a campfire fueled with camel dung. This part of the world has long been an Anglo-American preserve, thanks to Aramco, the oil pipeline company that was a joint Saudi-American partnership. Indeed, on my first visits to the kingdom, the messages preparing my arrival in the capital to see His Majesty and other high Saudi officials had to be transmitted to the Saudi government by American officers of Aramco. They controlled the only means of communication, inside or outside the country. Ultimately, we established our own channels and our own close contacts with the top leadership of government and intelligence in the kingdom.

For some time, we had been reporting to the Saudi government at the highest levels that arms of Soviet origin were entering the kingdom illicitly from South Yemen, the Communist-dominated principality to the south. The island of Socotra, off the shores of (communist dominated) South Yemen, was the largest Soviet base outside the frontiers of the empire! The Soviets had every interest in destabilizing Saudi Arabia because of its enormous oil wealth, Western dependence on Saudi petroleum supplies, and the huge American presence in the kingdom. Other Middle Eastern nations were also becoming disenchanted with the Saudis for their dominance and control of the international oil market and their ability to set prices by controlling supplies. Jealousy and envy are potent motives in a region as volatile as the Middle East, though as host to the sacred precincts of Islam, the Saudis had long been somewhat immune to the more overt manifestations of this hostility.

The first alert of trouble at the Kaaba in November 1979 was sounded by a Moroccan pilgrim who was performing his devotions when he heard shots. Scores of terrorists—all fanatic extremists, encouraged by Iran's Islamic Jihad, anxious to destabilize, even overthrow, what they viewed as an increasingly secular and corrupt Saudi leadership—were embarking on an elaborately prepared and heavily armed operation to seize and hold the sacred Kaaba itself. Dashing from the holy places to the first telephone he could find, the Moroccan pilgrim called the Moroccan embassy, where, as chance would have it, the duty officer was a member of the Moroccan Intelligence Service. This captain immediately recognized the gravity of the situation and called Rabat. Within minutes, King Hassan II, himself a most devout Muslim who carried the title Commander of the Faithful, received the hastily decoded message announcing the violation of the holy places. By chance, he had in his presence Prince Abdullah Ibn Abdul Aziz Al Saud, chief of the fabled Saudi White Guard, which, apart from the army and the police, constituted the shield of the Saudi monarchy. A colonel from that crack unit turned out to be a principal organizer of this plot. Using a number of trained terrorists, he had assembled supplies for the rebels hidden deep in the labyrinthine basements of the Great Mosque of Mecca. Automatic weapons were concealed on the stretchers that ordinarily held the dead or dying pilgrims, carried this time not by family members circling the sacred Kaaba, but by the terrorist forces.

It was one of the largest terrorist actions ever mounted in the Middle East, certainly the largest ever mounted by Muslim against Muslim. The Saudis, on their own initiative, turned to us. They were aware we had been carefully monitoring their security problems and passing to them valuable, if often ignored, intelligence on the source of possible infiltration of arms and terrorist operatives into the kingdom. Moreover, the Saudis were keenly aware that precise, and especially discreet, action was essential—not a massive military intervention on the scale of Desert Storm. Indeed, our first advice was that no French military official be directly involved in the operation to root out the terrorists. A purely Islamic force had to intervene in a precinct as sacred as the Great Mosque and the Kaaba. Though our role had to be thoroughly concealed, we were able to provide detailed planning that enabled the Saudis to carry out this operation successfully. Concussion grenades and other specialized equipment were supplied by the French security services. It took days to clean out the terrorist forces from the labyrinth. But ultimately, stability was restored. The Saudis, nevertheless, remembered the lessons they'd learned then. While, wherever possible, they tried to maintain cordial relations with their neighbors, they never again fully trusted their security to any outside power, and their ties with the West were increasingly used simply to buy the most sophisticated armaments for their own protection. Even Operation Desert Storm does not belie this concern. American forces, and their potentially corrupting and destabilizing influence, were sent packing as soon as the immediate military menace of Saddam Hussein's Iraq was dealt with.

Some Saudi xenophobia helps explain the reaction to a suggestion I made in an audience with King Fahd a short time after the Kaaba operation. By that time, he had realized it was easier for terrorists to dishonor fifteen hundred princes of the Saudi family in a single stroke by desecrating the holy places than to assassinate them one by one, the way King Faisal had been murdered four years earlier in March 1975. All the meetings I had held with King Faisal and with Crown Prince Fahd, the heir to the throne, were conducted in the greatest secrecy.

King Faisal and I began our conversation in his chambers in the royal palace in Riyadh. He was dressed in a plain brown robe; he looked very simple, very humble, as he rolled his Muslim prayer beads in his fingers. Yet he was a world traveler and extraordinarily well read. As we began our conversation, he asked a question that had clearly been troubling him for some time: "How do you see my country in the future?"

"With Your Majesty's permission, I have done some thinking about this. My sense is that you will have great trouble by passing in one generation from the period when you were bedouins, men of the desert, to the postindustrial civilization where you find yourselves now. Your greatest danger is that you will lose the virtues of the desert without assimilating the ways of the postindustrial world. This gap will be very dangerous for you and very destabilizing, especially with your neighbors surrounding you on a different pace and timetable entirely. It is a time when you may lose your soul, and more."

His Majesty looked at me very intently and said, "You have understood. The most dangerous thing that can happen to a nation is to lose its soul. This is my most important problem." Some years later I had another conversation with Crown Prince Fahd, the future ruler of the Saudi Kingdom.

"You know, we have all the money in the world," he sighed. "We have all the oil, and with oil at thirty-eight dollars a barrel, as much money as we can ever need. But we have by no means enough men or soldiers to defend our vast territories."

Some months later, with Crown Prince Fahd, we went over the same problem after he told me that they had money and some ideas but no manpower.

"Well, Your Highness," I suggested, "we have been giving considerable thought to this problem as well. And there is one possible solution to your dilemma. The British are in the process of disbanding right now several battalions of Gurkhas. The Gurkhas are the most superb fighting men in the world. They are tough physically, they are mountain people from the slopes of the Himalayas. And onto this toughness has been grafted British discipline, spit and polish. They're fabulous. I've seen them operating in Africa and at the Battle of Cassino during the Allied thrust on Italy during the Second World War. They are not antiterrorist specialists, but they are super, outstanding fighters. If I were you, Your Highness, I would hire a brigade of these very cheap mercenaries—no political entanglements, no religious problems—and station them in the middle of the Red Sea, say in Bahrain, with a few helicopters and fast boats. I'm not saying this alone will prevent the entire Soviet Army from marching down through the Middle East if they set their mind to it. But dealing with any other threat—I will guarantee you peace for ten years."

Crown Prince Fahd smiled slowly. "I like it. It's a great idea." Then he paused for a moment and frowned. "But, my dear Count, this is impossible. You know, it is a question of Arab honor—they are not our own."

The failure by those nations that oppose the use of terrorism to react coldly and unemotionally with whatever weapons or forces will do the job most efficiently is precisely why terrorists have always been so successful.

The key imperatives in counterterrorist operations are speed and cooperation. The efficiency of the operation at the Kaaba is a powerful argument for the establishment and maintenance of some form of international police force that can react quickly and surgically. Whether it is in an advisory capacity or in the form of active participation, regardless of who is under attack, such a force is indispensable in putting down the actions of today's modern terrorists and those who control them. The Western intelligence community attempted to address this need for a powerful, rapid, and effective response to terrorist operations throughout the 1970s and in the 1980s, and we are addressing it continually today. But there are many forces working against us.

The primary factor impeding our efforts to develop an effective and lasting response to terrorism has been the absence of cooperative operations by any two Western nations, let alone multinational actions of any significance. Indeed, the only large-scale endeavor to have been undertaken in the recent years prior to Operation Desert Storm, which was far more a conventional military move than a counterterrorist offensive, was the joint Franco-Belgian-Moroccan operation in Zaire in the late 1970s.

The vast African nation of Zaire, the former Belgian Congo, is four times the size of France. It is the single wealthiest nation in black Africa in terms of its natural resources. The Congo River represents a source of hydroelectric power beyond all comparison with European rivers. But the nation is riven with tribal rivalries. Only the powerful leadership of General Mobutu Sese Seko was able to hold it together through brute force. Shaba Province, once known as Katanga, with its concentrations of copper, diamonds, cobalt, manganese, cadmium, lead, tin, oil, is the principal source of supply of four of the eight strategic minerals critical to the Western defense effort. It is the richest of the provinces in that wealthy nation. For years, various forces have tried to split Shaba from Zaire—a catastrophe in our view since it would have left a fabulously wealthy Shaba and a struggling, though strategically situated Zaire. Such a Zaire would have been deeply vulnerable to forces ranging from the Soviet Union to Qaddafi's Libya.

In May 1978, 4,000 former Katangese gendarmes returned from Angola, where they had been working as mercenaries helping the Communist-backed Angolan government. They were ordered by their Angolan paymasters to lay siege to the fabulous mines of Kolwezi in yet another effort to promote an uprising that might split off Shaba Province and perhaps even overthrow President Mobutu Sese Seko. Some 120 Europeans were massacred, along with hundreds of other local citizens.

Through intelligence sources, we learned about this operation even before it was mounted. It was clear from its scale that some external government backing was involved—certainly the Communist-led government of Angola, its Cuban supporters, and by extension the Soviet Union as well. Moreover, the attempted invasion was receiving at least moral encouragement from Qaddafi's Libya, which was anxious to promote instability in a part of the world where such unrest could prove to be a major opportunity for expansion of Libyan influence. With all those forces arrayed on the side of the invaders, it quickly became clear that two elements would be essential to neutralize the action: beating off the gendarmes, and restoring law and order. To accomplish this, a multinational force including Europeans and Africans had to be assembled; then a full-scale paramilitary operation needed to be mounted—and well prepared in advance by detailed intelligence work. To gather the manpower, we first went to work on the Belgians. Zaire, after all, was the former Belgian Congo, the cornerstone of the Belgian overseas empire. Still, we had to beg them to come in. There was clearly resentment that France was playing such a key role. Moreover, the Belgian decision to join the intervention was made so late that without the French and Moroccan forces, large numbers of civilian lives would have been lost.

Even before the multinational force was assembled, we dispatched agents of the SDECE, who were the first to arrive in Shaba.

Some were disguised as cooks and hairdressers. Some wore the more formal military uniform of the feared French Foreign Legion, the purple berets. Landing at night, as did all our field operatives, they fanned out through Kolwezi. We quickly discovered that the thirty Cuban advisers accompanying the Katanga mercenaries had fallen back immediately to the other side of the frontier that Katanga shared with Shaba Province.

While our operatives were preparing the groundwork for the full-scale invasion by our paratroop regiments, I left for Morocco to persuade King Hassan to supply Moroccan infantry, as accomplished as the Gurkhas, for the operation. It was essential, I believed, that this be perceived as an African operation in Africa and a multinational cooperation among our Western allies.

My relationship with King Hassan II was such that it was not necessary for me to ask for an appointment. I just arrived. Accompanied by my aide-de-camp and one of my generals, we traveled to the *kaida,* the great tent Hassan often used on his farm outside Fez. The only coded message the king had received from me was one telling him of my arrival.

As we approached to within fifty yards of his *kaida,* the king emerged, made a quarter turn, and spotted the three of us. And then there happened something quite extraordinary, which to this day remains inexplicable to me. He raised his right hand, wagged it, and said, "No, I will not go." He already knew the purpose of our visit. I have no idea how he knew. I had told nobody about my project and the reason I wanted to see him. Without question his intelligence service was equal in many respects to ours. There is no question he also had a sixth sense, a third eye, a sort of perception of events and people that was quite extraordinary—a sensibility that could bring him great power. And at that moment, I needed him, because who else could assemble and dispatch troops for an operation like this within a few hours? So I walked the fifty yards to the tent.

"Your Majesty, we need you," I began. For the next twenty-five minutes, I explained the strategic situation to him—the necessity of preserving Shaba and Zaire for the West, the prospect of the African continent severed at its waist should a collapse follow inertia.

The king recognized immediately that he had an extraordinary geostrategic responsibility, and he did not hesitate. He waved his hand and everyone else left the tent. "Give me the phone," he commanded. "I agree."

I moved to get up and leave so he could speak in confidence. But he ordered, "No, this is your operation. You're in charge. You stay."

Within minutes he had commitments from four African chiefs of state—from Gabon, Senegal, the Ivory Coast, and Togo. Each committed a small force to be led by the Moroccans and backed by the French and ultimately the Belgians. Finally, he turned to General Dlimi, his principal aide.

"How much time will it take to send our men?" he asked. The answer was a matter of hours. No red tape, no field headquarters, no bureaucrats. This was action by a committed leader against what was effectively a large-scale terrorist operation that would become more difficult to dismantle with every passing moment.

We were called on to provide the air transport that got eleven thousand troops on the ground in Shaba in a matter of hours. We used Transalls, the last kind of plane you'd want for an operation like this, because they were instantly recognizable as aircraft of the SDECE. Moreover, because they were propeller planes, it was a miracle that the first paratroops out weren't hacked to death by the propellers of the Transalls that followed. But they were the only planes available on such short notice. Still, the operation went off without a hitch, though the French Foreign Legion paratroopers had new chutes they had never used before.

From start to finish, the action was an enormous success. The Katanga mercenaries retreated back into Angola. The mines of Kolwezi were saved and hundreds of lives of Westerners and Zairians alike were spared.

The success of this early Zairian operation eased the path for future such rescue missions, assuring the peace in this vital corner of Africa. Such missions allowed us to guarantee the safety of our own and other Western nationals—most recentlee in September 1991, when Zairian troops, who had not been paid for months, revolted, looting and pillaging the capital of Kinshasa and other provincial cities. A joint Franco-Belgian paratroop operation assured the evacuation of foreign nationals, including several thousand Americans. These missions also served notice to outside powers who might covet the riches of this nation that any interference in Zaire's internal affairs would be strictly and swiftly dealt with.

But such combined operations relied on joint intelligence, and execution was and still is rare indeed, despite the growing perception that allied efforts are as essential. We are not and have never been organized to fight terrorist activities wherever they might occur. This must change.

11

Organizing Against
the Apocalypse

n the days before the Fourth World War, the Soviet bloc took maximum advantage of our inability to co-ordinate effectively our intelligence activities and our intelligence responses. Today, terrorists and their backers continue to exploit these weaknesses.

The task of a major intelligence service is not merely to have a good idea of the way others function in one's own country and else-where, but to be generally aware and sensitive to what is going on in the world at large. One of the principal weaknesses of Western nations, in their methods of organization and analysis, is that they are unable to deal with a global adversary with a global perspective, whose theater of operations is the entire planet. All too often, we are content with a local or regional, tactical view, a Francocentric view, an American perspective—representing wishes not reality. We wish desperately for a tiny corner of our world to stand for the whole. Instead, we should be cultivating a global, strategic view. Where we do not have the resources or the understanding, we should be pre-pared to place our security in the hands of our allies who do have the capacity that we lack.

There have been repeated cases of disasters or near disasters caused by suspicion, disbelief, incredulity, or simply a failure of communications between intelligence services that should, by ide-ology and sympathy, have been closely cooperative.

For example, in May 1981, Pope John Paul II might have escaped the bullets of Ali Agca entirely had Vatican and Italian intelligence authorities dealt with the information French Intelligence passed along to them.

Long before hard information on the actual assassination attempt reached us, we had speculated closely on the value to the Soviets and their allies of a dead Polish pope. Studying various scenarios, using our best modeling, putting ourselves in the shoes of East European leaders, we concluded that there were four substantive reasons for wanting this pope dead.

First, because he came from the East, the pontiff had a deep understanding of just how the Communist mind worked. And there was nothing the Communists hated more than someone who understood their mind-set and operations. An angel cannot imagine what hell is like, only demons who have been there can. This pope has always grasped what his predecessors from the West have never really understood—the profound differences and the similarities that coexisted in the religions of Catholicism and communism.

The second reason for an attempt on the life of John Paul II was the mission this pope announced publicly from the moment of his installation: to bring all elements of the Catholic Church back into the fold. That included those Catholic prelates and priests in the East who had been all but coopted by the Communist regimes, who had served as instruments of dominance over their subjects.

The third reason we identified was the likelihood that if this pope was killed, his successor would be an Italian—a prelate far less involved with the evolution of an Ostpolitik in the East, far more concerned with operations of the Vatican itself, and less interested in developing a Catholic presence in parts of the world where the Soviets were seeking to implant their own secular religion based on Communist dogma.

The final reason is the most basic. The pope was the ultimate symbol of Polish resistance to Soviet communism—the flag, the father, the very soul of Polish nationhood. In Poland, a nation of supreme strategic significance to the Soviet Union, situated as it is along the main communications and rail links between Russia and Germany, three quarters of the faithful attend mass regularly because of religious conviction, still more attended services because they symbolized resistance to a hated occupation force—Soviet Communists. Even leaders of the Polish Communist party would secretly travel to villages hundreds of miles from their home to baptize their children in violation of every canon of communism. A pope dedicated to destabilizing the Communist system would be poison to the Kremlin rulers of that era.

So we were fully prepared for the arrival in January 1980 of hard intelligence that the Soviet leadership had decided to kill the pope. The alert came from a tip I received from Eastern Europe. Moreover, as the tip confirmed all our advance analysis, it had all the appearance of truth.

I dispatched to the Vatican two of my most trusted aides—among them General Maurice Beccuau, who was my personal doctor and adviser, and a civilian member of the top leadership of French counterespionage. Their audience with Vatican officials was arranged by a senior French bishop, a veteran of the Second World War Resistance. Although diplomatic etiquette warranted that the pope, a head of state, should have been briefed by me of this pending threat, if I had gone personally, the terrorists mounting the operation would certainly have been alerted and altered their plans.

My two secret emissaries traveled to the Vatican and laid out their information to the pope's most trusted aides. They in turn presented it to the Holy Father, who, they were told, immediately dismissed it out of hand. His life, he said, was in the hands of the Lord. I have a great deal of respect for this conviction, though I believe there are times when it would not be inappropriate to give the Lord some earthly assistance. Nevertheless, we never raised the matter again.

It is certain that given the close relationship between the Holy See and the Italian state, Vatican security officials discussed our warnings with authorities in Rome. I have never ceased to question whether the Italian authorities ever took sufficient measures to protect the Holy Father.

There have been repeated visits to me through the years by investigators looking into the entire affair of the attempted assassination of Pope John Paul II. Recently, a senior official of the French Criminal Police came to see me, which indicates that the investigation is continuing to this day. But the first visit was from the investigating magistrate Ilario Martella, who was leading the Italian inquiry into the assassination attempt, not long after it occurred on May 13, 1981. He arrived with a list of thirty questions, which, because of my oath of official secrecy to the French state, I was largely unable to answer. But we did discuss a number of issues, including my conviction that Agca was not an isolated fanatic or even one assisted by an ad hoc network of Bulgarian drug runners and criminals. Ten years after the attempt on the Pope's life, Martella came to see me again in Paris, October 1991.

The evidence I presented Martella demonstrated that Bulgarians were used frequently for the worst kind of work—"wet work," or assassination. As the nation most loyal to, and most ethnically and culturally congruent with, the neighboring Russians, they were often perceived by the leadership of the KGB as appropriate for many delicate, yet hardly intellectual assignments. That's one key reason why we were constantly on the lookout for Bulgarians in Paris or elsewhere. Bulgaria was also a prime staging area for the transfer of arms between the Soviet bloc and key terrorist organizations. Because it lay along the main truck routes between Europe and the Middle East, which passed through Turkey and across the Bosporous, terrorist operatives often stopped off in Varna, Bulgaria, to load up on arms and munitions en route to what turned out to be their principal European headquarters during much of the 1970s and into the 1980s—namely, Paris.

So throughout the 1970s and 1980s, we kept close watch on the East European allies who were often pressed into service for the kind of terrorist and intelligence activities the KGB did not want to perform. Moreover, cooperation between Soviet and East European intelligence services, controlled directly from KGB headquarters on Dzerzhinsky Square in Moscow, was total, from top to bottom, including collection of raw intelligence, analysis, and of course operations. Their cooperation contrasted sharply with ours in the West, which has often been fragmented and has disintegrated to an open competition among services. Our cooperation was sporadic at best— relying on personal friendship and contacts, and then only on a case-by-case basis.

Our enemies depended on institutional directive and on established division of labor that was firm and immutable. Rumanians were used for intelligence work in the oil-producing nations; because of their country's oil reserves at Ploeşti, they had developed expertise in the petroleum industry, which helped them to infiltrate that industry in other countries. They were also useful in certain Romance-language countries because the Rumanian language is the only East European dialect with Latin roots. Officers of the Rumanian Securitate were also seen in French-speaking regions of Africa. Polish agents were often to be found in northern France, because several hundred thousand Polish coal miners or descendants of Polish miners have found their way to the French mines over the years. Because of the Poles' long closeness with Catholicism, Polish security became adept at infiltrating the Church in France. These agents were directed to gather information ranging from detailed status reports on coal reserves to strategic targets for behind-the-lines attack in the event of war. They were also instructed to track disaffected expatriates who might communicate with contacts back home—and, more important, serve as potential external sources of funds for dissident activities and subversion within the Soviet bloc.

East Germans were used extensively at the highest levels in West Germany because it was so difficult to distinguish one German from another. Chancellor Willy Brandt of West Germany was on close personal terms with Captain Gunther Guillaume, who turned out to be an officer in the East German Intelligence Service, and who had access to all the secrets of the Federal Republic of Germany. He had spent years slowly and patiently penetrating the West German bureaucracy, cultivating the loyalty and friendship of Brandt—the man who was first mayor of Berlin, and ultimately chancellor. After Guillaume fled back across what was then the border between East and West Germany, he was promoted to major in recognition of his devoted service to East Germany and the Kremlin.

We were not, of course, the only intelligence service monitoring the activities of our East European opposite numbers or Middle Eastern terrorists operating in the West. It was important for Western intelligence agencies to cooperate closely with the Mossad, the Israeli intelligence agency, because of its extraordinary expertise in the Middle East and Middle Eastern elements operating abroad.

For a variety of reasons, the Israeli Secret Service is highly efficient. First, with members of the Jewish state coming from all over the world, they have an enormous linguistic reservoir and capability, as well as a deep knowledge of nations on every continent and every ideology. Second, they have been all but continually at war for a half century and therefore must remain constantly vigilant. The Israeli nation and people are among the most important targets for many terrorist organizations. This feeling of being constantly under siege has always prevented any deep political or military cooperation with foreign military or intelligence services. But this siege mentality has also led to a respect for nations the Israelis have perceived also to be under terrorist attack. And this mind-set proved invaluable on many occasions.

The Israeli Secret Service was among the first agencies to realize that Paris had been chosen by a number of leading terrorist groups as their European headquarters. From George Habash, who flew the Tripoli–Paris route like a businessman flying the Washington–New York shuttle, to the Turkish People's Liberation Army, the Iranian National Front, the Japanese Red Army—all had their representatives in Paris and its environs. Even before the Ayatollah Khomeini showed up in Neauphle-le-Château, Turkish terrorists (the feared Gray Wolves) and Iranians were operating in Paris alongside the notorious terrorist Carlos (Illych Ramirez Sanchez). Germany's Red Army Faction, Italy's Red Brigades, along with the IRA, and of course the Spanish Basques were in and out of the French capital on a regular basis. Our own internal security operatives were watching all these people. So was the Mossad.

Moreover, the Mossad fully understood how important it was to meet terrorism on its own turf wherever necessary. Their agents were salted everywhere. Senior Israeli intelligence agents, doubling as journalists based in Paris, dealt with their colleagues at *The New York Times,* CBS, *The Washington Post,* not to mention *L'Express, Le Figaro,* and *Paris Match.* The information they shared with their Western colleagues was generally accurate—and served as a critical counterweight to the violence that terrorist leaders used to move world opinion. It was, and remains, essential that terrorist leaders be perceived for what they are—not as courageous freedom fighters, but rather as simple, though deadly, foils or tools of the insidious dictators.

Although our relations with the Mossad were warm, we maintained our closest day-in, day-out intelligence relationship with the British external intelligence service, MI6, and the British electronic monitoring services at Cheltenham. Our relationship was especially close in the Southern world, where we had both once maintained colonies with overlapping but congruent interests, and so continued to cooperate long after our empires had dissolved.

At one time, during one of our periodic lunches, the head of the British Secret Service, Sir Maurice Oldfield, told me, "Look, I want to have a man in a harbor in Africa." He named a West African country that was a former French colony. "You have people there, don't you?"

"Of course," I replied. "We've had people there since the days when it was a French colony. Now, it's a place where there are a lot of Soviet rest and recreation activities. They often bring in their fishing trawlers. Their fishermen love to ogle the French tourists in their string bikinis."

We both smiled because we knew that all these fishing boats were in fact heavily equipped by the Soviet naval fleet, the "fishermen" were Soviet naval officers.

"What if we were to put one of my men in there alongside yours?" Sir Maurice asked me.

"Why don't you do that," I replied. "Especially if you have a fluent Russian-speaking counterespionage agent who can function well in Africa. Because I don't."

After lunch, we looked at the dossiers of three British officers he had brought with him. And we chose the agent together. This was something all but unheard of in the West, even today, yet it was the way we always worked.

This kind of personal rapport was vital. Every six months, I made it my business to attend the joint luncheons held in London, Paris, or Munich with the heads of the three principal intelligence services in Europe—the British MI6, the West German Bundesnachrichtendienst (BND), and the French SDECE (now DSGE). Our joint get-togethers were not kept secret from the Americans. The Americans were simply excluded.

Each of the European intelligence services specialized in one area or another. Wherever we could, we shared intelligence—whether or not it was ultimately believed or acted upon. Our specialty was Francophone Africa, North Africa, the Middle East, and certain areas of Southeast Asia where we once had colonial interests. The British specialized in their areas of Africa and the Middle East, and their electronic intelligence on Eastern Europe was truly unparalleled. The West Germans were especially active in East Germany, while also monitoring the activities of East German agents in much of the rest of the world. And all of us kept as close tabs as possible on what was then the most formidable enemy for each of us—the Soviet empire.

The smaller European nations also had their own areas of particular expertise and often proved quite useful in specific cases. The Belgians, with a small service headed by a magistrate, specialized in the former Belgian colonies including the Belgian Congo, now Zaire. Among the Scandinavians, the Norwegians with their vast North Sea reserves, specialized in oil and OPEC. They also had the closest listening posts to the Soviet Northern Fleet base at Murmansk and engaged in regular exchanges of intercepts with the British at Cheltenham. In Luxembourg, the intelligence operation was small but highly efficient, run by a French-trained officer. The grand duchy is full of foreigners and for a nation of its size had far too many East European diplomats. KGB agents stationed in Paris, barely an hour away by car, often found their way to Luxembourg to augment their already large station there. It was a place where people met and plans were laid.

The Italians had close ties with Libya, but they were not to be fully trusted. Because of Qaddafi's large financial investments in Italy (he was a substantial investor in Fiat, among other enterprises), money was flowing from Libya all the time. Qaddafi also tried to buy every Mediterranean island between North Africa and Italy. On Pantelleria, heavily fortified by Mussolini during the Second World War, Qaddafi bought everything he could, including the goats.

On Malta, for a thousand years an island of strategic significance in the Mediterranean between Italy and Libya, Qaddafi bought up every piece of property available, except the British military base. And so Malta became a major terrorist staging area. In November 1985, an Egyptair Boeing 737 that was hijacked on a flight from Athens to Cairo was forced to land here, its hijackers seeking refuge. The attempt was quite simply too brazen, however, and the Maltese authorities had no choice but to allow Egyptian security forces to storm the plane. Egyptian President Hosni Mubarak personally blamed Qaddafi for masterminding the attack. The incident was but one of many conflicts between these two nations.

Qaddafi himself also had large numbers of his own operatives in Italy whom we knew were exchanging information with Italian intelligence. Italy was the only European country in which this kind of relationship existed; it was the only real intersection between the intelligence services of the South and the North.

Spanish intelligence was especially active in the Middle East and was particularly interested in monitoring economic developments in the Southern world. As a major Mediterranean power, not to mention the only West European nation to be occupied for more than seven hundred years by Arab forces of the jihad, Spain has always turned its attention heavily to North Africa and the Middle East. There are still Moors in Spain who trace their ancestry to the ancient Berbers recruited thirteen centuries ago by Arab generals in Algeria and especially Morocco.

The Dutch, a serious people, were especially valuable in dealing with their former empire in Southeast Asia—now Indonesia. Today, Indonesia is a member of OPEC and one of the world's most populous nations, and Muslim as well. The Dutch, more than any other intelligence service, also know about the operations of Royal Dutch Shell, one of the world's true multinationals. We were not especially interested in Royal Dutch Shell as an institution. But when a revolution was afoot in an area where it maintained substantial holdings, as happened during the attempted Communist takeover in Indonesia in 1965, that company, and by extension Dutch intelligence, monitored developments closely. Surinam is another nation where the Dutch and French had interests for years. France's Ariane rockets are launched from Kourou in neighboring Guiana. During Surinam's decolonization period, from 1973 through its finally acquiring independence in November 1975, we were concerned that the transition to self-government be peaceful and stable, especially without the interference of Cuban communism under Fidel Castro. My British counterpart, whose nation was also concerned about the Caribbean, came over to Paris from London and raised the issue of potential instability in that corner of the world.

"Have you spoken directly with the Dutch about it?" I asked him during our meeting. He said he had.

Together, we French in neighboring Guiana, the Dutch in Surinam itself, and the British in their corner of the Caribbean cooperated closely in monitoring the entire transfer of power to self-rule in Surinam. Joint river patrols were organized along one frontier to prevent infiltration of potentially disruptive opponents of the independence process, particularly Cuban-backed agents. As a result, Surinam became an independent nation in an orderly and peaceful fashion.

Physically, all the major European intelligence agencies maintained a permanent representation in each other's capitals. The British monitoring services were especially vigilant in passing along via a confidential teletypewriter link any "Sigint," signals intelligence, or "Elint," electronic intelligence, they managed to snag from the network of stations they operated from Turkey to Cape North. In December 1981, when the Polish Communist government used force to break the big strikes at the Gdańsk shipyards where Solidarity had been born, the British suggested that I might want to travel that night to one of their monitoring stations somewhere in Europe. I agreed and headed there immediately. When I arrived, the chief of this operation installed me at a console. On my left was a Polish interpreter, on my right, the commander of the station. For hours, I listened, riveted, to the conversations between the Polish tank commanders who were on the road that night.

"Be careful," one would warn, "there's an oil leak after the second tree on the right. Slippery. Use caution."

On the huge-scale map in front of us, we were following the progress of the tank column toward the shipyards as if we were there. Eavesdropping in this fashion on the Red Army was also a means of assessing the morale of the troops. Late in the evening of the Solidarity operation, when their officers had left them alone, the noncommissioned officers chatted among themselves over their radio links, complaining about the weather, the bad living and working conditions, the lack of food, their family problems. And these were elite troops—who would have been among the lead units in any frontal assault on Western Europe.

In recent years, I've given considerable thought to just how such monitoring capabilities could be used in the new context of the Fourth World War against such weapons as terrorism or drugs. There are certainly some real differences between the forces of the Third and Fourth World wars, especially in their means of command, control, and communication—the traditional three Cs of strategic doctrine. Terrorists, for the most part, do not use the same kind of detailed, battlefield-level communications to plan these attacks. But we have discovered that monitoring communications from embassies of Southern nations who support terrorist activities—particularly the Libyans, Syrians, and Iranians—has led to some dramatic breakthroughs. Logistics were discussed by radio for the bombing of La Belle discotheque in Berlin on the night of April 5, 1986, when a Turkish woman and an American GI were killed and more than two hundred others, including a number of American soldiers, were wounded. Electronic monitoring of radio traffic between Tripoli and the Libyan People's Bureau, or embassy, in East Berlin established Libyan complicity. The monitoring led to identification of the sources of the bombing, but alas, the data were not interpreted with sufficient urgency to have prevented the catastrophe. Such an incredible amount of electronic "traffic" is generated by such monitoring that important information often remains on unmonitored tape recordings until some incident causes them to be replayed by an analyst. The few successes are often due to chance encounters, the experts performing work as laborious as the monk-scribes of the Middle Ages, though today sophisticated monitoring devices that key in on preselected words or phrases can improve the odds on picking up the epiphanal conversation.

But beyond hard intelligence, we leaders of West European intelligence also discussed at our periodic meetings a number of potential plans at the operational level before they ever reached the political levels of our heads of state or government.

"We could destroy the Libyan armed forces, and perhaps even provoke a military coup against Qaddafi," I suggested at one of those liaison lunches I held with my British counterpart. "But we need the cooperation of the Egyptians and the Israeli Air Force. The Egyptians would embark on a saber-rattling operation on the frontier they share with Libya. The Libyans would respond by moving a substantial portion of their air force and armored corps to the border regions. Then the Israeli Air Force, the Israeli fighters marked with Egyptian insignia, would arrive at the crack of dawn and *phhhfft!* And if you want to worry about world opinion, you could take some of the destroyed Libyan tanks, move them to Egyptian territory, then take a hundred Libyan corpses, Kalashnikovs and all, and lay them down on Egyptian soil."

The operation never happened, of course, though there was enough tension from time to time along the Egyptian-Libyan frontier to have given appropriate cover for it. But my European colleagues loved the imagination and panache of the planning.

As Europe moves toward becoming a continent without barriers in 1993, it is clear that more than imagination and panache and some shared aperitifs will be needed to establish the sort of cooperation that will truly discourage terrorists, drug runners, and other criminals from taking maximum advantage of this new Europe.

The leaders of East and West who in November 1990 put their signatures to the red-leather-bound document they called the Charter of Paris for a New Europe were undoubtedly sincere in their proclamation that "Europe is liberating itself from the legacy of the past." And they quite rightly pointed out the tie between this document and the Treaty on Conventional Armed Forces in Europe, which substantially reduced the military forces facing each other down on what was once a vast divide between the Communist East and democratic West. But the fact that thirty-four countries ranging from San Marino and Liechtenstein to the United States and the Soviet Union signed the Charter of Paris did not by any means signal the kind of front-line cooperation in intelligence matters that could make Europe an impossible battleground for the terrorists and drug runners who are fighting their own dirty but violent little wars on our turf, probing our weaknesses from day to day, destabilizing our societies, and demoralizing our citizenry.

Indeed, from the moment when a united Europe first became the dream of politicians and businessmen, it became a nightmare for intelligence agents. The then head of Interpol, a distinguished British police officer, Raymond E. Kendall, expressed grave concern that an end to frontiers, a common passport, and free movement across borders would only facilitate the work of terrorists, drug runners, and all sorts of criminals.

But the fact is that frontiers are not where most terrorists are caught. Only the careless amateurs are snagged by a random check of a car that turns out to be carrying a trunkful of automatic weapons and plastic explosives. Terrorists are nabbed by long, tedious, methodical police work, by the kind of penetration of small cells that may take years, by chance tips from disgruntled lovers. But Europe and its intelligence agencies must be sufficiently organized to take advantage of each of these opportunities.

On one visit to Kinshasa, the capital of Zaire, I had dined at the presidential palace with President Mobutu and we were seated on his terrace beneath a magnificent full moon. After a long silence, Mobutu erupted into a great laugh that only he could manage and said, "You know, my dear Count, you Europeans could be very great indeed if you would just forget your tribal system."

That is where Europe now finds itself—still mired in its tribal system, struggling desperately to emerge from it. We have embarked on what could be called the first phase of true "Europeanization" so gingerly. We "admitted" new members to the inner circle only after the most profound soul-searching. Many French were afraid that countries like Greece or Portugal, with their backward economies, would drag down the other members of the European Community. What if their hordes of impoverished workers were to engulf our factories, throwing our own citizens into the streets? None of that has happened, of course. The hordes that engulfed northern and central Europe came not from the newly admitted nations of southern Europe, but rather from former colonies in Africa and the Middle East.

Europe is what it is today thanks in a large part to one man—General George Marshall—and the generosity and vision of the Americans. The Marshall Plan, developed after the Second World War, helped to pick up a war-torn Europe and dust it off, but it was a country-by-country undertaking. When the French government asked me to accompany General Eisenhower as his aide-de-camp on his tour of France at the beginning of the Marshall Plan era, Ike could see that it would work from a French point of view. Eisenhower's snapshots of each of the other nations he visited— Britain, Belgium, Germany, Italy—were equally distorted by the ethnocentric perspectives of each of those nations. He was observing the results of the last of the classical wars we may ever fight. The wars we are now battling are revolutionary wars—much different indeed.

Both the old organization of Europe under NATO and the new organization of Europe under the European Community share many of the common traits of what might be called the first phase of the New Europe. How we handle the second phase is the most critical, the most delicate, and—while I don't want to appear too apocalyptic—I fear may well determine the success or failure of Western civilization as we know it. For if we fail in this second phase, those poised on the geographical fringes of our civilization are already prepared to step in. The terrorists that the more malevolent leaders of the Southern world are using today as their surrogates are merely an avant-garde.

The second phase of the evolution of Europe must encompass the integration of the key blocs that exist, and have existed since the Second World War, on the east and the west of Europe—the United States on the west across the Atlantic, and old Soviet bloc nations on the east. In some respects, this second phase of East-West integration in Europe has already begun. Already, the two Germanies have been rejoined for the first time in forty-five years. This reversal of the historic separation of the two halves of Europe began for one key reason. Gorbachev, desperately trying to rescue his own very sick economy at home, had to cut loose the nations of Eastern Europe, formerly communist dominated, and later the countries of the Soviet empire. This is an enormous challenge. Yet each of those countries has very different characteristics, different needs. Each represents a different challenge, certainly from a political and economic perspective, but from an intelligence viewpoint as well.

East Germany, or what was the German Democratic Republic, needs the help of all the countries of the West, but especially that of the former West Germany; for Germany is one state, with one language and one culture—comprising some eighty million Germans, an enormous bloc itself in the middle of Europe. In fact, though their living standards and economy are inferior for the moment, East Germans include the Prussians and Saxons—renowned for their hard work and military abilities. The West Germans in their hearts are delighted to have them back. And no other European nation has either the resources or the incentive to nurse what was East Germany back to health.

This impressive economic, social, and political strength is by no means shared by the other countries of Eastern Europe. There will be more difficulties there. Hungary and Czechoslovakia are not far behind East Germany in their readiness for absorption into the economic and social system of Western Europe. They are small nations that are comparatively well developed, with Hungary somewhat ahead of Czechoslovakia. Yet privatization in Czechoslovakia promises growing inflation. And in Hungary, a similar move led to 30-percent inflation, resulting in a standard of living that was falling even as the show windows of stores were overflowing with goods that no one could afford to buy. Together with Austria, one of the most economically advanced nations in Western Europe, Hungary had been part of the powerful Austro-Hungarian Empire, which dissolved after the First World War. So the Hungarians should be ready, at least psychologically, to become full-fledged members of the European system once again. We must accept that and help it become an economic as well as a political and social reality.

Poland, of course, is an entirely different situation. An economic basket case, it appears entirely willing to plunge headlong into a democratic political experiment that we can only hope will succeed. The Polish mentality certainly makes this difficult. The Poles are a stubborn and strong-willed people. A dozen Poles will present as many different ideas on how to govern their country; and so in an entire nation, you have an enormous capacity for chaos. Unemployment for the first time hit 5.5 percent, or more than one million Poles out of work. We can only hope that calm and reason will mark the policies of his successors. But for the moment, at least, there is little we in Western Europe can do to accelerate the process of economic growth.

Rumania should have been an easier case. In fact, it is an even more troubled nation. Under Ceauşescu, the Pol Pot of Europe, it had become an economic invalid despite its oil reserves and a resourceful, clever people who proudly call themselves a Latin island in a sea of Slavs. Yet their nation has been torn and fractured by years of dictatorship and the bitter revolution that deposed Ceauşescu. Prices of many goods were rising at 300 percent in the first year under the new regime. In Bucharest, people waited in line for hours to buy meat, gasoline, and other staples. Water was periodically shut off. It may be a very long time indeed before Rumania can return to a state of equilibrium that will allow any integration into Europe.

The same, alas, is true of Yugoslavia, which since the death of Tito, the leader and glue that held together this disparate and artificial nation created out of the leavings of the Austro-Hungarian Empire, has become violently unstuck. Today, it finds itself in a position not dissimilar to Rumania's, torn by bitter and violent ethnic conflicts that have only been accentuated by the contrast between the relative wealth of Slovenia and Croatia in the northwest and the profound poverty of southern Serbia, Macedonia, and Bosnia. The fragile federation appears to be breaking apart entirely.

The challenge to European unity posed by a fragmented Yugoslavia pales by comparison with the challenge posed by the fragmentation of the rest of Eastern Europe and the Soviet empire itself. The process of disintegration of a Soviet Union assembled with blood and held together by terror for three quarters of a century, touched off by the inexorable economic pressures from a West prepared to outspend the Kremlin at every turn, has taken the once monolithic land of Marx and Lenin in directions that Gorbachev seemed never to have envisioned when he first began to cut loose his satellite states. It was a testament to the sickness of the Soviet regime and of its own economy with what alacrity the Kremlin allowed the nations it once dominated, especially East Germany which it also feared, to leave the Soviet bloc, and indeed how easily it allowed the bloc and finally its own union to dissolve. Clearly there were multiple dynamics at work here—an enormous pent-up hostility among peoples enslaved for three and four generations, the final failure of the Soviet military machine to match NATO in military, technological, or economic terms, made most apparent in the development of the next generation of high-tech weaponry including the much-maligned "Star Wars" space defense system. These forces all combined to break apart into increasingly tiny fragments a union that once seemed unshakably monolithic and cohesive.

I followed each of the East European countries closely during my years as head of the French Secret Service and in the period of turmoil that has followed. As the second phase of European integration begins, each of these nations represents as enormous a challenge from the intelligence perspective as it does from any political, economic, or social point of view.

There are several benefits that apply broadly to the arrival of a democratic system in Eastern Europe. No longer will terrorists have that open back door into Europe through an environment that was hospitable to any enemy of the West and whose closed societies made it difficult at best to monitor subversive activities. No longer will terrorists be able to count on routine access to the first-rate munitions and weapons produced by some of the former Eastern bloc countries. No longer will terrorists be trained by official agents of police states and have direct access to the latest techniques of violence and mayhem.

Embassies of Libya, Syria, and Iran in such capitals as East Berlin had provided logistical support for terrorists, and full communications links behind the protection of the East German Communist government and its powerful and feared secret police, the Stasi. The tenuous links that existed between the two Germanies were particularly useful for terrorists. The common language and culture allowed the freest possible movement between Communist East and democratic West, while the controls on the Communist side of the Berlin Wall provided what was effectively a one-way mirror that allowed the authors of destruction the sanctuary they craved. Moving through the wall, travelers found that their papers were scrutinized only on the eastern side, and those individuals with the proper escorts or papers could pass quite freely. Once in West Berlin, it was an easy plane or train ride to just about anywhere in Europe.

As a result, a range of Middle Eastern terrorist groups, but especially West Germany's homegrown terrorists like the Baader-Meinhof Gang, used East Germany like Alice's rabbit-hole into another world. Their safe houses, not to mention their sources of false documents, money, and carefully protected exit and entrance routes, were in the East. When five West German terrorists were arrested in Paris in 1980, notes they were carrying disclosed that they had access to a large store of pistols, machine guns, hand grenades, and explosives in East Berlin.

The East German secret police of course enjoyed many of the same advantages as their terrorist guests for much of the post-Second World War era. Sharing a common language and culture with their West German brethren across the frontier, the feared Stasi was able to infiltrate with impunity the highest levels of German government and industry. Their enormous intelligence apparatus functioned with virtually equal effectiveness on both sides of the Berlin Wall.

Most of this activity ended when the wall came down and Berlin became the capital of the one Germany. Middle Eastern embassies in East Berlin that had once fueled terrorist activities originating in their home countries were closed. And the West German Interior Ministry was given the express task not only of dismantling the East German intelligence and secret police apparatus but of tracking down Stasi officers and soldiers and uncovering their most flagrant abuses. Still, many such officers and terrorism specialists, particularly those posted to wealthy Middle Eastern countries like Libya, simply removed their badges and turned into "free-lance consultants." They remain in place today, trading their expertise for large quantities of hard currency. Their paymasters are the same—they are paid out of the oil revenues of Libya, Syria, or Iran. The checks are simply deposited directly by these governments in Swiss bank accounts instead of traveling through the bureaucracy in East Berlin.

There were similar moves to dismantle the intelligence machines across the rest of newly democratized Eastern Europe. In Czechoslovakia, the election of President Vaclav Havel, the onetime dissident playwright and poet, led to the immediate unraveling of the secret police apparatus—particularly the arm that dealt with Middle Eastern or West European terrorist groups. Relations with the governments that supported them became equally tense, though many of these Southern countries restrained their anger in the interest of retaining access to the high-quality arms and munitions that continued to roll from Czech armament factories.

The quiet, secluded spa of Karlovy Vary was once known as Carlsbad when it served as a watering hole of the world's jet set. In the hills surrounding the elegant resort, the Czech sugar barons, merchants, and industrialists of the Austro-Hungarian Empire had built their lavish mansions. After the Communist takeover in 1948, all of those estates became property of the state. Some were used as plush retreats for the Party elite; others became training facilities for terrorists, ranging from Italy's Red Brigades to the most militant Palestinians. Behind doors carefully guarded by members of the Czechoslovak secret police, these terrorists received advanced training in the ways of the West and the use of the sophisticated, Czech-made explosives and weapons they would ultimately be using in their operations.

Even Yugoslavia, the "least Communist" of the East European Communist states in pre*glasnost* days, was not immune from participation in terrorist activities or giving terrorists sanctuary. Yugoslavia fancied itself "nonaligned"—and so constantly attempted to navigate between both blocs. Many of the countries with which Yugoslavia was most assiduously promoting its ties had by then moved firmly into the enemy camp of Yugoslavia's West European neighbors. Yugoslavia's resolutely nonaligned status often meant giving aid and comfort to some of the less savory elements. If there is any country in Eastern Europe where the unwinding of the old Communist machine in recent years has made less difference in terms of its tolerance of such activities, Yugoslavia would appear to be such a place. First, it is heavily preoccupied with its own internal problems, which are bordering on civil war. Second, its strong attachment to the principles of nonalignment remains unwavering. And that movement itself continues to be preyed upon by terrorists anxious for official sanction and support.

Through the last two decades, the Palestine Liberation Organization has maintained some representation in Belgrade (as it has throughout the rest of Eastern Europe and in Paris as well). So it should have come as no enormous surprise that after Abul Abbas engineered the bloody hijacking of the Italian cruise ship *Achille Lauro,* he wound up in Yugoslavia. It was a classic case of each nation for itself. The terrorist's first stop was Italy, where United States Ambassador Maxwell Rabb made frantic requests to the Italian government to hold Abul Abbas for extradition to the United States. Instead, Italian authorities ignored the American pleas and immediately transferred the terrorist leader to a plane heading for Yugoslavia, where he was received with open arms. And within hours, he was relaxing in a PLO safe house in Belgrade, blithely participating in telephone interviews with Western correspondents in Paris and Tunis where the PLO maintains its headquarters. Finally, when the diplomatic heat grew too intense even for the Yugoslavs to take, Abul Abbas disappeared again, onto a JAT (Yugoslav) airline flight bound for Damascus, blending back into the terrorist firmament where to this day he remains a star.

For forty years, we devoted all our energies to monitoring the activities of the agents of each of the East European countries. We understood how they operated, identified them as individuals, and followed them as they moved from station to station. We observed their contacts, and when their activities became particularly flagrant or their networks particularly dangerous, we rolled them up whenever possible—expelling them from our countries, arresting our own citizens who were most deeply involved with them. So how do we suddenly change our mind-set from seeing those East European governments as enemies to viewing them as friends, and shift our spotlight to the terrorists and drug traffickers who will be our enemies for the next forty years? Only with the help of our friends and our allies.

CHAPTER 12

Enemy into Friend, Friend into Ally

The singular challenge to Europe for the next generation and beyond will be to turn our principal enemy since the Second World War into a friend, and to transform our principal friend into a true ally in the fight for victory—indeed for our mutual survival in the Fourth World War.

At the heart of this challenge is whether we can understand the fundamental nature of the two societies—the transformed and fragmented society once known as the Soviet and the American—how they think and function, how their evolutionary processes work as well as what forces have brought on their revolutions. This challenge has been multiplied in its complexity by the fragmentation of what was once a Soviet Union which exists no longer. The emergence of a dozen or more Soviet nations, some of them micropowers, each with its own highly individualistic language, culture, history, identity, and especially worldview, poses a challenge of monumental dimensions to the intelligence and security services of the West and to our diplomats and politicians as well.

In the decades since the Second World War, we invested considerable time, energy, and manpower in understanding and dealing with the forces that drove the two superpowers. Yet throughout this period we were failing miserably in two key respects—first in understanding and coming to grips with the powerful internal forces that today are driving the powers that have emerged from the Soviet empire; second in dealing with the former Soviet Union and the United States as superpowers themselves. We failed for one central reason—for most of the time that we were at war with the Soviet empire, we counted too much on the protection of the United States. Neither offered Europeans a fundamentally healthy relationship. Never did we approach either power, our friend or our enemy, clear-sighted, evenhanded, able to stand on our own feet. With each of them, Europe is essentially a party in a painful divorce—we must learn how to be our own person before we can have a healthy relationship with someone new. For Europeans to understand and reach some deep accommodation with the two superpowers or the powers that are emerging from the ashes of the Soviet empire, it is essential. But especially, we must begin to redirect our complex systems of intelligence that have been trained so long on the superpowers to the new enemies that surround us on all sides—indeed, who are among us already.

Communism was born with the century; it is dying with the century. That is not to say that all Communists will be good democrats by 1999. Habits accumulated over generations are difficult to break. Of what immediate value is private industry when the concept of the profit motive must be taught, as we teach grammar to a second-grader? Those who were schooled on communist theory and practice must be taught the most fundamental concepts of market economics and democracy as we enjoy them and as they do not understand intuitively. Yet the people of what has been known as the Soviet Union must also return to some basic values that are very deep in the Russian, not the Soviet, soul—or for that matter the Latvian, Lithuanian, Estonian, Moldavian, or Ukrainian soul.

The values that are being substituted for communism as Russia grapples with democracy include those of the Church. We are already seeing a phenomenal return in Russia to the traditional Orthodox Church. For most of this century, while under the bloody thumb of Soviet Communism, the Russian Orthodox Church has jealously guarded its deepest secrets, what could be called the mystery of the Church, what Russian men and women have always sought as a path to peace of mind—which has been passed down through the years by the priesthood and the true believers. The Communists understood such a need for mystery. I have always believed that their fundamental mistake was promising that the ultimate reward for their faithful would come on this earth. That removed the mystery in the short term, and communism was doomed. It failed to deliver on its promises of secular prosperity and well-being, and the world was able to observe and ridicule that failure. The Orthodox priests and patriarchs understood that you can never remove the mystery from the Church, otherwise you have nothing. Though the Church never served as the core of opposition to Communist rule, because of its deep mystical components, and its promise of relief in the hereafter from the troubles and hardships of today, the Russian people are returning to their religion in droves. Percentagewise, there are more Christians, those who actually and regularly worship, in Soviet Russia than in France.

We must understand one other fundamental characteristic of the former Soviet Union that will help us toward some workable and peaceable coexistence. The Russians of the Soviet empire are 137 million out of 288 million people. If you add the other European Slavs like the Byelorussians and the Ukrainians, now independent countries, whose interests may diverge from those of the Russians themselves, you are at a little over 200 million. For the Soviet empire, much of that population, for the moment, is west of the Urals—in European Russia. But the bulk of the landmass is outside Europe entirely, where the most rapid population expansion is taking place. As the Soviets discovered to their deep dismay during their invasion of Afghanistan, they have within their borders in this Central Asian region a new form of conflict between a European nation, Russia, and the heroic freedom fighters of Afghanistan defending their sacred soil.

We have monitored all of these pressures and trends as best we could. The ethnic Russians never functioned very well in the harsh conditions of the Virgin Lands—the vast empty steppes of Asian Russia—from the time Nikita Khrushchev tried to develop them. But give those lands to, say, Uzbek women and they will do very well. They prosper in what for outsiders are remote and forbidding territories. And the numbers of these non-European people are multiplying at a frightening pace. The most rapidly growing populations on the other side of the Urals have no real place to go. They cannot go to the East because of the Pacific Ocean and Japan. They cannot go to the South because the Chinese and Indian empires and the territories of Islam are there. To the west are the already dense populations of European Russia. Our principal problem for the future is likely to be managing these powerful demographic forces.

Twenty years ago, I said to Pyotr Abrasimov, then ambassador of the USSR to France and a member of the Central Committee of the Communist Party, "You are once again the bogatir—the great warrior with a huge sword and chain-mail suit—who protects the European world from the Mongol hordes."

In the vast Asian regions, part of what was the Russian Empire and, after 1917, the Soviet Empire live different kinds of people who are of course not western Europeans. Among them, in the South of this enormous land mass, are sixty million Moslems who, now liberated from communism, are rapidly going back to their old religions and culture.

The United States had fought, and lost, what might appear to have been a South-North conflict in Vietnam. But it was not. North Vietnam, a province of the former French Indochina, had fallen prey to a radical Communist dictatorship supported by the Soviets and more or less by the Chinese Communists. As a result, it was a government with a cold war—a Third World War—mentality and ideology to match. Its theology was communism and power, not God and the Messiah. This was a war with clear geographic boundaries, fought with terror tactics, jungle guerrilla tactics that we were forced to learn, more or less successfully, and weapons that were familiar to the West, even if we never figured how to defeat them. But the Vietnam War had one value for the United States. It accustomed the American people to the need to go to battle with, even risk defeat at the hands of, what appeared to be a lesser power. And while the Americans found it somewhat less than gratifying psychologically, their prestige has largely remained intact. As a result, it became that much easier for them to take on other, even more deadly, skirmishes, most recently in the Persian Gulf against Iraq.

The war in Afghanistan for the Soviets served some of the same psychological purposes that Vietnam served for the Americans. It was the first war the Soviets had ever lost. But of even greater significance, it was also the opening of the process of decolonization of the Soviet empire that was to lead ultimately to the dismantling of much of the East European system built up since the Second World War. In this respect, the end of the Soviets' East European empire, indeed the Soviet Union itself, was the last gasp of the Third World War, an end to the Soviet capacity for the old cold war-style East-West confrontation.

In Afghanistan, two critical factors led to the public Soviet declaration of withdrawal. First was the rising tide of popular opinion back home that managed to break through even in a nation never known to allow public opinion to influence any strategic decision.

Too many young men, the flower of Soviet manhood, were coming home in body bags. The second factor was purely economic. The war was becoming too great a drain on a Soviet economy that was already reeling. Gorbachev was prepared to cut loose his close allies, relinquish his cordon sanitaire, the East European nations his predecessors had subsidized at incalculable financial and human cost since the Second World War. So how could he justify to himself or his supporters the cost of a war for control of a remote, Muslim nation far removed from the traditional Communist camp, though Gorbachev still was financially supporting the Kabul regime. It ended only in January 1992.

At the beginning of the decade of the 1990s, money became the touchstone for the Soviet policy at home and abroad. Cost-effectiveness became the Soviets' ultimate litmus test, a new standard. We must understand how the KGB may be equipped to function in the new arenas of the Fourth World War, just as we must understand the strengths and weaknesses of our American allies.

There is no hard evidence, for instance, that the Soviet intelligence or military apparatus is being suddenly and totally dismantled. Restructured, yes. Each of the breakaway republics appears to have been given control over its security apparatus, left over from the KGB, which remains under its own control. But it would also appear that at the central KGB and GRU directorates it is largely business as usual with respect to foreign intelligence and operations. We must remain equally vigilant for the appearance of intelligence agents in each of the dozen or more legations that may be expected in our Western capitals from the newly formed nation-states of what was once the Soviet Union. In the meantime, in one form or another, the KGB and GRU remain everywhere. Their reach and influence, at home and abroad, can never be exaggerated. Though the curtains have been drawn back on the glass facade of the Soviet mission to the United Nations on East Sixty-eighth Street in New York, in critical flashpoints of the world there remain in place agents who years ago burrowed deeply into each of their host countries and continue poised for the moment when they may be called upon. Those agents remain in place as well at key posts in the Southern developing world, and in the Northern, Western democracies.

Operations of the KGB and the GRU military intelligence apparatus were going at reduced speed, under new leadership, especially in the United States, two years after Communist leaders were ousted in Poland, Hungary, Czechoslovakia, and East Germany, even after the Soviet Union itself unraveled. Indeed, there is some evidence that under KGB sponsorship, the feared Stasi, the East German secret police, continued to operate in a deeply undercover form in what was East Germany before reunification. Hundreds of native members of the security apparatus who took their orders directly or indirectly from the KGB buried themselves deeply underground in all the East European countries, reporting only to KGB control agents. Others fled to the mother country itself to continue their activities in the employ of the Kremlin. The interest of the KGB, a trait shared with their intelligence counterparts everywhere, is to help some of their people who are loyal to them stay in power, both in the security services and in the governments themselves. We call such individuals assets, sympathizers, or fellow travelers, but some are full-time agents, well paid, highly trained, and skillful. Those individuals in many respects continue to be the way that the Soviets project their power abroad—into the Western democracies that were their enemies throughout the cold war.

This kind of game has been played as long as there has been espionage. Look, after all, at what happened to the Nazis after the Second World War. Hundreds stayed on in disguise and became members of the Stasi. It was an ideal way to continue to project Nazi power. Alas, for their sake, the Second World War only too quickly gave way to the Third. Rather than a return of Hitler's Reich, they found themselves trapped into working for the very enemy they once so heartily despised. The Communist system made effective use of many Nazis who merely changed their black armbands for red ones, and easily and quickly adapted to the new realities. The West profited from their expertise to a lesser extent. As we move from the Third to the Fourth World War, there will inevitably be similar shifts in loyalties. Call it opportunism or survival, we must make certain that our Western, or Northern, intelligence organizations are the chief beneficiaries.

The Soviet Secret Services must still be approached with great caution, as one would approach a wounded, but still-powerful bear. Western intelligence must continue to monitor Soviet intelligence activities. Where the Soviets are operating, who their friends are, and what actions they are taking, is still knowledge of enormous importance.

The collapse of the Soviet economy today is itself a cautionary tale about the futility of pumping vast sums of cash into a desperately inefficient economy controlled not by market forces but by incompetent and narrow-minded government bureaucrats.

The decision to no longer jam Western radio broadcasts was an important first step by the Soviet government in opening Russian society to Western political and economic concepts—a fortuitous action that allowed Soviet citizens and their leaders to understand how flimsy was the August 1991 coup that nearly ended *perestroika*. More than fifteen years earlier, I had urged the President of France to begin transmitting Radio France International to the Asian republics of the Soviet Union, in hopes that it might be seen as somewhat less threatening than the CIA-backed Radio Liberty and hence have a greater chance of reaching our intended audience. We had been monitoring developments in those areas for years, long before the invasion of Afghanistan, and understood the revolutionary power building up in those regions that are so far from the Kremlin. Now, French broadcasts, alongside their American, British, and German counterparts, received loud and clear, are an open window on the West for the most remote Soviet Asian village. This is only the first step in the long and tedious process of reeducation of an entire civilization to a strange new way of life.

It has always been difficult to work inside the Soviet empire itself—for intelligence or any other purposes—doubly difficult in the Asian regions. While we maintained a large embassy and staff in Moscow and a smaller consular staff in Leningrad, it was difficult to travel, to build and maintain friendships or even contacts with the Soviet people, let alone with their rulers. The situation was totally asymmetrical. In the West, the Soviets had managed to infiltrate scores of agents into regions of France where they had never maintained any diplomatic representation, and to operate in parts of Paris where it was difficult, if not impossible, to control them.

The UNESCO world headquarters in the heart of Paris is a classic case study. UNESCO is an extraordinary listening post. There, diplomats and spies rub shoulders with specialists in various social, educational, and cultural disciplines from every continent. It is a window into every member nation of the United Nations. Each of the major secretariats has had more than its quota of Soviet agents through the years—agents who travel on UN diplomatic passports and operate with immunity in France or wherever they are posted. For ten years, the director of UN personnel in Geneva was a Russian—a colonel in the KGB—with full access to the personal dossier of every United Nations employee. You don't need many agents like that.

At UNESCO in Paris, a senior member of the press section was also a Russian and a KGB agent. During the 1980s, he served as one of the leading escorts of Western journalists and television crews who visited UNESCO headquarters—watching every camera angle, listening to every question. French authorities had no control over the activities of such individuals. All we could ultimately say was, "We don't want this chap in our country anymore." But those words were hardly ever uttered. For every such individual we removed, they removed one of ours. Moreover, we were then faced with the daunting task of discovering which Soviet had assumed the functions of the one we had expelled.

Back to the time of Peter the Great, throughout the rule of the Romanoffs, long before the arrival of the Communists in power, the Russians devoted enormous energies to a fundamental understanding of the West. We Europeans have attempted to do the same with respect to the East. We have succeeded on many levels in deepening our understanding—we are, after all, from the same continent, sharing many of the same ethnic, if not political or cultural, backgrounds.

Over the years, while Leonid Brezhnev dominated the Soviet political scene and as his health deteriorated, an increasing amount of our attention and energy was devoted to understanding just how ill he was. One day, Brezhnev paid a visit to Denmark and we arranged an interesting cooperation with the local intelligence service. We found that with their help we could have an apartment directly below the one where Brezhnev was staying. Tapping into the pipes that led from his private bath, we were able to collect everything that came out of his body so that it could be analyzed. We discovered, to nobody's surprise, that he was an alcoholic—but truly a profound alcoholic.

With that in mind, on his state visits to Paris, the French protocol office made certain that the bars in his suite at the Trianon Palace in Versailles, where he often stayed, and at the Élysée Palace, where the official meetings took place, were well stocked. On what turned out to be his last state visit to France, the first meeting was held at 4:00 P.M. The Élysée Palace made sure there was every kind of drink in the world on hand. There were thirty different kinds of whiskey—Scotch of every variety, rye, Canadian, Irish. If he'd said, "Sake," we would have asked which brand. He asked for the only beverage that was not available—coffee! He wanted a cup of coffee and milk. But the kitchen at the Élysée, it turned out, was closed; the cooks who prepared lunch had gone out for a walk and not yet returned to begin work on dinner. We finally improvised.

Throughout Brezhnev's visit, French Intelligence watched his every move—what he ate, how he was acting, how he felt at lunchtime, if he got red in the face. We had specialists who looked at him carefully. And cameras, too. That afternoon of the first meeting, we were already monitoring him. He was a very heavy man, more or less limping, kept upright by two aides. After the session returning to the Trianon, he got out of the car, walked very ponderously toward the entrance. But the moment he closed the door to his apartment, he trotted, nearly ran, to the bar. And poured himself a killer shot of vodka au poivre—pepper vodka. Any but a Russian stomach would have turned inside out.

We made major efforts to collect this kind of intelligence—understanding the enemy—a skill that will be central to intelligence battles. So it comes as no surprise that we were enormously frustrated when the political leadership paid little attention to the kind of information we were able to provide—when President Giscard d'Estaing would slip off to a summit in Warsaw with President Brezhnev without even the most basic of briefings from his intelligence agency. These kinds of lapses were not only frustrating, but dangerous. In this, at least, we shared some of the characteristics of our American counterparts—frustrations never experienced by our Russian colleagues, who found that their intelligence was always taken with the utmost seriousness and sought after at every opportunity at the highest levels. Nevertheless, when our advice was sought, it was understood and considered carefully.

Not so among our American allies, whose political leadership, and even intelligence leadership, has on so many occasions abdicated its responsibility to itself, not to mention to its allies. The Americans must come to realize the errors of their past ways. If the United States is to prove effective as our focus of attention shifts to the far more complex and subtle issues of the South-North War already under way, the American political leadership must also school itself in the arts of subtlety as practiced by our new enemies.

From my earliest days of dealing with the American intelligence establishment, it has been painfully clear to me that there was a critical, systemic flaw in the organization of gathering, analyzing, and acting on intelligence. This defect has affected the Americans' ability to function against the Soviet empire and its Eastern allies in the Third World War, and it is preventing American intelligence from operating effectively in the Southern world. At the heart of this failure is the inability of the top leadership of the United States government to understand just what the intelligence community itself is reporting—what it all means. An objective understanding must precede any action that might be taken with a hope of a successful outcome. Even more dangerous are the repeated attempts to use intelligence for political purposes, to skew the diplomatic or political agenda to particular views for partisan reasons. Truly objective and unbiased assessments of international situations and world leaders can never be presented in such an atmosphere.

At one point during my first meeting with President Reagan in California, the President-elect asked me, "Just how do guys like the Ayatollah function, how do they think?"

I said to myself quickly that I had better not go too deeply into the history of the sons of Allah and how some became Shiites and some became Sunnis.

"The only thing I would like to stress, Mr. Reagan," I began, "is that these are not the kinds of people you want to have normal diplomatic striped-pants work with. They do not see like we do; their inner system, their compass, is not like ours. May I describe how I see them by telling you an extraordinary story that took place in France in the thirteenth century?"

Mr. Reagan nodded. So I told him about the Siege of Béziers. "Before the battle began, the representative of the pope said a mass for the troops and offered them benediction," I said. "And he concluded with this phrase: 'Soldiers, kill them all, God will recognize his own.' It is a phrase that every French schoolboy knows. So they butchered by hand, one by one, every inhabitant of the town of Béziers. The pregnant women they cut open so that none of the heretics could survive. It was like killing twenty thousand sheep. Mr. President, God must have had a difficult time recognizing his own."

President Reagan understood the point of the story—that for many of our new enemies—as fanatically religious serving as soldiers of Allah as were the troops at Béziers serving the will of the pope—human life has simply a different meaning than it does for us.

But I have never been convinced that either he or any of the six directors of central intelligence with whom I dealt during my term as head of French security ever fully understood how the Islamic nations think—or how the Soviets think, for that matter. It's not easy to reach such understanding in the two or three years that most directors of central intelligence generally hold office.

The deep lapses in understanding that marked the leadership of the professional intelligence community were even more intensely duplicated in the civilian leadership of the United States.

During one of my visits to Washington, I called on the chairman of the Congressional Joint Intelligence Committee, intending to brief the congressman and some of his top staff on the latest developments that we had been following, particularly in the Middle East. I asked him for a map of the Middle East so that I could more graphically illustrate some of the points I was making. Immediately next to my office in Paris, a cartographer was stationed, concerning himself with nothing but maps. Yet in Washington, it took twenty minutes for the head of this committee that has the responsibility for overseeing the entire American intelligence establishment to find a map of the Middle East—an aide, one of 108 staff members of the committee, finally returning with a basic map the size of the page of a small book. How is it possible to understand the world if you do not even know the shape of it?

From my years of contact with my civilian and military counterparts in the United States, it's difficult to choose the most telling evidence of the vast gulf in comprehension that separates Europeans and Americans dealing with intelligence and strategic or military analysis, especially of the third world.

But there was one memorable encounter in Paris at the height of the Vietnam War in 1968 with General William Westmoreland. We were in the drawing room of the apartment of Pierre Damelon, who was a *préfet*—a very high French civil servant—and a dear friend of mine. The general was on his way back to Saigon to resume his position as commander in chief of American forces in Vietnam. We struck up a conversation that evening.

"Well, how are things going?" I began.

"Oh, very well," he replied brightly.

"That's very good"—I smiled—"because as for myself, I don't really have the same impression from the outside."

"I'll show you why," he shot back. From his pocket he pulled a three-by-five-inch index card that had some figures neatly typed on it. "We have put out of commission five hundred thousand Vietnamese, dead or captured. Now, how about that?"

"Excuse me, General, I am not impressed," I replied, as a cloud passed over the general's face. "May I explain. You are the commander in chief. You have lost five hundred thousand rifles. What do you do?"

"I send a message of procurement to Washington: 'Send five hundred thousand rifles.'"

"That's it," I said. But I was never really sure he got it. General Westmoreland, like his colleagues almost to a man, never really made any effort to understand the mind of his enemy. To the North Vietnamese, five hundred thousand men are nothing but five hundred thousand replaceable weapons. More are requisitioned. Then more behind that, and more again. Still, I'm sure the general was thinking, "This smart aleck, he's sitting on his ass in Paris and I'm fighting a war."

"All right, so what would you do?" he finally blustered to me.

"You must always play to your own strength, not to your enemy's," I began. "And one of your greatest strengths, because of your navy and air force, is your weather bureau. Yes, meteorology."

"What about the weather bureau?" he asked quizzically.

"Me, I would wait for the day of the most intense monsoon of the year. And you have the technical means of knowing that. And that day, I would bomb all the dikes of every river in North Vietnam."

He gasped. "But you would kill two or three million people."

"What is war about, General?" I asked. "Saving civilians was not what you had on your minds at Hiroshima and Nagasaki, but have you forgotten that lesson?"

Westmoreland turned his back on me and stalked off. One of America's great military leaders had failed to learn two of the most fundamental lessons of the Third World War, one of the few lessons that is directly applicable to the realities of the Fourth. He had failed, first and foremost, to get inside the mind of his enemy. And he had failed to understand what was indispensable and what was dispensable to those whom he was battling. Manpower was dispensable and all but infinitely fungible. Land, and the infrastructure that protected that land, was indispensable and irreplaceable.

In so many ways, Westmoreland, like most of those of his generation of military leaders in the United States, and in the Soviet Union as well for that matter, was still fighting the Third World

War, in which the enemy came from their own mind-set, with values that were part of their own personae. Of equal gravity, they were fighting with many of the same tactics in both defense and intelligence that I observed being used in the Second World War. Clearly, Vietnam would have been the ideal setting to try out new tactics and new concepts that might prove valuable against an enemy that none of us truly understands. Yet it was only the rarest military or intelligence mind that attempted to know the enemy more profoundly than he could ever know you.

Nevertheless, there were some isolated Americans through the years who understood the need to get inside the mind of the enemy. Late in 1953, shortly after Admiral Arthur Radford took over as Chairman of the Joint Chiefs of Staff, we talked in Washington about Indochina, where we French were in the process of committing many of the same errors the Americans were to commit years later. He asked me what he should know if his military were to become involved in Vietnam.

"Each nation has its problems," I replied. "Historically, America always worries about its manpower. That's why you invented the mechanical combine to harvest your crops. We French can lose two hundred men, it's no big deal. But you Americans, no. If one American soldier gets killed, it is a national tragedy. One thing I have learned is never go into the Asiatic continent with an army. The enemy can stand any number of dead. We can't. Stay on the high seas and in the air where you are strong. They build a bridge, destroy it. They build another bridge, destroy it. They build a fifth one, destroy that. This is the essential lesson. Always fight your own war, not your enemy's."

The fact is that neither major power has ever truly been organized to fight the Fourth World War as we are coming to know it—but the Americans, in my opinion, are the least prepared of all. Few of the heads of American intelligence with whom I came in close contact during my years in office ever fully understood some of these most basic axioms of war or espionage or geopolitics in the age of South-North conflict.

Perhaps the one who came closest was George Bush, whose mission, in the barely twelve months he held the office of director of central intelligence in 1976 and 1977, was to reorganize the American intelligence community, restore to it some of the respect it had lost as a result of a series of fiascos, and revive some of its effectiveness as a player in what was then the cold war. Any success, of course, would have enormous long-term implications for the Americans' ability to function in the intelligence environment.

Mr. Bush was introduced to me by the French ambassador to the United Nations in a handwritten note. "He is a real gentleman," the ambassador wrote to me, "born of an old New England family who has had a respect from birth for the kinds of fundamental moral values that we both share."

Shortly after this note arrived, George Bush turned up in Paris. It was March 1976. From the first moment, we got along famously. Our first meeting took place in my office at our headquarters, over a wonderful lunch prepared by our French Navy chef. I still remember the soufflé. Bush was accompanied by his principal aide, General Vernon Walters, who was and remains one of the most extraordinary diplomats and intelligence analysts in the West. Alas, their hands were very much tied by the corrosive and systemic failings of the American intelligence system. Our discussion during that first meeting consisted largely of a general review of the world situation, particularly in the wake of the American debacle in Vietnam and the takeover by the Communists, which had happened barely a year before. I was particularly anxious to establish some joint system of cooperation with the Americans, similar to the loose working arrangements we had with our European allies. But Bush was cautious. He had just recently taken on his new functions and he was clearly sensitive to the realities of power in Washington.

"Look, none of us can ever be strong alone," I said, trying to convince a man for whom I already had enormous respect. "If we continue to operate one by one, piecemeal, we will never be strong enough. But together, that is a different story. Together, we are very strong."

Still, Bush reserved judgment. Two days after our meeting, he headed off on the remainder of his first European swing—to Munich, Brussels, and London. When he returned to Washington, I quickly received a charming, handwritten note:

> Dear Friend:
>   Perhaps this is too informal, but this is how I feel. Thank you for your enormous hospitality. I came home feeling deeply about the importance of our relationship and about our common purpose. The luncheon was spectacular, but the conversation and getting your impressive views on the troubled world surpassed even that delecta-

ble soufflé. An added dividend was Barbara's great feeling
of warmth for your charming wife. Please come our way
soon so we can continue what I hope will be a terrific relationship. To you and all your people, my thanks.

Sincerely,
George B.

Alas, there is a yawning gulf between feeling deeply about a
common purpose and embarking on joint operations. Indeed, Bush
did not reply to my suggestions on that score until July, when I
received a second handwritten note:

I found the proposal you conveyed to me most interesting,
and very much appreciate the spirit that prompted you to
make it. As you know, the proposal raises a number of
policy problems which must be considered. However,
please be assured that your views about future cooperation between us are being studied very carefully.

Clearly, George Bush had discovered that he could not take on
every problem at once. First, he had to resolve the problems with his
own Central Intelligence Agency before he could even consider opening discussions about coordinated actions with any of America's
allies. And with barely a year in office, he was only able to take the
first steps toward solving the problems plaguing America's own intelligence capabilities.

Many of those problems are endemic to the way American intelligence is organized and supervised. Of paramount concern is the
problem of secrecy. Intelligence operations live and die by secrecy.
The public spotlight has never been conducive to mounting actions
that require surprise, subtlety, or conspiratorial invention. Moreover, when more than one country is involved, it is often necessary
to guarantee more than the traditional levels of secrecy to prevent
embarrassing domestic and international consequences from premature disclosure of actions. The problem for the CIA begins with
the very process of planning an operation. The number of internal
and external committees that participate in the decision-making
process for each operation is staggering. At least one hundred individuals are involved in such committees on any given project, which
means that the press and public are likely to become aware of an
action even before planning is completed. The oversight process, as
well, is an open, running sore. Since the intelligence oversight com-

mittee of the Congress includes members and staff of both the Democratic and Republican parties, it is likely that one side or another will disapprove of any given operation and use the media to torpedo it before it can get off the ground. And that's assuming the CIA director himself doesn't kill it first.

Admiral Stansfield Turner, director of central intelligence under President Jimmy Carter, had perhaps the most corrosive influence over the agency in this respect. He never ceased to amaze me. At the height of the cold war, with the Soviets invading Afghanistan, targeting the pope for assassination, and subsidizing many of the most deadly terrorist operations, Admiral Turner paid me his first visit in Paris.

"Call me Stan," he opened our conversation. I cringed. "In today's world, do you think communism is still something to be feared?" He might as well have asked about the real deadliness of Abul Abbas's terrorist group, or whether the ayatollahs of Iran were indeed single-minded fanatics.

So I giggled. But he was serious. Deadly serious. As far as I was concerned, our conversation had begun and ended there. "Jesus, this is the man," I thought, "who serves on the National Security Council and who helps to form the opinion on world affairs of the President of the United States. Yet he can ask the head of an allied intelligence agency whether communism under Brezhnev, Chernenko, or Andropov is a threat to the West?" If the head of the CIA began by questioning the power and tenacity of his country's principal enemy of the previous thirty-five years, against a backdrop of the broader public agenda in America of the 1970s of a generalized mistrust of the intelligence community, there was little hope for the integrity of the agency, its operations, or its analyses. When I was asked about Admiral Stansfield Turner, new head of the CIA, I answered: "Well, I guess he is a good sailor."

It was not surprising that the Carter administration all but succeeded in destroying America's human intelligence capability. In part, that was a reaction to the involvement of several CIA "resources" in the Watergate break-in—that ill-fated attempt during the Nixon administration to derail the American political system by subterfuge. After the revelations of Watergate, and the arrival in power of Jimmy Carter, the crisis of American intelligence deepened and intensified. There is no doubt that large segments of the American public did begin to question whether its intelligence agencies would only operate abroad and not interfere in domestic political affairs. I have long believed, in fact, that use of foreign intelligence resources for domestic political ends can only undermine confidence in and ultimately destroy the national security system. Events in the United States in the middle to late 1970s only served to reaffirm my belief.

Intelligence comprises two principal branches—"Humint," or human intelligence; and "Elint" and "Sigint," or electronic and signals intelligence. Each is vitally important. Without the latter, we are blind and deaf. Without the former, we are dumb. The Carter administration dispersed the personnel of the American intelligence services but left the technology intact. In that area—the spy satellites and electronic monitoring through the National Security Agency—the Americans have always had an unparalleled capability. However, by eviscerating the human resources, the United States became incapable of properly interpreting what monitoring picked up and at the same time acting on it. Carter, the consummate technocrat, always felt far more comfortable with devices than people.

This focus on electronic data-gathering might have been of some value in the military and intelligence realities of the Third World War, the East-West conflict. But in the South-North War, human intelligence plays a much more significant role. Our new enemies are backward nations. Their communications are often primitive. The thought processes are intricate and involve personal dynamics that are essential to understand and penetrate. The decisions and the calls to action are communicated with the utmost discretion. There is no role for electronic intelligence until the die is cast—until the troops begin to move or are already under way, until the terrorist is launched and irretrievable, the courier already delivering his plastic explosive to the unsuspecting target. Human intelligence can intercept him at the source. Electronic intelligence can only signal an alarm—and often, too late.

Carter failed to realize that international intelligence is not purely the technical means of gathering data; he also failed to realize that at the other extreme, contrary to popular opinion, intelligence is not merely a matter of lying all the time, of skulduggery and dirty tricks. It is quite simply a question of the rapport among people—whether you have their confidence or not, though clearly such relations are facilitated by confidence rather than suspicion or ambivalence.

My hope for the future enlightenment of the Americans springs from two sources: first, my certainty that international terrorism will finally find its way to their shores. That is not something I would wish on my most mortal enemy, let alone my friends. But if the terrorist threat has the effect of shaking up the American people, and especially their leadership, then perhaps it will be of some value. The Americans, until now, have led a relatively charmed and sheltered existence. Terrorist incidents involving Americans or American property have all happened far from the territory of the United States. One explanation is the extraordinary vigilance of the Federal Bureau of Investigation, not to mention the fear that the mythologized FBI strikes in the hearts of terrorists everywhere. Another explanation is the physical difficulty of operating in the United States, so far from the terrorists' home bases in the Middle East, and the relative ease of operating in Europe, where equally violent and high-profile ends can be achieved at much lower cost and risk.

Many of these circumstances may be changing, though. With international terrorism now nearly two decades old, its leaders have become adept at, even smug about, operating in any type of environment. The FBI is beginning to look no more threatening than France's DST or Great Britain's MI5. The United States may soon seem a soft and tempting mark. And it will take only one successful terrorist operation there to convince the terrorist international that the United States is a promising new and virtually untapped well of targets for their violence.

The second source of my optimism that the Americans may become more realistic intelligence allies is the continued expansion and internationalization of the drug trade. Drugs—for the most part products of the Third World that find their markets in the North—are merely another form of terrorism, another weapon in the Fourth World War. The drug trade may indeed be more disruptive, more pernicious in the long run, to the survival of our Western society than any terrorist activities. While terrorists may maim or kill hundreds in a single incident, drugs penetrate the inner soul of millions, make of each individual another person, deprived of his or her faculties, the very ability to function.

The drug cartels have long targeted America as their principal battleground. While Europe is in many respects the perfect Western breeding ground for terrorists, America has the perfect environment for the growth and operation of the drug trade. The United States has the wealth to finance the production and distribution of the drugs and a deeply troubled and violent underclass with nothing to lose and a constant need to escape from its daily misery. Early on, the masters of the drug cartels realized that their road to riches was a simple matter of being on every American street corner with this instant escape.

The Americans have come to realize that drugs can arrive on their shores from virtually any direction—and pose an intelligence challenge every bit as real, indeed more real on a daily basis than international terrorism. True multinational intelligence cooperation—in terms of gathering, analyzing, and above all acting on information—is perhaps the only viable means of targeting the major international drug cartels.

The leadership of those cartels is every bit as adept as the most wily and battle-hardened terrorist in the fine arts of deception, smuggling illicit cargo, shifting transportation routes, as well as in the use of violence. Any drug enforcement agent will testify, as would his counterterrorist or secret service counterpart, that the most substantial arrests and seizures, the most serious disruptions to the operations of the cartels, do not come from random searches at frontiers or airports. To undermine these operations, it takes intensive intelligence gathering, undercover penetration, patience, skill, and contacts.

The Americans are just coming to realize that they have made many mistakes in targeting both drug traffickers and terrorists over the years. That was due in part to their impatience—a problem that has long existed in their intelligence operations—and also to their bad choice of friends and allies. Repeatedly misguided attempts to find easy-fix shortcuts to penetrating the mysteries of the Third World have led Washington to enlist such truly inappropriate and insidious allies as Manuel Noriega.

If it is proved that Noriega was on the U.S. payroll, then it was a shameful mistake. After all, who better to monitor the activities of the international drug cartel than a fellow traveler? In fact, it was more like asking the fox to monitor the chicken coop. What a wonderful position that fox is in to select the fattest, most succulent chicken for his evening meal, and with the blessing, indeed the connivance, of the farmer! Never use shady characters.

We should always be very careful whom we hire, since such decisions reflect directly, often irrevocably, on the individual who is doing the hiring. My own philosophy has always been that when you have something particularly dirty to do, you hire a gentleman to do it. If a gentleman is persuaded that what we are contemplating is an act of war, and by extension an act of patriotism, then we will find some very good people to work for us. By contrast, if we hire a hoodlum or thug, then eventually we will be compelled to kill the thug in one way or another because we would be blackmailed by him. Certainly, this principle would hold true for any such activity involving South-North intelligence operations, where penetration of alien cultures and systems is so much more complex and sensitive than any we have attempted during the past three world conflicts.

At one of our early meetings, I expressed this philosophy to George Bush, without any direct reference to the hiring of Noriega. Now, years later, the worst nightmare has come to haunt the Americans—a protracted and messy jury trial following a lethal and embarrassing military operation in Panama—all designed to get rid of the rat they should never have hired in the first place. The entire Noriega operation was one fiasco after another. If you do, after all, hire the rat, and are ultimately forced to get rid of him, then by all means do so quickly and permanently. Bringing Noriega back to face "justice" in the United States is such a decidedly wimpy American idea. Such a concept of justice has no place in much of the third world. The Panama operation went bad from the opening salvo— Noriega fleeing as American troops landed in his country, while Washington posted a $1 million reward for his capture. Offer $10 million for Noriega dead or alive and another, more nefarious rat would take care of the Americans' problem entirely—with a neat body bag dumped on their doorstep. In a case like this, an "organized accident" is cheaper.

In many respects, though, the thought processes that went into the alliance with Noriega are perhaps even more dangerous than the selection itself. Over the years, the Americans have so wanted, so desperately needed, to be loved that it has frequently clouded their judgment—resulting in alliances with those who profess eternal loyalty and fidelity, but whose motives are somewhat more venal. It is one of the greatest weaknesses of the American intelligence system—probably of the American character—this awful tendency to want always to be loved. When an American has met you twice, he is fully prepared to call you "my old friend," or "my good friend," while this friend may in fact want nothing more than to destroy you. Beware of such an individual. Treating you to a fine lunch and a cigar by no means makes you his close friend, or his confirmed ally. Such a friendship may prove to be very fickle indeed.

The Soviets—especially their agents—do not share this American trait. One characteristic of the Soviet intelligence agent has always been his strong identification with mother Russia herself. Like most patriotic Russians, he has a deeply ingrained sense of his country's power and majesty, a sense that the Russian people will outlast time, and especially that they will outlast the West, but above all a sense that his ultimate responsibility is to understand his enemy before his enemy can conquer him. It is not necessary to love this enemy or to be loved by him or her—all that is needed is comprehension. All the Russian agent wants is to be feared, as do third world terrorists and their mentors. For as long as I have dealt with them, Russians, like terrorists, have had only the burning desire to win—to succeed—against their western enemies of the Third World War or against the forces of terrorism and drugs and religious fanaticism that are our enemies in the Fourth World War.

The Russians are beginning to experience at home a drug problem, though they have not yet encountered the horrors of terrorism on their own territory. A sort of "Red Mafia" has penetrated every level of Soviet life and wields enormous power and influence. Whatever restraint may remain on its freedom to operate is the same restraint that prevents terrorists from targeting the Soviet Union as they have targeted Western Europe. The Russians do not yet boast the truly open frontiers that would allow terrorists the kind of easy access they have to our major population centers in the West. There is still a most powerful, effective, and influential KGB that keeps track of every foreigner, even if it has relaxed the strictest surveillance and intimidation of its own citizens. But it must be known that the conservative communists have put aside billions of dollars to continue their secret war throughout the world, like they did between the First and Second World wars.

With respect to the terrorists, there is a further restraint—the legacy of years of cultivating the vineyards of terrorism. The subsidies to terrorist nations and the teaching of terrorist leaders continue to provide a modicum of protection for Russian interests. But the older terrorists, those who remember just how much they owe to their Soviet comrades—in money, materiel, training, and moral sustenance—are already dropping from the scene. Their newly minted successors will have no such feelings. They have no loyalty to some distant master in East Berlin or Moscow. Their loyalty now is to their paymaster. And the paymaster resides in Damascus or Tripoli, Baghdad or Teheran. Communism is no longer part of the core curriculum.

The drug lords are the ones who capitalized most profitably on the bitter dregs of the first war the Soviets ever lost. The real legacy of Afghanistan, alongside the body bags and the grieving widows, was the junkies. For the first time, the cream of Soviet manhood tasted the heady drafts of cocaine and heroin. As had their American predecessors in Vietnam, Soviet soldiers by the thousands became new customers of the drugs. This was, of course, a key element of my suggested plan for winning the Afghan war that I had presented early on to President Reagan and that foundered in the bureaucracy of the American security apparatus. Flooding Soviet barracks with drugs was intended to sap their morale and their power as a fighting machine in Afghanistan. Effectively, the drug merchants acting for their own motives did our work for us!

And when the soldiers returned to their homes in Moscow or Kiev or Leningrad, thousands brought the habit with them—the physical craving they'd developed in a vain attempt to escape the horrors they experienced in the remote Afghan hills and valleys. When they returned home, drugs became a means of shutting out the deprivation they found in the Soviet Union they'd left behind; at the same time, drugs allowed them to blank out memories of the atrocities they'd practiced in their far-off war. As Soviet society became more open, the availability of drugs began to feed the demand. And demand began rising in pace with the supply.

The KGB for the time being has little understanding of the complexities of the international drug cartels. Of course, the converse could be said of the drug cartels themselves—only just getting their feet wet in the vastly different operating environment of the Soviet Union. But the learning curve for a drug enforcement agent is a long one in this complex world. Moreover, the abilities of the KGB to function in this new milieu have been sapped enormously by the turmoil and disorganization throughout the Soviet Empire—particularly Moldavia, Georgia, and the Baltic States, as well as the Asian republics where in-depth operations have always been difficult.

Still, the Russians are coming to understand a fundamental truth that political leaderships in the West have only recently begun to accept. The only truly viable means of neutralizing the major drug cartels, as well as the most dangerous terrorist groups, is to internationalize the war against them—not to mention the intelligence activities that monitor them—and to target the nations that harbor them, the governments of the third world that appreciate their utility as weapons in the present and future South-North War.

The first step, no different from any other intelligence operation, is to understand the enemy. The drug barons themselves are not terrorists of the kamikaze type. As independent contractors, they lead extremely comfortable lives, thank you very much. They love money and everything money can buy, and have no interest in relinquishing their life-style very easily. Indeed, their aim is not to destabilize the Western democracies or the Soviet system in the interest of any religious or ethnic fanaticism. Their aim is, plain and simple, to make money—lots of money—and spend it lavishly on themselves. If they also serve the political ends of governments that sponsor them, or harbor them, that is merely an added fillip.

Once we understand their motives, the most effective tactics to neutralize them become quite clear. Just as I suggested to President Giscard d'Estaing that we target the Corsican terrorists with a select hit-list, one by one, until they get the message, so should we target the leaders of the drug cartels. The operation would be equally simple and fully deniable. First, there would be the establishment of what would appear to be a vigilante organization of extraordinary power and apparently unlimited funding. It would be a multinational organization backed secretly by the heads of the drug enforcement operations of the leading customer nations and would operate under an assumed name.

International police cooperation and superior intelligence work, of course, would be necessary for any such operation to succeed. Moles inside the key cartels, intimate knowledge of the movements and weaknesses of their leaders on a minute-to-minute basis are all vital to the success. Moreover, each failure only serves to reinforce further the sense of invulnerability of these leaders among their minions and among those who hunt them.

If we are to have any hope of victory in the Fourth World War, we must understand that while cooperation is the most complex weapon, it is the most lethal one.

EPILOGUE
A Club for Decent People

hat we are calling the Fourth World War marks a return to some of our most primitive origins in so many respects. The medieval mentality of an Iranian ayatollah is effectively defining the strategic concepts of the twenty-first century. We must be fully prepared to accept the new rules of engagement, to arrive at a new balance of power, or terror, in order to assure the peace. The concept of Certain Destruction that will define the new stability of the postnuclear age must quickly take its place alongside that of Mutually Assured Destruction that guaranteed the peace of the nuclear balance of terror. Certain Destruction is the new strategic concept that will prevent the global destruction of a Fourth World War. The threat is truly awesome in its reach and scope. It requires a whole new strategic system to address and cope with it—a system of conventional weaponry and unconventional tactics that is capable of ensuring the peace the way the nuclear balance has ensured the peace for the past half century. The world is a substantially different place than it was even five years ago. New political and military alignments are changing the balance of power and the balance of terror as well. All of our institutions—political, military, and especially intelligence—must keep pace with those changes or we are lost. Above all, the threat of the Fourth World War is the reason we need a club.

It might, perhaps, be called the Decent Peoples' Club—and have as members those nations who believe in respect for the individual, for the right of all of us to live our lives as we wish, to prosper or fail according to our talents and desires; and who above all will ensure that their neighbors are left alone to fulfill their own destinies. This club should become the gendarme of the world. For as the world explodes from five billion people today to the more than eight billion it is estimated will populate our planet by the year 2025, each individual will need desperately some assurance that there can be at least a modicum of freedom from random, unpredictable violence perpetrated by fanatic dictators and drug barons alike.

Our club must have a global franchise to protect human life. At issue is, fundamentally, the very survival of civilization as we know it. The club's members would be the true power of the Northern world—the United States, Europe, and Japan—plus our friends the Decent People from the South. Each member would pledge an elite force of one hundred thousand men, all essential land, air and sea equipment and logistical support, and whatever funding might be required for a given operation. A central commander would be designated, a permanent headquarters staff and intelligence directorate established. In this respect, the club would not be much different from NATO—the North Atlantic Treaty Organization—but without the "North Atlantic." For under a binding treaty similar to the alliance agreement that established NATO, ratified by the appropriate body in each country, all members of the club would pledge to take whatever action the leadership decided was necessary and appropriate. Often the leaders of the club would have to be prepared to act with lightning speed and total secrecy. There might be no time for consultation with parliamentary committees, not a moment to spare for political soundings or votes of confidence. Indeed, the results of the most successful operations might never become known. But the slightest hesitation could have frightening consequences for the future of civilization.

Indeed, NATO, and especially the American administration that has taken the lead, has begun to move in the direction of rapid response that is the tactical foundation of the Decent Peoples' Club. The restructuring of NATO currently under way is designed to establish a highly mobile quick-response brigade-size unit of five thousand troops that could be on the scene in an emergency with full equipment within seventy-two hours, backed up by a rapid-reaction corps of fifty thousand to seventy thousand troops available within five to seven days, under British command. The unit would include one British heavy armor division of fifteen thousand troops based in Germany; a second British division of light armor, paratroops, commandos and marines; and two multinational divisions; as well as an

American division that would also provide all planes, helicopters, and airlift capability for the entire corps.

But this NATO move is in reality only the first hesitant step toward the kind of unified political and military capability that can guarantee a lasting or sustainable peace. France has still effectively excluded itself from NATO, since it is not a member of the organization's military command. The French administration has continued to press for the impractical alternative of a purely European force, under European command, thereby ignoring most of the imperatives of the South-North War we are now fighting. NATO must expand, not contract, its legal sphere of activities, which at this writing remain confined purely to Europe and the North Atlantic. But it must expand as well its political will to intervene in crises wherever Northern interests might be endangered.

The unilateral decision by the Bush administration in September 1991 to dismantle the American short-range nuclear arsenal and to move toward substantial nuclear disarmament was clearly an important strategic move in retargeting nuclear forces. The signal was clear—the Northern countries will in the future maintain a nuclear capability sufficient only to act as a deterrent force against aggression from unpredictable and irrational foes. Instead, resources will be redirected toward the kinds of forces capable of sustaining the doctrine of Certain Destruction—quick, surgical strikes that excise a cancer before it has a chance to spread widely.

As we have discovered repeatedly during the early years of the Fourth World War, when we hesitate, we are lost. Tentative steps, halfway measures, will not work in the new global environment. The military forces deployed must possess overwhelming means. They must strike fear into the hearts of tyrants who have never before known defeat. They must not only appear to be invincible, they must be invincible.

The Decent Peoples' Club is not a device to freeze out certain powers. Nor is it a thinly disguised effort to eradicate enemies of its member nations—the checks and balances of competing political imperatives in the various nations would ensure that it does not degenerate into a club of vengeance. Nor should much time and effort be expended on debating the choice of a commander from one nation or another. During the Gulf war, none of the nations pledging troops objected for an instant to the leadership of General Norman Schwarzkopf.

Nor would the club itself be a totally restricted and closed community. Many other decent nations would likely be called on for specialized assistance as their intelligence or military capabilities made them obvious choices in one crisis or another. The club would purely and simply be a means of making sure that one mad dictator or one renegade nation would not destroy the rest of the planet.

Yet the target of our club would not be any single individual—for instance, neither a Saddam Hussein, nor a Kim-Il-Sung, nor a Muammar Qaddafi, nor a Hafiz al-Assad. Its aim would simply be to assure that no individual, no nation, could build a threat to the rest of the world, especially a nuclear threat. If such a threat became real, the club would intervene with military force to take it out—in a simple, surgical strike of mammoth and unequivocal proportions.

In every case, of course, the consequences of intervention would be carefully weighed and the decision to act be based on the best possible intelligence. Before launching Operation Desert Storm, the United States administration was deeply misinformed not only by its allies in the Western and Arab worlds, but also by its own intelligence specialists. All predicted a quick demise for Saddam Hussein and his entire political-military apparatus. But the widely anticipated uprising never materialized. Saddam Hussein lingered on as a cancer in his own country and the entire region—a cancer that began growing again even before surgery was completed.

What we are discussing here are threats beyond individual frontiers. We are not suggesting that the world should be remade in our own Western image. The club would be in no sense an effort to establish a new world order. Hopefully, as the will to reduce such threats became part of the established international order, military actions would become less and less necessary, fewer and farther between.

All we want is to give every country the freedom to create its *own* destiny as long as it does not seek to impose that destiny on its neighbors. The leaders of all nations must understand that if they accumulate nuclear, biological, or chemical weapons and threaten to use them offensively as a challenge to the established order, to civilization beyond their own frontiers, those weapons and the ability to use them will most certainly and definitively be destroyed.

The Decent Peoples' Club would be, effectively, the ultimate deterrent. If properly structured and deployed, it would ensure the implementation of the strategic equilibrium by the policy of Certain Destruction, which will prevent a global inferno from emerging from the Fourth World War—the equilibrium of terror—just as the policy of Mutually Assured Destruction prevented an inferno from developing in the Third World War.

Let us suppose that next year, we learn that some weird dictator is six months away from completion of an atomic bomb. What do we do? Have him sign the nuclear nonproliferation treaty? So, in this case, the plant and its entire capability to produce a nuclear weapon would be destroyed instantly and definitively by the Decent Peoples' Club. When American jets bombed Tripoli in 1986, it had little or no impact on Qaddafi's ability to mount terrorist attacks. Indeed, the mission failed even to find and destroy Qaddafi himself. Instead, the bombs fell in some residential neighborhoods and killed some old women and children—a fact that Qaddafi used most effectively for propaganda purposes. But even this misguided and apparently ineffectual action did have one important consequence—it gave Qaddafi pause. For some years after this bombing, Qaddafi became somewhat more restrained in his use of terrorism, his distribution of subsidies to terrorist groups, his whole range of dealings with the terrorist international. In short, even this ill-conceived mission did affect his will, if not his ability, to invoke the terrorist weapon. Striking the oil fields, removing his source of funding for terrorist operations, would have destroyed his ability to invoke terrorism as well.

Such an action is precisely what the United States and its allies tried to take against Saddam Hussein in the Persian Gulf. Yet the allies have been criticized in some quarters for targeting a leader who may be anathema to the West (and the North)—but who is a hero in much of the Third World. It is certainly true that Saddam Hussein is a figure of some popularity in his own country and beyond in some quarters. We members of the club would have no problem with this. He could do whatever he chose within his borders—as long as his people tolerated him. He could crown himself emperor for life, he could proclaim a conversion of his people to Shintoism or Shiism. But he could not build plants for the manufacture of atomic, biological, and chemical weapons, could not seize the territory of a peaceful neighboring nation without provocation, could not menace for an instant the world beyond his frontiers.

In fact, what we have had in the Persian Gulf was effectively the first operation of our Decent Peoples' Club, writ large. And the operation reveals both the plan's strengths and its weaknesses.

First, the club would need to move quickly—a central reason for restricting its membership and compelling action without consultation. The panoply of nations contributing troops, materiel, or simply moral support to Operation Desert Storm was so vast that it severely restricted any nimble diplomatic or military maneuvering. In the end, a frontal assault was really the only alternative available, though it pulled up short, leaving a deadly residue—an Iraqi nuclear weapons program that must still be eradicated.

Second, club forces would need to move wherever possible clandestinely using small, surgical strike forces to take out the specific threat. The fact that Saddam Hussein was forced to face down publicly the entire military might of the Northern and parts of the Southern world only compelled him to dig his heels in deeper, extending the conflict. Saving face is a powerful motive for any dictator, or indeed for a ruler of any stripe.

Above all, the club would need first-rate intelligence, instantly available to its military and civilian leadership. During the Gulf war, the conflicting intelligence estimates of the Central Intelligence Agency, the Defense Intelligence Agency, and battlefield intelligence units, particularly on bomb damage assessments, only led to confusion at the operational levels—General Schwarzkopf's principal complaint.

The first stage in the formation of the Decent Peoples' Club might well be a worldwide intelligence effort coordinated by the intelligence directorates of the club's members. The action or operations units of these intelligence services might become the interim military arm of the Decent Peoples' Club. Imagine a surprise surgical strike by a unit like Britain's Special Air Services on Libya's most productive oil fields or Syrian-controlled terrorist training facilities in Lebanon's Bekáa Valley?

The club could accomplish a lot without even firing a single shot. One important contribution might be the establishment of an international tribunal for the prosecution of terrorists and their backers, staffed by the club. Each terrorist would be tried before this special court—placed, for the sake of argument, in Nuremberg, Germany, site of the war crime trials of Hitler's henchmen. The accused would be tried in person if captured, in absentia if not, and the results broadcast worldwide on the BBC, Voice of America, Deutsche Welle, and Radio France International.

"Mr. X, you have been tried and convicted of terrorist activities.

You are on the books now. We are coming after you for the rest of your life. One day we will get you."

Such a sentence would have enormous deterrent effect, especially after the first criminal was identified, seized, and executed or imprisoned.

His or her colleagues would begin to think, "I still have forty or fifty years to live, and this powerful organization is going to pursue me for the rest of my life. There must be a better way to spend the rest of my days than in flight."

We must prove to these international outlaws that we are serious—that we have a will and determination that will outlast them all. Threats will not work on fanatics, but they will work effectively on those in the pay of governments that control and direct the fanatics. Investigators of the Libyan- and Syrian-backed bombing of Pan American Flight 103 over Lockerbie, Scotland, identified the professional handlers employed by Qaddafi who directed his intelligence agents and the members of the Palestine Liberation Front General Command. All of their names should be on the lifetime watch-list of the Decent Peoples' Club.

The kind of war the forces of the Decent Peoples' Club will be fighting will be very different from any we have fought in the past. There are a number of reasons for this—the very different nature of the enemy, and his most unorthodox strategy and tactics. The forces of terror that are launched against us are often difficult to uncover in this landscape against which they have camouflaged themselves. By contrast, when we arrive in their capitals, we are immediately spotted by the most untrained eye.

We cannot disguise ourselves among them, which makes retaliation and the implementation of Certain Destruction that much more difficult.

There was a French explorer of the last century, René Caillie, who spent years in disguise in North Africa. He was never discovered. Until one day he was in the desert and thought he was truly alone. So he urinated standing up. The Muslims never do that; they crouch. He was observed, and they chopped off his head. One little slip—and like that, you lose your head.

In the southern part of the United States there is the same potential for extraordinary unrest that exists in many European nations. America has within its borders Hispanic and Islamic communities capable of concealing forces that are potentially explosive. A succession of American governments has quite simply failed even to address the problem.

It is our arrogance and neglect in these matters that will ultimately be our downfall when the first shots of the Fourth World War are fired in anger in Europe or in America. The profound failure to penetrate these newly arrived communities will have the gravest consequences.

Certainly, all intelligence services understand the need, value, and difficulties of infiltration. The Allies made use of it throughout much of Europe in the Second World War. It was the cornerstone of the Resistance movement in France. At the end of the Second World War, as the Third quietly kicked in, Stalin moved infiltration to a higher plateau, infiltrating the West with agents masquerading as defectors or disenfranchised émigrés. But today's infiltrators, rather than merely agents for intelligence gathering, will become the engines of destruction and battle as well. The Fourth World War will be a terrorist war.

In effect, some of these foreigners in our midst—those who practice or espouse terrorism—can become the missiles that during the Third World War might have destroyed nations but, because of the strategic scenario of Mutually Assured Destruction, ultimately guaranteed the balance of terror. The difference today is that there is no five-minute launch time delay; the human missiles of the Fourth World War are here already! Against them, we have no antimissile defense, no Star Wars or Patriot missiles to target them. Above all, we do not even have the retaliatory capability to guarantee the Certain Destruction that the Fourth World War and its new strategic realities mandate. We must develop an ability to retaliate if these human missiles are launched by hitting and destroying their bases. And with improved intelligence capabilities, we must develop the kinds of distant early warning systems that will alert us to their launch.

Certain nations will use terrorism more effectively, more predictably as an instrument of war and military or state policy than other nations. Today, it is clear that Libya, Syria, Iran, North Korea, and Iraq are among the principal terrorist nations. Moreover, there are traditions in each, deep historical forces, that make them more likely than others to turn to terrorism as a weapon against the North.

Today's terrorist weapons are merely more sophisticated versions of the dagger. Terrorism today is not merely throwing a hand grenade into a crowded cinema in a large metropolis or assassinating an American senator. It could include putting poison in the water supplies of Paris or New York, planting a nuclear device in the heart of a great city of Europe or America.

Until now, we have been lucky. Until now, terrorists and fanatics of all types have been largely artisanal. That is to say, they are well organized. They have little or no chance of getting caught. But there have been no precise targets established for political reasons by their sponsors. Terrorist leaders are merely given quantities of money or materiel and told, "Do whatever you want to do, just make life difficult for your enemies out there in whatever fashion you choose."

But our luck will not hold out forever as the Fourth World War is truly joined. The next stage is the one we are entering now. It is the stage in which terrorists become the precisely targeted international weapons that can truly turn them into powerful instruments of state power and military force. We are entering the period when terrorist leaders will be given by the government that underwrites and commands them all but unlimited quantities of money and arms with the following instructions:

"Now you are organized. You are an army. You will make life very difficult for the enemy in this way, at this time, and in this place precisely. These are the targets we have chosen. You will destroy them."

It will still be a subtle kind of warfare, but more insidious and dangerous.

Our plea today is an urgent call to action. Today, what is at stake is the world order as we know it.

Index